C000157339

Matthew Bell is a mechanical engineer by trade but spends every spare moment writing about Sheffield United Football Club. He has edited the United fanzine 'Flashing Blade' for over twenty years and has written a weekly column in the 'Green 'Un' since 1993.

In 2010, along with Gary Armstrong, he co-authored 'Fit and Proper? Conflicts and Conscience in an English Football Club', the definitive account of the recent history of Sheffield United.

He was co-editor of 'Blades Tales' and 'Blades Tales 2' and has written articles for 4-4-2 magazine, the 2003 Sheffield United v Arsenal FA Cup semi-final programme and Yorkshire County Cricket Club.

Reviews for "Fit and Proper? Conflicts and Conscience in an English Football Club":

"The best book ever written about Sheffield United" - www.s24su.com

"With the country's fifth-largest city home to two League One sides, many a neutral has asked how Sheffield football has reached such a state...... the answers are to be found in this book" – When Saturday Comes

"A litany of the disappointment, broken promises and occasional euphoria that has been the supporters' experience down the years" – Sheffield Telegraph

"Provides a superb insight to the goings-on at Bramall Lane and makes one wonder how the club ever functioned during some of the more sobering experiences of boardroom politics" - A customer review on amazon.

Red, White and Khaki

The Story of the Only Wartime FA Cup Final

Matthew Bell

peakpublish

Peakpublish
An imprint of Peak Platform
New Bridge
Calver
Hope Valley
Derbyshire S32 3XT
First published by Peakpublish 2011

Printed in India

A CIP catalogue record for this book is available
from the British Library

ISBN: 978-1-907219-17-7
www.peakplatform.com

Dedication

This book is dedicated to all sportsmen who have met untimely deaths, whether in armed combat, in pursuing their sporting dream, or by sheer accident. The world would be a less interesting place without them and their kind. It is especially dedicated to Jimmy Revill, the first Sheffield United footballer to be killed on wartime active service.

It is also dedicated to those players of Sheffield United Football Club who played so hard to win the FA Cup in the most traumatic football season in history. Little could they have known that their club would lift only one major trophy in the next hundred years - and that just a decade later. Before undertaking this research these men were merely names, but in the course of reading countless newspaper reports they grew into long-lost friends. I feel as if I know every one of them personally.

Acknowledgements

The author is indebted to Sheffield Central Library for the use of its extensive archives of newspapers and other material held for public viewing in the Local Studies Library, and also to its always courteous and helpful staff. On the wall of the stairwell of Sheffield Central Library is a quotation from son of Sheffield Michael Palin. It reads: 'There is no institution I value more in this country than libraries.' Wise words indeed.

Thanks are also due to my editor - my brother Iain - who, as a football fan and unparallelled student of military history of the first half of the twentieth century, was the ideal person to cast a fresh eye over the manuscript. That is despite the fact that he supports Sheffield Wednesday.

Finally, no book covering the history of Sheffield United can be written without the considerable assistance of the numerous invaluable and incomparable reference volumes produced by Denis Clarebrough and Andrew Kirkham, respectively the club's historian and statistician. Thanks also to Denis for his kind loan of several photographs.

CONTENTS

FOOTBALL AND WAR

The Football Association was formed in 1863, the Football League twenty-five years later. They are the oldest governing bodies of their type in the world. Organised association football was developed and codified in Great Britain, from where it was exported to most corners of the globe by British workers, traders, soldiers, sailors and expatriates. Throughout the period of rapid growth and soaring popularity of football - and sport in general - in the late 1800s, Britain was also a world-leader in another area of human contest: the country was almost permanently at war. Many of the conflicts in which Britain was involved at that time will be familiar only to avid students of British history; British forces were engaged in military action in such obscure locations as Bhutan, Ghana, Nigeria and Zanzibar. Arguably, just the two Boer Wars, from 1880 to 1881 and 1899 to 1902, would be known to most people.

All the while the people of Britain carried on their everyday business as usual. They worked, slept, ate and relaxed unconcerned by the activities of British soldiers thousands of miles from home. Their valuable free time might well have been spent watching football matches, especially if they lived in one of the great industrial cities of the north or the midlands. They might have read in newspapers about wars in Africa and Asia – if any news filtered through – and if so, it would have had little or no impact on their lives. Their primary day-to-day worries would not have included whether or not the British Army was making progress in Sudan or Abyssinia; at the forefront of their minds was earning enough money to provide a roof over their heads, put food on the family table and, hopefully, to retain enough of their income to indulge in their favourite pastimes. Those faraway wars perhaps did not seem real, except to the unfortunate families informed that their father, brother or son had lost life or limb.

All this was to change in August 1914. Now came a war that affected every single member of the population of Britain. Instead of a conflict in some far-off, unheard of place, this war was being fought on land just a couple of dozen miles from the British shoreline, inside British territorial waters and in the airspace above British soil. It involved countries - allied and enemy - that were Britain's near neighbours. This war certainly was real; it was worryingly close to home. If events turned against Britain, foreign forces would step on to English beaches in great numbers for the first time in a thousand years. There was fear, and a real danger, that Britain might actually be invaded, apprehensions that persisted until the war was won.

When the First World War began, politicians were keen to convey the idea that there should be 'business as usual' at home. Commerce, industry, entertainment and recreation were meant to continue undisturbed, but that was never going to be possible. When there is fighting almost within hearing distance and there are food shortages and rising prices and long lists of the dead, wounded and missing printed in the daily papers, life can never go on 'as usual'. In *Apartheid* era South Africa there existed an expression frequently used by opponents of that country's re-admission to global sporting competition: 'There can be no normal sport in an abnormal society'. The same phrase can be applied, to a large extent, to a country in the throes of a major war. If society cannot continue 'as usual' it is, by definition, an abnormal society. It could be justifiably argued that the playing of sport, particularly the most popular sport of professional football, is one of the most powerful barometers of 'normal' life, so if it is accepted that prevailing circumstances force society to become 'abnormal', how could it be possible for professional football to go on? But, for the first ten months of the First World War, football did go on.

As soon as war was declared, some sections of the population held the belief that sport and entertainment, especially professional football and its associated mass appeal, were vital for maintaining the morale and spirits of the general public. If the working man had no means of occupying his scarce hours of leisure, what else would he do? He would read the reports of the war in the newspapers and worry and fret, said some, and what good would that do? Or he might replace watching football with the consumption of beer, said others, which was an even more awful scenario to contemplate. Football must carry on to prevent either situation arising, they said, and, don't forget, the Government had told its population to carry on 'business as usual'. To play football was therefore to follow instructions. But there were plenty of others who demanded that the game must be stopped. Their arguments were twofold: first, how could tens of thousands watch and play football when many thousands of their contemporaries were dying in battle? It was morally reprehensible. The second part of the argument was that if people were denied the opportunity to watch or play football, they would instead enlist in the forces and serve their country. If only it were that simple.

Each of these viewpoints had its merits, though neither was compelling, and football defended itself by insisting that matches provided the ideal conditions for encouraging recruitment to the services and raising money for the various war relief funds. After all, where else did thousands of people gather in one location and form a captive audience for recruitment campaigns? In addition, it was claimed that football supplied more volunteers for the army and navy than all other sports combined. Unfortunately for football's case, very few of these volunteers were well-known names from the more famous clubs. However, such arguments were sufficient to hold back the critics for a while, until it became clear that football grounds were not such prolific breeding grounds for recruits after all. The call for football to be stopped regained momentum, and as clubs suffered financial hardship due to rapidly falling attendances, it appeared that the game's opponents might get their way, not through legislation or choice, but because some stricken clubs may not last the season.

That football did make it through to the end of the season in the face of such fierce opposition, with all fixtures completed on schedule and without any clubs going bankrupt, was not far short of a miracle, reflecting great credit on the game's rulers, football club directors and, to a lesser degree, players and spectators. Their collective stubbornness overcame all obstacles, very much against the odds. Then, when it became obvious that the war was not going to be 'over by Christmas', as some had predicted, the football authorities took a decisive step, correct both morally and financially, to cease professional football until the fighting was over. Twenty-four years later, at the outbreak of the Second World War, the Government and football's governing bodies were mindful of the storm stirred up by the continuation of the game in 1914/15, and cancelled the young season immediately. There were no arguments this time.

This, therefore, is the story of the indomitable men who, from August 1914 to April 1915, fought tooth and nail to keep the game going in the face of stern opposition from politicians, military men, the clergy, authors, poets, temperance workers, historians, academics and large parts of the press and the general public. It is also the story of the only time in English football history that the FA Cup has been played for, and won, in a time of World War. In particular it is the story of one city and one football club: Sheffield and Sheffield United FC. In the early twentieth century Sheffield was one of Britain's major centres of armaments manufacture and iron and steel production and therefore its citizens were chief players in the war effort, even when they were not fighting on the front line across the English Channel. It could be said that their role was almost as crucial as that of the gunners manning the artillery made in the city.

Sheffield is also the birthplace of modern football. It is home to the world's oldest football club, Sheffield FC, founded in 1857, and the second oldest, Hallam FC, founded in 1860. Sheffield FC formulated the first set of written rules of the game in 1858. The world's first inter-club football match, between Hallam and Sheffield, took place at Hallam's Sandygate ground on Boxing Day 1860. Sandygate is the world's oldest football ground in continual use, and the world's oldest professional sports ground, Bramall Lane, first used in 1855, is also in the city. Bramall Lane staged the world's first floodlit football match, in 1878. The world's first cup tournament, the Youdan Cup, sponsored by a local theatre owner, was staged in Sheffield in 1867, won by Hallam in a final held at Bramall Lane. The same year the world's fifth oldest[1] professional football club, Sheffield Wednesday, was formed.

Sheffield United FC was founded in 1889 to make more use of the Bramall Lane ground for football. Sheffield Wednesday, who previously played their more important matches at the venue, moved to a new ground a quarter of a mile away at Olive Grove in 1887, resulting in a loss of income for the Bramall Lane Ground Committee. Then, following a Cup semi final tie at Bramall Lane between Preston North End and West Bromwich Albion in March 1889 that produced an attendance of 22,688 and receipts of £558 1s 6d, the Ground Committee realised the popularity of professional football in general and of the new Football League competition, which attracted crowds higher than all but the biggest Cup games. A mere six days later Sheffield United Football Club was formed to play professional League football at Bramall Lane. Over the next dozen years the club became one of the most powerful in the country, winning the League once and the Cup twice by 1902. There followed a lean spell, but by 1914 United were once again on the rise. It was their misfortune that this resurgence coincided with the start of the most horrifying war in world history. Despite the circumstances, Sheffield United went on to become the winners of the FA Cup in that fraught season, forever darkened by the constant shadow of massive death and destruction.

It is a unique story, and Sheffield United is therefore a unique football club. The 1915 FA Cup final was held on April

---

[1] Some claim that Sheffield Wednesday (or 'The Wednesday' as they were known until 1929) is the third-oldest professional football club. Stoke City FC's official foundation date is 1863, but there is evidence to suggest that the current club was formed in 1868. Chesterfield FC claim 1866 or 1867 as its year of formation – there is evidence for both dates – but that club was Chesterfield Town. The current club came into existence in 1919. The Wednesday can lay claim to be the oldest sports club in the world – it was founded as a cricket club in 1820 – and to be the employer of the world's first professional footballer, Scotsman James Lang in 1876.

24. The same day, during the Battle of St Julien that took place near Ypres in Belgium, the Germans used chlorine gas on allied forces; 3,508 Canadian soldiers were casualties, over one thousand of them dead. In this most terrible of wars, such a number of killed and wounded in one place on one day was not unusual. It was against this harrowing background that the 1914/15 football season kicked off, progressed and was completed, and Sheffield United's captain George Utley lifted the FA Cup. When he did so, there was no celebration. It was not the time for that.

CHAPTER ONE

AN INVENTION OF TRADITION

The last two decades of the nineteenth century and the first of the twentieth were a time of unparallelled innovation and development in the fields of science, technology, engineering, transport and domestic products. A thirty-year period brought the first car, the first motorcycle, the first electric tram and the first aeroplane. Wireless communication, radar, the cathode ray tube, X-rays, neon lighting, the gramophone record and stainless steel were invented or discovered, the last-named by Harry Brearley in Sheffield in 1913. More everyday items such as the ballpoint pen, the vacuum flask, the zip, perforated toilet paper, the electric iron, the disposable razor blade and the crossword first saw the light of day.

As well there being access to a whole host of new gadgets and devices, other areas of life were experiencing great change. Modifications to working patterns, instigated by the expansion of the right to vote, the growth of trade unionism and enhancements in safety in the workplace allowed working-class people increased leisure time and an improved quality of life. Activities and facilities therefore developed and grew to enable them to fill their additional free time enjoyably and healthily. Additionally, advances in health care and the provision of improved medical services contributed to a better lifestyle for working-class people. The city of Sheffield, like most other industrial cities, could boast many new hospital facilities to look after the health and welfare of the population. For example, the Royal Hospital, on West Street, was completely rebuilt in the early 1890s and included a new dental wing. The Royal Infirmary, on Infirmary Road, was extended in 1884 and further in 1900, and an isolation hospital at Lodge Moor on the very edge of the city was founded in 1888. The Children's Hospital moved to its present site on Western Bank in 1881 and was extended in 1902.

There also existed a simultaneous growth in state- and community-provided social services due to the ever-expanding body of professional men, such as medical officers, teachers and factory inspectors, the birth of self-confident working-class organisations independent of politics and the fact that influential middle and upper classes were becoming increasingly aware of, and shocked by, the poverty that existed in parts of their cities. Friendly Societies were formed, into which employers and employees paid subscriptions that were used for mutually beneficial purposes, by means of the provision of sickness benefits, pensions, insurance and payments to the unemployed in times of recession. By 1911, the various Friendly Societies in Sheffield had a combined membership of some 90,000 citizens, whilst the three Co-operative Societies in the city, formed in the late nineteenth century to provide consumers with both groceries and a share of profits, could boast more than 50,000 members by 1914.

In turn, education reform led to increased literacy, which generated greater readership of newspapers by the common man and raised his interest in all kinds of previously out-of-reach subjects, such as politics, the arts and, notably, sport.[2] They had a lot to read about too, as the late nineteenth century was a boom time for codified sport, with teams and leagues

---

[2] At the turn of the century there were twenty-five newspapers in London alone devoted entirely to sport.

being formed at a rapid rate. There were also opportunities for the entrepreneurial organisers of sport, in the form of a massive new body of keen consumers to whom their games could be sold, and once again Sheffield was at the forefront of this new form of commerce.

Concomitant with this economic and social diversification was the development of modern systems of transport. Motorised vehicles and even bicycles were beyond the scope of the lower classes, but mechanised means were now being provided for them to get around, albeit at a cost. Britain's railway network expanded from 15,500 miles in 1870 to 23,400 miles in 1910, making possible for the first time rapid travel between most major towns and cities. Urban roads were widened and re-surfaced (a form of asphalt was first laid on some roads in Sheffield in 1907) to provide more accessible and speedier routes for horse-drawn vehicles, but the new surfaces did not meet the approval of all, as there were complaints that they caused horses to slip. From 1885, electric tramways began to appear on the streets of British towns and cities. Sheffield had had a horse-drawn tramway since 1873, running from Lady's Bridge to Attercliffe, Brightside and Tinsley, after which the routes were extended to Heeley, Nether Edge and Hillsborough. These lines were used for the city's first electric tram in September 1899, which ran from Nether Edge to Tinsley, via the city centre, and by the end of that month further electrified lines were constructed to Walkley and Pitsmoor. The same year an electricity generating station (which now forms the premises of an industrial museum) was built at Kelham Island adjacent to the River Don, specifically for the use of the tramway system. All the city's tram routes were electrified by 1902 and by 1910 the network covered thirty-nine miles, with its main depot near the railway station, at Leadmill.

At the end of the nineteenth century everything was therefore either already in place or in the process of being introduced for the cultivation of perfect conditions to produce an expansion of spectator sport and other forms of mass entertainment. In effect, the working classes were now being asked to pay for their shorter working hours, and they did so willingly. They filled those extra hours voraciously: football and cricket quickly became the two most popular sporting pastimes of the working man, and were soon virtually national institutions. The Football League was founded in 1888 and the first official County Cricket Championship took place in 1890, although a semi-formal inter-county competition had been in place since 1873. As towns spread outwards into rural areas, in the 1880s and 1890s many golf courses were designed and built on former farm or estate land, whilst municipal parks and recreational areas were set out in towns and cities, often on land donated by wealthy philanthropists from their extensive properties. Away from outdoor recreation, a glut of new theatres, music halls and, later, motion picture houses was built to satisfy the burgeoning demand from the masses for affordable entertainment.

The city of Sheffield was in the vanguard of such progress, largely thanks to its world-leading heavy industries of iron, steel, railway wheels and rails, armour plate and munitions manufacture. By the turn of the twentieth century Johnson Cammell and Company, at its Cyclops Works on Savile Street/ Carlisle Street, John Brown and Company, at its Atlas Works on Savile Street East, and Naylor Vickers and Company, at its River Don Works on Brightside Lane, each employed more than five thousand people. In 1895 these three companies combined supplied 23,000 tons of armour plate on Government contracts and ten years later Cammell's produced what was believed to be the heaviest casting ever made at the time, weighing eighty-four tons. Such work made for healthy profits - in 1902 Vickers reported a surplus for the year of £501,292, a sum worth over £40 million today. When John Brown's merged with neighbouring company Thomas Firth and Sons in 1908, one of its first research projects was to investigate a method of overcoming the problem of high-temperature erosion of artillery gun barrels. In charge of this task was metallurgist Harry Brearley, who found that adding chromium to standard carbon steel produced a material that was resistant to corrosion. This he termed 'rustless steel', a name later changed to the more mellifluous 'stainless steel'. Another steel producer, Hadfield's Limited, at its Hecla Works,[3] specialised in the manufacture of manganese and silicon steel for electrical transformers, railway crossings and digging machinery, and, from 1914, for tank tracks and soldiers' helmets. Between 1894 and 1914 the company's workforce grew from 530 to 5,690 and its capital expanded from £135,750 to £700,000.

The number of inhabitants of Sheffield shot up from some 336,000 in 1881 to over 454,000 in 1911, the year its population surpassed that of Leeds (445,000). Boosted by boundary changes and an influx of immigrants from Scotland, Ireland and various parts of England, in the ten years since the previous census Sheffield's population had risen by 11.14 per cent, that of Leeds by 3.97 per cent. The economy of Sheffield was taking off, whilst at the same time living and working conditions, sanitation, health and housing improved considerably. The landscape, layout and buildings of the city also began to change beyond recognition. Granted city status in 1893, Sheffield's central hub immediately found a new location. Prior to this time the main hive of activity of the town centred on the area surrounding the original Town Hall (which remains, but - internally - in an almost derelict

---

[3] Now the site of the Meadowhall Shopping Centre.

condition) on Waingate, and the markets, on the slopes leading down to the confluence of the River Don and the River Sheaf. A replacement Town Hall, designed by architect Edward Mountford, whose most notable achievement was the later Old Bailey in London, was to become the city's new focal point. It was Mountford's first major project of this nature, his Edwardian Baroque-style building rising above Pinstone Street and Surrey Street between 1890 and 1897. When finished, the City accountant revealed that the total cost was £182,128 15s 5d. Queen Victoria visited the city in celebration of its completion. The holders of the city's purse strings were not afraid to release them: as soon as the Town Hall was completed they authorised the rebuilding of the Midland Station at a cost of £215,888.

The ground had been laid for such infrastructural changes from 1875 onwards, when a road improvement scheme was sanctioned and funded by the town corporation, mainly for the reason of facilitating transport in the city centre. Pinstone Street and Leopold Street were constructed by 1879, and Fargate was widened in the 1880s. The 1875 plan also incorporated a proposed widening of High Street, but disputes with property owners delayed any modifications until 1895. In all, eleven major streets were widened and three new streets created, producing Sheffield's unusual linear commercial area that stretches from Lady's Bridge north of the centre to Moorfoot in the south, a distance of around a mile and a half. The street improvement scheme, the consequent demolition of many eighteenth century residential and industrial premises and the acquisition of former open land allowed space for the erection of several buildings that today still provide some of the city's more distinctive landmarks, such as the Victoria Hall on Norfolk Street, the colourful Royal Exchange Buildings at the outbound end of Lady's Bridge, Channing Hall and Montgomery Hall on Surrey Street, the Fitzalan Square main

Post Office, Parade Chambers at the junction of Church Street and East Parade, Cairns Chambers, on the corner of Church Street and Vicar Lane, the Yorkshire Bank on Fargate and the School Board offices on Leopold Street, all built between 1880 and 1910.

In other ways the new city centre was a very different place to modern-day Sheffield. St Paul's church stood on the site of the current Peace Gardens on Pinstone Street, before being demolished in 1938. The City Hall on Barkers Pool and Graves Art Gallery on Surrey Street were still many years in the future, but in the early years of the twentieth century major changes were taking place that would make the city more recognisable to the modern citizen. Slums in the Crofts area near to West Bar were cleared and improved housing provided, such as early corporation-built flats (1903) in the triangle bordered by Hawley Street and Townhead Street and the imposing 1912 Common Lodging House towering over the current West Bar roundabout. The same period also saw the construction of the city corporation's first council houses on Hands Road, Walkley, and the first extensive out-of-town housing development, the Flower Estate at High Wincobank, comprising 617 dwellings, both begun in 1903. The new tram routes were also providing impetus for house building and extension of the suburbs. In 1899 the *Sheffield Daily Telegraph* observed: 'Cottage houses are rising like exhalations all around; the trams are proving the great building agent, and what were not so long ago wind-swept fields are now beehive colonies. In Crookes, houses are arising as though by a magician's wand.' The previous year Alderman G. Franklin had written about the criteria the city planners considered when discussing new housing developments in Sheffield: 'When they looked at the difficulties which beset corporations dealing with crowded and unhealthy areas, such as existed in Sheffield, they would see the ultimate connection there was between an adequate, efficient and cheap tramway service, and the question of the housing of the working classes.' In a short period from the early 1890s the former rural communities of Meersbrook, Millhouses, Sharrow, Fulwood, Walkley, Crookes, Firvale, Tinsley, Catcliffe, Darnall and Intake became engulfed by the fast-expanding city. These new suburbs were followed in 1901 by the incorporation into the city of the Hillsborough and Norton parishes. By 1911 plans were in place to develop the Bannerdale, Abbey Lane, Ecclesall, Wadsley and Rivelin Valley districts. Housing reform gained more widespread support in Sheffield than in almost any other comparable city: in 1912 three of the nineteen planning schemes proposed in the whole of England and Wales were in Sheffield. The same year the British town planning expert Professor Patrick Abercrombie wrote: 'The Sheffield of to-day is doing fine work and in many ways is taking the lead of big manufacturing cities in the application of Town Planning principles.' This era of great construction also produced a number of new churches, suburban libraries and numerous characteristically stone-built Sheffield Board schools that still punctuate the city's suburbs, at Meersbrook, Heeley, Carterknowle, Attercliffe, Netherthorpe, Pye Bank, Carbrook, Manor Lodge, Lowfield, Firs Hill, Low Wincobank, Owler Lane, Hillsborough, Hunter's Bar, Walkley, Bole Hill and elsewhere. There was therefore a significant increase in the number of children receiving full-time education, from 61,122 in 1892 to 83,589 in 1914.

Alongside new housing and schools came the requirement for a reliable supply of clean drinking water, which was central to an improvement in health and sanitation. To this end, construction of the Howden and Derwent reservoirs in the Derbyshire Peak District commenced in 1901 and 1902 respectively, to provide water for Sheffield and the cities of the East Midlands. The Nether Hallam Health Association was founded in 1899 (renamed the Sheffield Health Association in 1904), with one of its major aims being the abolition of 'privy middens',[4] which were recognised as the single most common source of disease and infection. 'In probably no other large City in the country is the condition of the privies so prejudicial to health as they are in Sheffield,' wrote the city's Medical Officer in 1898. The installation of water closets in houses had begun in 1892 and was speeded up from 1898, so that by 1914 some 11,000 privy middens had been removed. Furthermore, by March 1914 105,800 of Sheffield's 107,300 houses had piped water. Despite such actions, only 18,400 houses had baths, 17,000 Sheffield families still lived in back-to-back houses, another 8,000 in dwellings considered to be unfit for human habitation and 11,000 further privies remained in use.

However, the position regarding health and sanitation had improved considerably over the preceding thirty or so years. Other welfare measures introduced included the monitoring of cows to regulate the supply of uncontaminated milk, the compulsory registration of births, the establishment of better midwifery and maternity care, and the provision of free meals for the neediest children. Another important consideration was a relative reduction in the consumption of alcoholic beverages as the number of public houses in Sheffield fell from 55.4 per 10,000 inhabitants in 1893 to 35.4 per 10,000 in 1913. As a result of such social change, the city's mortality rate decreased from 20.9 per thousand people in the years 1891-1895 to 15.9 per thousand in the period 1911-1915. This figure was slightly above the national average, but it was still a notable achievement.

As well as more free time, an increasing number of people had plenty of disposable income as wages rose in some

---

[4] A privy midden was a communal pile of human waste, or a dungheap, deposited either directly or by the emptying of chamberpots and other lavatory receptacles.

industries,[5] therefore ways had to be found for them to spend both hours and money. Four new theatres were built in central Sheffield in the late 1880s (only the Lyceum in Tudor Square still stands), then with the advent of moving-film techniques picture houses began to spring up around the city. The first was the Tivoli, on the corner of Union Street and Norfolk Street in the city centre, opened in 1905, followed in the next few years by, amongst others, the Cinema House, Barkers Pool, the Palace, Union Street, the People's Electric Palace, Shalesmoor and the Don Cinema, West Bar. Outside the centre, picture palaces were built at Landsdowne, Walkley, Park, Langsett Road, Wincobank, Woodseats, Tinsley, Brightside and in many other districts. The People's Theatre on Staniforth Road, Darnall, commenced showing movies in 1906 and impressed its customers in 1913 when it was amongst the few in the city to show films using the 'Kinemacolor' process, which involved the use of black and white film projected behind synchronised alternating red and cyan filters to produce colour images.

Connoisseurs of screen and stage were well catered for, but for those desirous of a healthier lifestyle away from the city's notorious air pollution, comparatively fresh oxygen could be breathed in various parks and gardens. The Botanical Gardens on Clarkehouse Road had been open since 1836, but until 1898 were available to subscribers only, except for four gala days per year. From 1873 poorer folk could use Weston Park, the first municipal park in the city, with the Mappin Art Gallery within its grounds, and from 1875 the thirty-five acre Firth Park to the north, on land formerly part of the Page Hall

---

[5] Wages in Sheffield increased from the 1880s but fell during a dip in the economy in 1893, before then reaching a peak in 1899. They declined during another economic downturn from 1902 to 1905, then remained steady until another recession in 1908-1909. They then climbed again, only reaching the 1899 level in 1913. In the same period overall manufacturing output rose more than did wages.

estate and donated to the city by steel magnate and philanthropist Mark Firth. The forty-three acre Meersbrook Park was opened in 1885; five years later art critic and social thinker John Ruskin housed his collection of art, minerals, prints, manuscripts and books in Meersbrook House within the boundary of the park. Also in 1885 Endcliffe Park was developed to provide a linear passage along the Porter valley from close to the city centre directly to the Derbyshire moors. High Hazels Park at Darnall, Hillsborough Park, Millhouses Park and Norfolk Park followed between 1894 and 1912 on land purchased from or donated by private owners. Several of the parks sported bandstands, around which local people would congregate on public holidays, such as Whitsuntide, to picnic, play and listen to brass band music.

If a Sheffield citizen's preference was for water-based relaxation rather than the open air, male swimming and bathing enthusiasts had enjoyed the use of Glossop Road Baths since 1832, before a ladies' pool was added when the site was purchased by the city in 1895. Glossop Road also housed Turkish Baths, which were available elsewhere in the city centre at public bathhouses on Norfolk Street and Arundel Street. Similar facilities were provided at Attercliffe Baths on Leeds Road in 1879, Upperthorpe Baths on Daniel Hill in 1895, Park Baths on City Road in 1902 and Heeley Baths on Broadfield Road in 1909. The number of bathers making use of these amenities rose from 267,000 in 1899 to 709,000 in 1914. The public of Sheffield had never been cleaner.

The 1880s, 1890s and 1900s were also a time of increasing interest in golf. There were only twelve golf courses in the whole of England in 1880, but by 1887 there were fifty. The figure rose to over one thousand by 1914. Three of the earliest golf courses in the Sheffield area were on the very edge of the city and north Derbyshire. Hallowes Golf Club (formerly Dronfield Golf Club) was instituted in 1893, closely followed by the Abbeydale and Hallamshire clubs. The Abbeydale course was designed by the well-known golf course architect Herbert Fowler[6] in the mid 1890s, and in 1896 the Hallamshire Club negotiated with the land-owner Duke of Norfolk's agent and tenant farmers to secure one hundred acres at Sandygate on which to lay out a course. Hallamshire was considered fine enough to stage the Yorkshire championships in 1908. Lees Hall Golf Club at Norton opened as a nine-hole course in 1907 and was extended to eighteen holes four years later. The Dore and Totley Club at Bradway followed in 1913 as the better-off folk of Sheffield enthusiastically took up the game. Golf would also soon be available to the poorer classes, as in 1914 Sheffield corporation acquired land at Tinsley, on which it was intended to construct a fifteen-hole municipal course. War delayed its opening until 1920.

Other sports were taking off by the early twentieth century: tennis, athletics, rugby, cycling, hockey, (lawn) bowls, fishing and walking, with clubs, leagues and societies being formed by working-class and middle-class people on a regular basis. For example, the national Cyclists' Touring Club was founded in 1878 to protect and promote the rights of cyclists, whilst Sheffield's first cycling tournament was held at Bramall Lane in 1888. One of the earliest cycling clubs in the city came about when a group of church boys from the Neepsend and Pitsmoor areas formed the Rutland Hall Cycling Club in 1908. Sheffield Phoenix Cycling Club and Sharrow Cycling Club also came into existence during this period. Bramall Lane was an important multi-sports venue - in 1885 it staged a tournament for the relatively new sport of lawn tennis. It was the affluent western districts of Sheffield that gave birth to lawn tennis clubs, such as the oldest in the city, Rustlings

---

6 A former cricketer and golfer, Fowler designed many golf courses in Britain and the USA. His most famous works are probably Walton Heath in Surrey and the eighteenth hole at Pebble Beach, California.

Lawn Tennis Club, founded in 1883, Brentwood Tennis Club, formed in 1908, and Fulwood Bowling and Tennis Club, incorporated as a limited company in 1910.

A small number of bowling clubs existed in Sheffield before 1900 (Hallamshire, Nether Edge, Meersbrook), but during the years 1906 to 1914 at least ten more were founded. For those who preferred less sedate activities, Sheffield in the 1880s was viewed as the English capital of 'pedestrianism', or professional running. Local sports entrepreneur Tom Bott, later to become a director of Sheffield United FC, put up the money to bring the now-famous Arthur Wharton to the city from the north east. Already an amateur sprint star (he held the 100 yards world record), accomplished goalkeeper (who went on to play, briefly, for Sheffield United) and cricketer, Wharton competed in handicap races around South Yorkshire for money, which was also the prime interest of the sport for spectators – betting on the outcome was far more important to them than the spectacle of the race. Soon, money proved to be the cause of division in the ranks of rugby players. The fluctuating rules of Rugby Union had reached some level of uniformity by the 1880s but the sport was split asunder in 1895 when accusations of professionalism at some northern clubs led to the formation of the Northern Rugby Football Union (Rugby League). Rugby Union had a foothold in Sheffield but Rugby League did not take root in the city. All the clubs that made up the new union were from West Yorkshire, East Yorkshire and Lancashire.

For the sports-loving people of Sheffield, the already established games of football and cricket held sway. Cricket had been played since the 1700s and was the original reason for the construction of a sports ground on Bramall Lane in 1854. Football came a few years later and was an immediate hit in Sheffield. For the football enthusiast there was, of course, Bramall Lane (Sheffield United) and Olive Grove, and later Hillsborough (Wednesday), for the professional game. Wednesday became a professional club in 1887 and joined the First Division of the Football League in 1892. Sheffield United, professional from the outset, became original members of the Second Division of the Football League, also in 1892. Football fans were spoilt for choice. As well as the two major clubs there were countless smaller teams to watch, including pioneer clubs Sheffield FC and Hallam FC, still going strong today. In his book *Football In Sheffield*, Percy Young listed the clubs that were members of the Sheffield Football Association in 1877:

Albion
Artillery and Hallamshire Rifles
Attercliffe
Brightside
Brincliffe
Broomhall
Crookes
Exchange
Exchange Brewery
Fir Vale
Gleadless
Hallam
Heeley
Kimberworth
Millhouses
Norfolk
Norfolk Works
Owlerton
Oxford
Parkwood Springs
Philadelphia
Rotherham

Sheffield
Surrey
Thursday Wanderers
Wednesday

The following year they were joined by Phoenix Bessemer, Ecclesfield Church, Burton Star, Dronfield Free Churches and Ebenezer. The rival Hallamshire Football Association included amongst its members Ecclesfield, Lockwood Brothers and Collegiate. Several years later, when it was decided to divide the Sheffield and Hallamshire Association Cup into 'Senior' and 'Minor' competitions, sixteen clubs were nominated for the former and sixty-six entered the latter. Football followers in Sheffield certainly had plenty of options when it came to watching a game in the city. Indeed, sports enthusiasts could revel in the pursuits available to them. They had never had it so good, providing they did not want to gamble or wield a gun. When Sheffield United purchased the Bramall Lane site from owner the Duke of Norfolk in 1899, the objectives of the new company formed to run the club and ground included the following statement of intent:

> *To promote the practice and play of cricket, football, lacrosse, lawn tennis, racquets, bowls, bicycle and tricycle riding, running, jumping, the physical training and developments of the human frame, and other athletic sports, games, and exercises of every description, dancing, concerts, theatrical and other entertainments, exhibitions; printers and publishers; and any other games but not including pigeon shooting or rabbit coursing, nor any race running for money.*

Social historian Eric Hobsbawm wrote that sport was 'one of the most significant of the new social practices' of the late nineteenth century. He opined that the period marked a decisive transformation in the spread of old and the invention of new. The codification of numerous sports gave them a public showcase and provided a means for extending activities hitherto confined to the aristocracy and the rich bourgeoisie. Importantly, sport was a mechanism for bringing together people of a similar social status, who otherwise lacked any such common or economic links (except for perhaps the public house), and provided a new role for women. Tennis and golf were slightly different to other sports in that they were not based on team effort and the clubs owned and looked after large pieces of real estate in expensive parts of towns and cities. They therefore attracted the upper and middle classes rather than the working classes and acted as social centres as much as sporting establishments, essentially for male businessmen in the case of golf, but for the well-off young of both sexes in the case of tennis. It was sport, therefore, that for the first time gave women a public role outside their previous function as merely wives, daughters and companions of males.

Even though sport was now available for all classes of society to enjoy, class lines remained and were characterised by two criteria: 1) amateurism and professionalism, and 2) in professional sports, the relationship between owner (employer) and player (employee). Amateurism persisted amongst the upper strata, which also provided the owners and sponsors of sporting clubs. The lower classes saw sport as a way out of menial, often dangerous, employment. Professionalism in sport gave them a fresh opportunity to make a living, at least for a short time during their younger days, provided that their health and talent were up to the task. For those whose physical attributes did not measure up there was a distinct shift from the participation in informal sports activities to the watching of (and perhaps betting on) those playing for money. Hobsbawm concluded that 'Class-specific sport among plebians rarely developed consciously as such. Where it did, it was usually by taking over upper-class exercises, pushing out their former practitioners, and then developing a specific set of practices on a new social basis (the football culture).' However, early in its life, the permanence and resolution of this new football culture were to be sorely tested by the events of the second half of 1914.

CHAPTER TWO

NECESSITY KNOWS NO LAW

When, on a Sarajevo street on June 28, 1914, a nineteen-year-old Bosnian Serb named Gavrilo Princip fired two shots from his Browning semi-automatic pistol, it set off a train of events that within a matter of weeks propelled most of the European continent into a state of war.

The targets of Princip's bullets were Franz Ferdinand, Archduke of Austria-Hungary, and his wife, Sophie, the Duchess of Hohenberg. The bullets hit home - both Ferdinand and Sophie were killed as they travelled in their car. The first bullet struck Ferdinand in the throat and as his wife tried to protect him she was hit in the abdomen by the second. Both died almost instantly. The motive for the assassination of the heir to the throne of Austria-Hungary and his wife was one of nationalism and independence. Princip was a member of an organisation known as 'Unity or Death', a group comprising Serbs and Bosnians. More commonly known as 'The Black Hand', the group was formed in 1911 to seek the union of Serb minorities within Austria-Hungary and Turkey with their kinsfolk living in already independent Serbia.

Already during the Archduke's drive through Sarajevo that morning there had been two failed attempts on his life by members of the dissident group, both involving hand-propelled bombs. The first, carried by Muhamed

Mehmedbašić, was not thrown as the conspirator lost his nerve due to the nearby presence of a policeman; the second was thrown a few minutes later by Nedeljko Čabrinović, but he mistimed his attempt and the bomb exploded underneath the car following that of the Archduke, injuring two of its occupants and several spectators. Princip, believing the chance had been missed, was ready to abandon the murderous plan but he was in luck - Ferdinand had given instructions that he wished to divert to the nearby hospital to visit those hurt in the bomb attack. As the driver stopped the car and reversed to change direction, he stalled the engine. Princip made the most of this unexpected opportunity and did the deed. Despite attempting suicide, he was captured along with five co-conspirators, but already the damage had been done.

Why did Archduke Ferdinand choose to visit a city in which he knew his life might be threatened by separatists? Forty years earlier Sarajevo had been not much more than a Turkish fort surrounded by dwellings, inhabited almost entirely by Moslems. Following the 1877-78 Russo-Turkish war, Bosnia-Herzegovina was given as a protectorate to Austria-Hungary as part of the 1878 Congress of Berlin, which reduced the power of the defeated Ottoman Empire. Austria, having won itself this deal by maintaining neutrality in that war, formally annexed the two provinces thirty years later as a result of the Bosnian people having the temerity to ask for an appointment of a European commission to investigate their claims of religious persecution and accusations that the administration conducted itself 'in absolute defiance of modern conceptions of justice'.

In 1914 Sarajevo was described as a city where 'alongside of the Mohammedan quarter are seen modern Germanised streets, beer-halls and cafés, shops full of costly wares, splendid public buildings and a fine railway station'. It boasted Europe's first city-wide electric tram system, commissioned in

1885. Austria-Hungary had brought lawfulness, modernity and prosperity to Bosnia, but not contentment. There was therefore a movement in Bosnia to re-align the country to its neighbour Serbia. Ferdinand vowed to win over the dissenters by a combination of severity and kindness, clamping down on any protest but pressing ahead with plans for modernisation and economic development. Already within the Austro-Hungarian empire were the Germanic and Magyar races and Ferdinand desired that the Southern Slavs of Bosnia-Herzegovina should join them under the Viennese crown. A man of strong convictions and principles, his visit to Sarajevo was designed to placate the Bosnians and promote his campaign for unity within Austria-Hungary. He knew the potential for danger in the city, but believed that if his presence positively promoted his objective it was worth the risk.

Certain that Serbia was behind the plot to murder the Archduke and his wife, Austria-Hungary demanded action, advising Serbia that it should investigate the matter. Serbia declined, asserting that it was no concern of the Serbian government. Austria then despatched a formal letter to Serbia, reminding it to maintain good relations with Austria-Hungary and to respect Austrian jurisdiction in Bosnia-Herzegovina. The letter, which came to be known as 'The July Ultimatum', also contained a number of demands and gave Serbia only two days to respond. The demands included:

- *A declaration condemning the propaganda directed against Austria-Hungary.*
- *The Serbian Government to undertake to suppress any publication that incited hatred and contempt of Austria-Hungary.*
- *All officers and others guilty of propaganda against Austria to be removed from the Serbian army.*

- Judicial proceedings to be taken against accessories to the plot to murder the Archduke.
- The arrest of certain Serbian officials alleged by Austria to be involved in the plot.
- Austrian delegates to supervise proceedings.
- Explanations to be given of unjustifiable utterances of high Serbian officials in Serbia and abroad.
- A prevention of the clandestine shipment of arms and explosives from Serbia to Bosnia.

Germany, apparently attempting to maintain an uneasy peace, issued its own statement: 'Austria drafted her note without consulting Germany, and Germany will do everything possible to localise the strife. Germany will keep her hands off the matter until some other power intervenes, and then Germany will only fulfill her duty as an ally.' However, it seemed that Germany's concern was a smokescreen. According to the *Sheffield Daily Telegraph,* that nation was 'in a war-like mood'. The newspaper's Berlin correspondent wrote: 'I have seen here many crises, but no war-like feeling. To-day there is a real war-like feeling; a belief that war is near, and a perfect readiness, and even relief, at the prospect. Germans as a rule never make patriotic street demonstrations. The law and practice are against that. Yet now, for five days the central thoroughfares, Unter Den Linden, Friedrichstrasse, Leipzigerstrasse, the broad central road through the Tiergarten, have been the scenes of demonstrative war enthusiasm. The enthusiasm of grown, responsible citizens, not of inflammable lads. In cafés and restaurants, German and Austrian national hymns and military songs are played to the verge of tedium.'

Serbia acceded to some of Austria's demands but not enough to satisfy Austria-Hungary and after receiving support from Russia, Serbia mobilised its military forces. Austria-

Hungary responded by breaking off diplomatic relations, followed on July 28 by a declaration of war against Serbia. Events now moved rapidly. Next, under the terms of the 1892 Franco-Russian Alliance, both these countries were obliged to mobilise their armies if any of the Triple Alliance of Germany, Austria-Hungary and Italy had already done so. Russia's call to arms then provoked similar action from Austria's main ally Germany, which declared war on Russia. On August 1 the Reuters news agency sent a cable to major newspaper offices. It read:

10-25PM. REUTERS TEL. GERMANY DECLARE WAR ON RUSSIA. ST PETERSBURG. AUG.1. T GERMAN AMBASSADOR IN T NAME O HIS GOVT HANDED TO T FOREIGN MINISTRY A DECLARATION O WAR AT 7-30 THIS EVENING. REUTER. 10-27

Much of mainland Europe - but not yet Britain - was now at war. Complacent Britain believed that it would never come to all-out conflict and peace would prevail. That mood soon changed and an acceptance of the reality of the situation hit home. Money markets in parts of Europe had already been suspended but to the shock of the British, who considered themselves immune to such volatility, on July 31 the bank rate was increased from four per cent to eight per cent, the next day climbing to ten per cent. In an unprecedented move, a notice was pasted on the door of the London Stock Exchange announcing a suspension of trading and was reported thus in the *Sheffield Daily Telegraph* of August 1, 1914:

The City yesterday had a day of sensations unexampled in living memory. The Stock Exchange, for the first time in its history, has

29

closed its doors, and that for an indefinite period. The bank rate has been doubled, and at the Bank itself, while there has been no rush, there have been extensive withdrawals of gold. The decision of the Stock Exchange Committee, presumably arrived at overnight, was posted about an hour before business for the day commonly begins. The notice created an intense sensation. The doors were besieged. The demeanour of the crowd was grave. These men at the financial heart of Europe had appraised the gravity of the situation.

Having sat in Cabinet session into the early hours of the morning and in an attempt to avert panic, the Government released a statement explaining that the position was not 'at present such as to justify any emergency action in regard to the supply of legal tender currency', adding, 'but in the event of further developments taking place necessitating Government action, the Treasury will be prepared to take such action immediately.' Now the British public had to take notice of a crisis that until then had caused them to enquire, 'What has Serbia to do with us?' Concerns over a shortage of money, food and other commodities were exacerbated when it was reported that three British steamers, a Norwegian steamer and several French and Danish ships loaded with barley intended for British markets were unable to sail from San Francisco because in the current financial and political predicament it was impossible for Lloyd's of London to arrange for their insurance.

Sir Edward Grey, the Secretary of State for Foreign Affairs, wrote to the French ambassador to Britain, informing him that Britain would offer its protection should Germany's navy move on the northern coast of France. Grey read his letter in Parliament:

I am authorised to give an assurance that if the German Fleet comes into the Channel or through the North Sea to undertake hostile operations against the French coasts or shipping, the British Fleet will give all the protection in its power.

Believing that the French Government was preparing an attack on German territory, Germany then declared war on France. German troops rode and marched into the Grand Duchy of Luxembourg and eastern France, with twenty thousand men said to have crossed the French border near Nancy. Belgium was next, after the German Chancellor Theobald von Bethmann-Hollweg told the British Ambassador in Berlin, Sir Edward Goschen, that he wished to send his army into France through Belgium, asking for Britain to remain neutral if such manoeuvres took place. However, the 1839 Treaty of London, which recognised Belgian sovereignty and neutrality, and signed by Britain, France and Germany, decreed that any violation of the country would result in Britain coming to its defence. The French Government had earlier made it clear that it would abide by the terms of the Treaty but when Britain put the question to Germany of maintaining Belgium's neutrality, the reply took the form of a delaying tactic: 'The [German] Secretary of State for Foreign Affairs could not possibly give an answer before consulting the Emperor and the Imperial Chancellor.' Unperturbed, Germany informed Belgium that it would treat it as an enemy if free passage of German troops across its territory was denied. The German invasion began on August 4 at Gemmenich, just across the border from the western German town of Aachen. At midnight that night, Britain declared war on Germany. Bethmann-Hollweg was reported to be unhappy that Britain had gone to war over 'a mere scrap of paper' (the 1839 treaty), but the fact was that it was now a pan-European war. In the Reichstag Bethmann-Hollweg tried to justify his country's actions, informing his fellow politicians that he feared France would have acted first had Germany not done so:

Gentlemen, we are now in a state of necessity, and necessity knows no law! Our troops have occupied Luxembourg, and perhaps are already on Belgian soil. Gentlemen, that is contrary to the dictates of international law. It is true that the French Government has declared that France is willing to respect the neutrality of Belgium so long as her opponent respects it. We know, however, that France stood ready for invasion. France could wait, but we could not wait. A French movement upon the lower Rhine might have been disastrous. So we were compelled to override the just protest of the Luxembourg and Belgian Governments. The wrong – I speak openly – that we are committing we will endeavour to make good as soon as our military goal has been reached. Anybody who is threatened, as we are threatened, and is fighting for his highest possessions can have only one thought – how he is to hack his way through.

In Britain, the Government made a proclamation to its public, stating the reason for the fateful move it had now made in response to Germany's invasion of Belgium:

His Majesty's Government informed the German Government on August 4th, 1914, that unless a satisfactory reply to the request of His Majesty's Government for an assurance that Germany would respect the neutrality of Belgium was received by midnight of that day, His Majesty's Government would feel bound to take all steps in their power to uphold that neutrality, and the observance of a treaty to which Germany was as much a party as Britain. The result of this communication having been that His Majesty's Ambassador in Berlin had to ask for his passports, His Majesty's Government have accordingly notified the German Government that a state of war exists between the two countries as from 11pm to-day.

August 6 saw the first British loss of life when the scout cruiser HMS Amphion struck a mine in the English Channel, having already destroyed the German mine-laying ship Köningen Luise. Some 150 Britons were killed, along with a number of German sailors rescued from the Köningen Luise. Immediately at the outbreak of war, the Prime Minister, H. H. Asquith, appointed Herbert Kitchener, the 1st Earl Kitchener, as Secretary of State for War. Lord Kitchener was a highly decorated Field Marshal in the army who happened to be on leave in England when war was declared. Asquith, who had been filling the position temporarily after the resignation of the previous incumbent, Colonel J. E. B. Seely, earlier in the year, saw Kitchener's military background as ideal for the role, despite his having no political experience. On August 7 Kitchener began a concerted recruitment campaign, in which he called for men between the ages of nineteen and thirty to volunteer for service in the army. The initial uptake was good, with 33,000, on average, joining each day. Towards the end of August Kitchener raised the maximum age of recruitment to thirty-five and by mid September the total number enlisted reached half a million. A month later Kitchener made a plea for more volunteers to replace the dead and injured, at the same time dropping the requirement for volunteers to be a minimum of 5ft 6in in height and to have a minimum chest measurement of thirty-five inches.

The Government also introduced a series of emergency measures. The August Bank Holiday, then held on the first Monday of August, was extended to Thursday, giving the banks and financial institutions time to adjust to the critical circumstances that had forced the suspension of the Stock Exchange. Honest debts were not to be chased, one pound and ten shilling notes were issued and the bank rate was cut to six, then five, per cent. The price of some foodstuffs had doubled almost overnight, so the Government guaranteed to underwrite the insurance of merchant ships, which initiated a degree of confidence in ship owners and traders, enabling supplies to begin to move again. It cost the Government a lot of money – British merchant ships were frequent victims of German U-boats throughout the succeeding months. The Government also took control of the railway system for, it said, the purposes of 'securing the public safety and defence of the Realm'. It was to be, as far as possible, 'business as usual'.

Despite such decisions taken to try to dispel anxiety and preserve the normal way of life during the conflict, the British people were going to have to quickly get accustomed to a state of abnormality. No one knew for how long that state would last.

CHAPTER THREE

A SPLENDID BODY OF ATHLETES

One of the fundamentals of a 'normal' society is that its people must have liberty to enjoy the participation in and the spectating of recreational and sporting activities. As the events of July and early August 1914 unfolded throughout the rest of Europe, the British characteristically carried on with their games and pastimes unmolested and unconcerned. The two great British summer sports of cricket and horse racing traditionally took centre stage, with tennis and golf also highly popular. There was no cricket Test series that year, but the County Championship was, as usual, keenly fought amongst the great counties of the north and south, and other high-profile matches, such as the Gentlemen v Players and the Varsity fixtures took place as scheduled in July. In racing, Durbar won the Epsom Derby in early June, whilst major and minor meetings continued throughout the country. Jersey-born Harry Vardon triumphed in the Open Championship at Prestwick Golf Club, taking home the grand sum of £50 in prize money. The Wimbledon Singles Championships were taken by Norman Brookes of Australia and Britain's Dorothea Douglass Lambert Chambers.

There was also much attention directed to the sport of boxing. Jack Johnson, the first black man to hold the undisputed world heavyweight title, had reigned for almost six years. Numerous 'Great White Hopes' came and went as the world looked to knock the arrogant upstart Johnson off his perch. One fight pitting together two possible candidates to do just that took place on July 16, 1914 at London's Olympia. The contenders were America's Ed 'Gunboat' Smith and Frenchman Georges Carpentier, matched together in a contest for what was termed the 'White Heavyweight Championship of the World'. Like today, boxing had its advocates and opponents, and three years earlier a High Court injunction, instigated by both moral and racial arguments, prevented a fight between Johnson and the British champion 'Bombardier' Billy Wells taking place at the Empress Theatre in London. The excuse was that the match might cause a breach of the peace. Now, however, a bout between two foreign white men was sanctioned. One writer, in previewing the fight, scoffed at the illogicality of it all: 'In this case the Home Office is not at all perturbed, which, if illogical, is true. Two whites may batter each other, but the risk must not be taken of a black battering a white. Which is not logic.' As it turned out, Carpentier was victorious, but other, more pressing, matters prevented him from challenging Johnson or anyone else for a while. At the outset of the war he joined the French aviation service and was later awarded two of the highest French military honours, the *Croix de Guerre* and the *Médaille Militaire*.

Meanwhile, the football season was approaching. With nothing so fulfilling as the winter game to occupy their summers, football followers eagerly awaited the latest instalment of what was still a young sport. It is difficult to comprehend today that in 1914 the Football League was less than thirty years old. Many people could easily remember the 1889 birth of Sheffield United Football Club; that sort of memory could be compared to today recalling what happened in the mid-1980s. In late July the *Sheffield Daily Telegraph* began to tap in to this rising excitement by advertising its own 'Football Guide':

THIS IS IT!

*THE REAL GUIDE IS THE 'SHEFFIELD
TELEGRAPH' FOOTBALL GUIDE WHICH
GIVES ALL THE LATEST AND COMPLETE
LIST OF TRANSFERS*

WAIT FOR IT - READY SHORTLY

----

*NEW FEATURES AND SPECIAL NOTES ON
ALL THE NEW PLAYERS*

ORDER IT AT ONCE - ENORMOUS DEMAND

READY SHORTLY

Early August saw its publication, and, according to its boastful publisher, the one-penny guide was 'filled with most interesting reading, for, unlike other guides, it is not a mere dish-up of tables and records'. Several pages were devoted to a full summary of the season's prospects, changes of rules, and player transfers made in both the Football League and the Midland League. It included around two hundred biographies of players joining new clubs and it was reported that the guide was sure to prove invaluable 'to all interested in the great pastime'.

However, would those interested in the great pastime be given the opportunity to put the *Telegraph's* vaunted booklet to any useful purpose? There was already talk that following the declaration of war, all unnecessary recreational pursuits should be cancelled forthwith. The argument in support of immediate abandonment was twofold: first, how could young men contemplate the idea of playing or watching frivolous sporting activities when thousands of their contemporaries were simultaneously being shipped to France and Belgium, many to meet a grisly fate? Second, if young men were watching and playing games, they would be less conducive to the idea of volunteering for military service.

Cricket and racing, both in the middle of their seasons, were amongst the first to feel the wrath of the objectors. During Yorkshire's County Championship game against Warwickshire at Edgbaston that began on August 6, the home club's committee met to discuss the continuance of the county programme. They decided to go on, unless British forces were to 'sustain material reverses', though how 'material reverses' were to be defined was not clarified. In addition, and probably more pertinently, the attendance at the first day's play was 'sufficiently indicative that at present people are still willing to patronise good cricket'. So long as the gate money flowed, cricket would continue. As the Warwickshire CCC decision-makers sat in session, the politicians of Austria-Hungary and Serbia did likewise. Their deliberations also resulted in a prolonging of the action: Austria-Hungary declared war on Russia; Serbia declared war on Germany.

The all-important Marylebone Cricket Club (MCC), the keepers of the laws and spirit of the game, concurred with their Warwickshire counterparts, the same day issuing a statement:

> *The Secretary of the Marylebone Cricket Club feels that no good purpose can be served at the present moment by cancelling matches unless the services of those engaged in cricket who have no military training can in any way be utilised in their country's service. If it can be shown in what way their services can be used the MCC would close their ground. Many 'out' matches have*

already been abandoned. Cricketers in England
would be sure to respond to any definite call.
(signed) F. E. Lacey, Secretary, MCC

In other words, the MCC was abdicating responsibility and would leave it to some higher authority – the Government – to make the decision regarding the complete abandonment or otherwise of sport as a whole. Some cricket matches on the southern coast had been called off, presumably for the sake of safety in case any naval battles were to take place in close proximity to the grounds. Additionally, clubs that fielded a lot of amateur players found themselves too depleted to play, as the amateurs tended to be amongst the first to volunteer for service. Matches involving the minor counties Devon and Dorset had succumbed for this reason.

Some could not contain their anger that cricket was still being played. 'Five Yorkshiremen of Keighley' wired a message to Tom Forrester, the Derbyshire captain, as they played Hampshire at Chesterfield. It read: 'Owing to extreme state of affairs we are surprised that you continue to play cricket.' Forrester did not respond. Why the 'five Yorkshiremen' did not cable their own county captain, Sir Archibald Woolaston White, 4th Bart, was not known. Perhaps it was because his name and title were too imposing, or too expensive to include in full in a telegram. The great former cricketer W. G. Grace added his voice to the debate, arguing for an immediate stop to the cricket season, even though there were only a few weeks to go. 'There are many cricketers who are already doing their duty, but there are many more who do not seem to realise that in all probability they will have to serve either at home or abroad before the war is brought to a conclusion. I think the time has arrived when the county cricket season should be closed, for it is not fitting at a time like the present that able-bodied men should play day after a day and pleasure-seekers look on,' stated Grace.

Despite such dissent from the famous and the ordinary man, a few days later it was announced that the annual Scarborough Cricket Festival would be held as normal - more or less. Half the profits - assuming any were made - would go to the Prince of Wales's War Relief Fund,[7] the other half being distributed at the discretion of the Mayor of Scarborough. All players - amateurs and professionals - invited to the festival agreed to make financial contributions to the fund. But the festival was not certain to pay its way and local boarding houses and hotels were not expected to do as well as usual as people were less inclined to travel. The prospects were worse still after the MCC withdrew from sending teams for two matches they had previously promised to fulfill, declaring that 'the continuance of first-class cricket is hurtful to the feelings of a section of the public'. Only the Gentlemen v Players fixture remained from the original programme, but eventually the MCC relented and two further games were played: Yorkshire v MCC and Lord Londesborough's XI v Marylebone Cricket Club South African Touring Team.

If the interest in the Scarborough Festival was not likely to reach its normal levels, at least interest in cricket generally was recovering. Certain newspapers, accused by others of 'war panic', had cut all references to the matches being played as soon as war was declared. Now cricket had recovered some of its lost column inches. Even the great cricketer Pelham 'Plum' Warner had changed his view: he took his place on the field for Middlesex's game at Lord's only days after calling for his

---

[7] At the start of the war, H.R.H. the Prince of Wales (who in 1936 became King Edward VIII) put his name to a fund (full title the Prince of Wales's National War Relief Fund) to be used to provide aid to people suffering financial distress as a result of hostilities, for example the families of soldiers killed in action. Its Executive Committee comprised several MPs, the Duke of Devonshire and other dignitaries.

county's match against Yorkshire at Bramall Lane to be called off. However, the County Championship was thrown into confusion when leaders Surrey elected to cancel their final two matches, away to Sussex and at home to Leicestershire. They had already been forced to move their penultimate home game from the Oval, which was under military occupation, to Lord's, north of the Thames. One newspaper announced that Surrey had won the title, based on average points per game (it was common at the time for each county to not play the same number of games), but another declared that they had forfeited it by failing to complete their fixtures. The MCC rule in force did not actually state that the club that finished at the head of the table would win the title. Instead, the rule read: 'After the close of each cricket season, the committee of the MCC shall decide the County Championship.' Of course it always ruled in favour of the team that finished top, but would Surrey's forfeiture cause the MCC to decide against them? Had Surrey lost the two games, their percentage of total possible points would have slipped a fraction below that of Middlesex, who had finished their matches (playing only twenty, whereas Surrey played twenty-six), but on the other hand they had to take just two points from the ten available (five points were awarded for a win, three points for holding a first innings lead in a drawn match and one point for a first innings deficit in a draw) to top Middlesex's percentage. It was commonly accepted that Surrey were the best team in the country and deserved the championship, which was in due course awarded to them.

In contrast to those who still saw sport as inappropriate in a country at war, there were many who believed it vital in order to maintain the morale of the population. If it could relieve tension, dispel anxiety and divert attention - if only for a few hours - away from the horrors of France and Belgium, it would be well worthwhile. 'Sport must go on because it is a national necessity,' was one journalist's opinion. Another wrote that sport would give 'everyone better spirits to face the inevitable defeats which are sure to come along prior to the ultimate triumph of our arms'. Supporters of the continuation of sport pointed to it as being a useful antidote to the stresses of war and a palliative for all the sadness. The first football authority to be faced with making a decision on whether or not to proceed was the Scottish League, whose junior clubs' programmes were due to start imminently, with the major clubs following on August 15. The League decided to go ahead, a decision that would certainly influence the governing bodies south of the border. *The Times*, in remarking that the continuation of professional football was the 'only subject of controversy' in Scotland, reported that over 200,000 spectators attended football matches on the first League Saturday in the country, adding: 'It certainly does seem strange that at a time like this huge crowds of able-bodied men should go, as a local newspaper remarked, "cheering their favourites as if the whole world were at peace".' Thomas Forsyth, the chairman of Airdrieonians FC, was opposed to the season proceeding as usual, arguing that it was incongruous that ten thousand of the finest trained men in Britain were 'playing games' when the country was so in need of volunteers to join the army. His appeal went unheeded. *The Times* report continued:

> *The difficulty, of course, is that professional football is not a sport at all. It is a business just as much as the running of a picture palace or a public house. The public in the great industrial districts [in Scotland] has been repeatedly urged in the last fortnight to go about its business as usual. So professional football goes on, with apparently the sanction of public opinion. Regarding the 10,000 professionals as merely*

*wage-earners, one ought perhaps to fasten the
responsibility on the 200,000 spectators and echo
the comment of a friendly critic: 'What a splendid
army of Scotsmen these would make.'*

Still, it wasn't all bad news: even as football kicked off in
Scotland, in Glasgow alone recruits for the army were signing
up at a rate of two or three hundred per day.

It was reported elsewhere that there was 'almost unanimous
opinion' amongst the English football authorities that the
season should commence as scheduled on September 1. An
unnamed 'prominent official' pointed out that unless matters
'took a very much worse turn' there would be no justification
for throwing several thousands of professional players out of
work, in the process entirely disrupting the arrangements of
clubs. The official added that football was now akin to a huge
business affair and clubs had entered into contracts with
players and grounds, arrangements that could not be legally
cancelled. For the first time an important official, although
anonymously, had raised the subject of the principal thinking
behind the desire to maintain the football programme –
economics. Morality remained a secondary consideration.

Another argument in favour of the continuation of sport
soon began to gain prominence: it was that such events could
be used to encourage military recruitment amongst the
spectators, and that large crowds would provide the ideal
opportunity for raising money for war relief funds (the main
one being the Prince of Wales's Fund), either by means of
donations or by some method of tariff directly related to gate
receipts. The Football League and the Football Association
were due to make pronouncements shortly: these statements
would decide once and for all the immediate future of football.

Other, smaller, sports were not faring so well. Swimming,
golf, Northern Union Football (Rugby League), Rugby Union,

tennis, hockey, cycling and motor cycling all had their own particular problems to contend with. Complaints had been made by swimming clubs about the haste with which many of their events had been called off, but they hoped that some fixtures could soon be re-arranged. Golfers, who tended to be drawn from the ranks of business and professional men, like the amateur cricketers were amongst the earliest to offer their services on the home front and, if young and fit enough, the fighting front. The Professional Golfers' Association decided to postpone the majority of its remaining tournaments, including the *News of the World* competition. However, the annual England v Scotland fixture would go ahead, providing that sponsors *County Life* and hosts the Mid-Surrey Golf Club consented. An admission charge was to be made, all proceeds going to the Prince of Wales's Fund. The P.G.A. had already made a donation of ten guineas to the fund. If golf courses were to be used infrequently or not at all, they were the ideal locations for rifle ranges, said one letter writer to the *Sheffield Daily Telegraph*, an idea duly taken up by Abbeydale Golf Club in the Sheffield suburb of Beauchief:

> *Sir, There are at the present time some thousands of golf clubs scattered over the British Islands, many of them being within easy access of large towns. Why should not the suitable ones be provided with rifle ranges which could be open to all men over the recruiting age where the use of rifles and the rudiments of drill could be acquired under the direction of military experts? If rifles are unobtainable for the moment, owing to the War Office demand, there is nothing to prevent a commencement being made by the setting up of ranges and by preliminary drill. By this means a large force of able-bodied men – married and*

single – probably a quarter of a million, could be
preparing themselves to play their part in the
defence of the country, should the situation arise.
Yours faithfully, A. GOLFER

The officials of the newly formed Sheffield Northern Union Rugby Club were especially unfortunate in their admirable attempts to establish the game outside its traditional hotbeds of West Yorkshire and Lancashire. For them, the war could not have come at a worse time, but they felt that postponing fixtures would serve no useful purpose, arguing that staging matches would 'help to distract the participants' and spectators' minds for a short time from the national anxiety and strain'. Their first public practice match was to take place at the Ball Inn ground at Heeley, which, in later years, would become Sheffield United's training ground. Like at other sporting clubs, the receipts were to go to the War Fund. A few weeks later, however, the club decided to disband, having been forced to cancel a game at Rochdale. The *Sheffield Daily Telegraph* bemoaned the unfortunate timing of the noble efforts of the club but, somewhat harshly, declared that 'the Cutlery capital is not yet ripe for the professional handling code of second-rate character'. Ownership of the club's players was to be taken over by the Northern Union, which would give any profits from their sale to other clubs to discharge Sheffield's liabilities, believed to be some £50.

It was noticeable that the amateur sports were the ones most willing to abandon fixtures and encourage recruitment to the services. The Amateur Football Association called off its programme, whilst the Rugby Football Union decided to cancel all international and County Championship matches, asking clubs to do likewise and transfer fixtures to the 1915/16 season, assuming, of course, that hostilities had ceased by then. The Rugby Union also issued a statement urging its players to volunteer for the forces, using the international players as an example:

> *Nearly every [rugby] football player is physically fit, and between the ages of nineteen and thirty-five, and all should, therefore, enlist. If, owing to special circumstances, some cannot enlist for services at the front, they can and should join some military organisation for home defence. It is added that all the members of last season's England Rugby team are attached to some naval or military forces, and the Rugby Union are approaching the War Office to ascertain if it would be feasible to form a corps of footballers to serve together. Rugby Union men desirous of joining such a corps are invited to communicate with the Rugby Union secretary, Twickenham.*

Meanwhile, over two hundred members of Sheffield and District lawn tennis clubs met at the Grand Hotel in the centre of Sheffield. The meeting was held to devise the most appropriate methods by which the clubs could assist the war effort and an appeal was made to each club to 'contribute to the last possible farthing' to the Prince of Wales's Fund. Not only that, tennis players were encouraged to put themselves forward for drill and shooting practice, that is if they were unable due to age, time or 'other good reason' (whatever that meant) to volunteer for active service, and despite the fact that the War Office was discouraging the setting up such *ad hoc* quasi-military bodies. The meeting unanimously carried the following resolution:

> *That this meeting considers it necessary that members of all clubs eligible to join the Army, but*

who are absolutely prevented by business
reasons, or by age, or any other ascertained good
reason, should be instructed in rifle shooting and
infantry drill, and that to effect this a committee
of this meeting be appointed to confer with other
athletic bodies in the city, and that a further
meeting of lawn tennis members be called to
receive a report of the committee.

Hockey was in a parlous state. Only five out of twenty Derbyshire Association clubs attending a meeting in Derby were able to fulfil their calendar. With such a small number of clubs able to play, it was agreed to cancel all scheduled fixtures and arrange games as and when possible. Like the tennis players, hockey club members were encouraged to familiarise themselves with the use of the rifle. The Derbyshire players' Sheffield counterparts were in a similar position, with numerous clubs out of action due to the unavailability of players. Many had given up the hockey stick for the rifle. The Atlas and Norfolk Works club had lost nine men and the Todwick club seven. Hockey clubs had large ladies' sections, which, of course, did not lose members to the service but the Creswell Ladies' Club stood firm with its menfolk. Both sections cancelled their fixtures. The Ladies' secretary explained why: 'So many [male] members have joined the army, while we hardly consider it "the thing" to continue when people are fighting for us.'

However, the Sheffield Pupil Teacher Centre Girls' Hockey Club, based in the centre of the city, was planning for 'business as usual,' said its Principal Mr A. J. Arnold. So was the Millhouses Ladies' Club, whose secretary stated: 'We expect to play all our matches in due course.' But there was bad news from Doncaster as the Woodlands Hockey Club asked to be put in touch with any Sheffield and District clubs they might be able to play, as so many in Doncaster had disbanded. For the benefit of all, the *Sheffield Daily Telegraph* listed all the local clubs that intended to fulfil their fixtures. They were: Sheffield Pupil Teachers' (Girls) Hockey Club, Millhouses Ladies, Woodhouse Secondary School, Firth Park Ladies, Leopold Ladies, Swinton Ladies, Wath Ladies, Ecclesfield Ladies, Sheffield Training College and Doncaster Woodlands (gents). Those temporarily disbanded were: Sheffield Atlas and Norfolk Works, Firth Park, Bolsover, Westbourne (Sheffield), Creswell (gents and ladies) and Todwick.

Equally as patriotic as the golfers, tennis players and hockey players were the cyclists. They were willing to forego their usual riding pleasures, instead wishing to offer their services to the Government in the form of a corps of riders. What exactly this corps would do by their own admission had not been thought out, but they were sure that whatever it was would be for the good of the country. The Sheffield and District Committee of the Cyclists' Touring Club suggested that the volunteers form a 'Cyclist-Constable' corps, which would ride within an eighteen-to-twenty mile radius of each designated centre, patrolling roads to relieve more important (but unspecified) men from such cumbersome (but again unspecified) work. Did they intend to seek out burglars, thieves and vagabonds, or German spies? Perhaps it shall never be known. Cyclists whose machines were propelled by means other than leg power faced altogether different challenges. Important to the successful operation of motor cycles were devices called magnetos, which generated electricity. Most magnetos in the early twentieth century just happened to be manufactured in Germany. How would enthusiasts procure new or replacement magnetos? They were advised to patronise English makers of these instruments, who would no doubt be smart enough to take advantage of the new opportunities provided. Petrol might also prove a problem, so big motor cycling events had already been cancelled, but the Sheffield and Hallamshire club intended to continue its weekend rides into the Peak District.

Now the more prominent sport of horse racing re-entered the picture. From August 7 meetings throughout the country were being cancelled - Kempton Park, Windsor and Stockton amongst the first - largely due to the uncertainty of rail travel and the availability of police. Perhaps some race horse owners, by definition amongst the more wealthy members of society, brought the contentious subject of morality into their thinking as several instructed their trainers to remove their horses from active training or send them to the owners' private studs. Consequently, many stable hands had lost their jobs. There was the added problem that Government agents were visiting trainers' yards selecting horses for use in the war. Reportedly, the agents commandeered a number of thoroughbreds, hunters and working horses from the Newmarket stables. Unlike humans, the poor beasts did not have an option when it came to volunteering for active service. Millions were to meet their deaths, forcing Britain to import as many mules from the Americas.

Despite the requisitioning of horses and the loss of grooms, the racing authorities pressed to get the already scheduled meetings back on the calendar. The directors of the Gatwick Racecourse Company decided to make an effort to hold the meeting of August 28 and 29. They said they had overcome the difficulty in providing sufficient policemen, and they hoped to arrange for the operation of a normal train service. They reminded trainers to send their horses earlier than usual; stabling would be provided for free. Entries for Lewes and Folkestone races were strong, indicating that these meetings would also take place. It was a different story at Doncaster, where the final Classic of the season, the St Leger, was due to be run in early September. The Race Committee was already £2,000 out of pocket as a result of cancellations and estimated that the loss to the town as a whole if the St Leger meeting was abandoned would be at least £13,000, a figure worth almost £1 million today. Besides the St Leger meeting, Doncaster racecourse made its money from the yearling sales, which attracted breeders and buyers from all over the world. However, due to the uncertainty surrounding the meeting, the well-known auctioneers had made alternative arrangements, so there was little chance of the sales taking place.

The Jockey Club stepped in to offer advice to the various race committees, first asking local stewards to give sufficient notice if they intended to abandon a meeting so that owners did not incur expense by dispatching their horses unnecessarily. However, the Jockey Club at the same time reminded course executives that they should only consider cancellation if it was imperative to do so, as any extended lapse in racing would result in a large number of people being put out of employment as so many depended upon it for their livelihood. Horse racing was an industry, and in the Jockey Club's opinion, the businesses connected with racing were at least as well worth preserving as any of the other industries in the country. Moreover, the horses on which the British army's cavalry was now dependent possessed sufficient strength and stamina to do the job entirely because of the breeding regimes and bloodlines produced by racing and its attendant businesses.

Whether or not it was because of the Jockey Club's advice, within a few days the situation at Doncaster had improved. The local Race Committee had apparently jumped the gun – they now declared that there was a full entry for the yearling sales. The racecourse stands and facilities were not required by the military and the railways were expected to be functioning normally. The Great Central Railway Company had promised to run excursion trains as usual, but the Great Northern Railway Company was unable to give the same assurance. Haydock Park and Yarmouth followed suit by confirming their meetings were on, but the upcoming Hurst Park meeting was called off. Owners sending horses to Haydock were reassured that the railway companies had plenty of horse boxes available. The *Sheffield Daily Telegraph's* racing correspondent 'Fortunatus' was happy at this turn of events, writing: 'The recent unavoidable cancellation of race meetings has already caused incalculable loss and hardship, direct and indirect, to a large section of the community. Since racing affects a vast number of commercial undertakings, it is of great importance that it should proceed without interruption, excepting when and where the paramount consideration of national defence would be interfered with.'

The entry field for the principal races at Gatwick (the County Handicap) and Manchester (the Prince Edward Handicap) were put forward as an example that racing was as popular as ever. At Gatwick, of thirty-one entries only nine had withdrawn, whilst Manchester's field of thirty-two had been reduced by exactly half, but it was pointed out that a long-course handicap race like the Prince Edward at the height of summer on invariably hard ground seldom attracted large fields. When the Haydock and Gatwick meetings were held attendances were surprisingly good, with the various enclosures well patronised. The only notable shortage was that of the colours of certain prominent owners, who were still keeping their horses away.

However, following its resumption racing still had many opponents. In early September the Jockey Club met at Derby House in London and issued the following statement to defend its stance:

The Stewards of the Jockey Club explained why they had thought it advisable to maintain racing where possible in spite of the present grave circumstances, and stated that they wished to ask the club if, in their opinion, racing should continue for the remainder of the season, the immediate question being whether the Newmarket Autumn meetings should be held or not, as the Stewards felt that if Newmarket were abandoned for reasons other than those connected with the public service, a general abandonment would follow. They further stated that they wished to make it clear that they had not encouraged racing for the sake of those who went racing for amusement, but because, having gone carefully into the matter, they were convinced that its cessation would have the immediate effect of throwing out of work a large number of people entirely dependent upon it for their livelihood. They considered that the interests of the nation were best served by such people being retained as far as possible in their usual vocations, as otherwise they might be impelled in the near future to apply for relief to funds which will be urgently needed for cases of unavoidable distress. Lord Coventry and the Duke of Richmond and Gordon having strongly supported the resolution of the Stewards, it was unanimously decided that the fixtures already arranged should be carried out where local conditions permitted, and where the feeling of the locality was not adverse to the meeting being held.

Those who did not wish to go to racing even if it continued would clearly have no need for their field glasses and were therefore asked to donate them to the army. Over two thousand such items were received in the first three days of the appeal and would prove invaluable in the field. Whilst discussions took place about whether or not sport should go on, news came through that two sportsmen had died on the battlefield. They were cricketers Captain Charles Hunter Browning,[8] who played for Eton in 1896 and 1897, and Captain Frank Scobell Nisbet,[9] who kept wicket in one game in the current season for Worcestershire. Many more were to follow. Such information did not prevent other sportsmen, professional and otherwise, from signing up for service. On the conclusion of Yorkshire County Cricket Club's season at Hove, professionals Roy Kilner and Major Booth enlisted together in the West Yorkshire Regiment (Prince of Wales's Own) ('Major' was the player's given name, not a military rank). In fact he became a Second Lieutenant but died on the first day of the Somme offensive at La Cigny on July 1, 1916.[10] Kilner served in Egypt before being sent to the Western Front in France, where he received shrapnel wounds and returned home for treatment in a military hospital. When recovered he worked as a mechanic at the Preston Garrison and took up his cricket career again after the war. It was estimated that by the spring of 1915 seventy-five per cent of all first-class cricketers had joined the services, but one who did not was perhaps the most famous player of the time. Jack Hobbs, who was knighted in

---

[8] Captain C. H. Browning, 36 Royal Field Artillery, died August 26, 1914, Grave Reference III. B. 5., Le Cateau Military Cemetery.

[9] Captain F. S. Nisbet, 36 Manchester Regiment, died August 26, 1914, Memorial Reference La Ferte-Sous-Jouarre Memorial.

[10] Second Lieutenant M. W. Booth, Grave Reference I. G. 14, Serre Road Cemetery No.1.

later life, cited family duties as the reason he did not enlist, but he caused a stir in cricket circles in May 1915 when he signed as professional with Bradford League club Idle (much league cricket continued throughout the war, though first-class cricket was stopped following the end of the 1914 season). Yorkshire CCC president Lord Hawke called Hobbs's decision to play professionally 'scandalous'.

Sportsmen of all abilities were enlisting. Charles Burgess Fry, the famous all-round amateur sportsman who played cricket and football for England and once held the world record for the long jump, was an honorary Lieutenant in the Royal Naval Reserve. W. L. Beattie, the captain of the Wakefield Trinity Northern Union Club, informed his committee that he would not play during the war. It was reported in Sheffield that half of the Blackburn (Wincobank) football team had volunteered, as had the local welterweight boxer Gus Platts.[11] Elsewhere, more formal arrangements for sportsmen to serve were proposed. The presidents of the Football League and the Northern Counties Swimming Association asked that all athletes over the age of thirty-five who were not eligible to serve in the regular army or Territorials form an 'Athletes' Volunteer Force,' intended to enable cricketers, footballers, rowers, athletes, cyclists, golfers, swimmers and other sportsmen to learn drill and rifle shooting together. As part of this scheme, in mid September a gathering of amateur athletes assembled at Stamford Bridge in London and in Manchester to compete in various events with the sole objective of raising money for the relief funds. The 'Athletes' Volunteer Force' idea was now extended to men eligible for enlistment who had not been accepted and to this end an appeal was made for all young Sheffield sportsmen in this category to present themselves for enlistment at a meeting

---

[11] In 1921 Platts became British and European middleweight champion.

at 'The Jungle',[12] at which various speakers were to explain what the duties of the attendees would be.

Various cricket officials wished to set up a 'Cricketers' Corps,' about which Lord Kitchener was said to be enthusiastic, providing a battalion of at least one thousand could be formed. The object of such a corps was to 'enhance the *esprit de corps* and to enable the men with a common bond of interest to serve together'. Each county club was asked to recruit within its locality, after which details of all such volunteers would be sent to the secretary of the MCC and subsequently presented to the War Office. Yorkshire CCC's president Lord Hawke was keen to assist, asking the county's many leagues and clubs to support the movement. A similar appeal to footballers was made by Lord Nunburnholme, Lord Lieutenant of the East Riding of Yorkshire. He advised that Lord Kitchener would authorise the formation of a special 'footballers' battalion' in his area, which would become part of the existing 7th Hull Battalion East Yorkshire Regiment. None of these units ever came to fruition in the suggested manner but within a matter of months both a Footballers' Battalion and a Sportsmen's Battalion were to be formed.

Another sporting subject of discussion was the Olympic Games. Still in their infancy, the importance of the Games in the amateur sporting world was increasing. The next event was still two years away but it was the scheduled host venue that was most significant - Berlin. Even if the war was over by then, how could sufficient peace, trust, faith and forgiveness

---

12 'The Jungle' was the former Alexandra roller skating rink near Hawley Street in the centre of Sheffield, close to where HSBC's Griffin House stands today. In November 1910 entrepreneur Frank C. Bostock took advantage of the space opened up by the early-century slum clearances to use the premises to provide entertainment for the local population. 'The Jungle' was primarily a menagerie of exotic animals, but then became a home for fairground devices and unusual shows and exhibitions. During the war it was used first as a recruiting station and later as a store for scrap iron and steel before it was melted down for use in munitions manufacture.

be found for the Games to be held in Germany? The *Sheffield Daily Telegraph* hoped that it could happen, and indulged in a touch of rhetoric: 'When this terrible fight for liberty and the overthrow of military power and force has been satisfactorily ended there will be a great revival of all the peaceful pursuits and recreations of the nations, and, instead of iron crosses for murderers, there will be real honours for valour and athletic supremacy.' And perhaps the country's current displays of patriotic desire of young men to get physically fit for the war would actually assist Britain's chances in sport, should the Games ever take place. *Field* magazine continued the rhetoric but went even further, belittling Germany's attitude to sport, criticising the comments of its leaders and stating that Germany could never again be trusted in any walk of life:

> *[Germany's] sole idea of physical exercise seems to consist of gymnastic performances and military drill, and anything more deadening than either (when taken by itself) it would be difficult to conceive. Sportsmanship is as alien to the German character as sport is to German authors. We know now that the elaborate friendliness of some of the German representatives on the International Olympic Council was as much a mask as all the rest. One of these gentlemen has since employed his time in a more congenial manner by spreading lies about us in the United States. And it is well that no such international sporting festival as the Olympic Games will ever be held in Berlin as was contemplated for 1916. The 'British Team' is indeed on its way to that city, more heavily financed, and better equipped than was ever thought possible. But it is not going for Olympic medals. We may doubt very much,*

after all that happened this summer, whether Germans will ever get any other nation to meet them in sport for several generations to come, any more than they can expect to be trusted in business matters or to be treated as fair foes on the field of battle.

So, as various sports remained in the public consciousness through their decisions to continue or abandon, football clubs began their preparations for the new season. During Yorkshire's County Championship match against Middlesex at Bramall Lane, Sheffield United's contracted players turned up at the ground for a roll call. They were all present and correct, unlike at some clubs, which had lost players to the army reserve. It was reported that serious training was to be started 'at once', while the players spent the afternoon admiring the batting style of Middlesex's Patsy Hendren, whom some of them knew from his footballing exploits as a professional at Brentford FC. Like Hendren, United's squad made a good impression on observers; they were said to be 'a splendid body of athletes' possessing 'healthy appearances and jovial good humour'. But were they any good at football? That would be seen in a few weeks, war permitting.

CHAPTER FOUR

MISCHIEVOUS RATHER THAN BENEFICIAL

Why is Britain at War?
For three reasons:-
To save her good name.
To save the life of Herself and of Her Empire.
To Save the Freedom of the democracies of Europe.
Fight for your Life.
Fight for your Good Name.
Fight, as Britain has fought before, for Freedom.
Fight for Humanity.

As soon as war was declared notices such as this began appearing in newspapers all over Britain, along with pleas for recruits to the armed forces. One stated: 'Your King and Country need you – A Call to Arms. An addition of 100,000 men to His Majesty's Regular Army is immediately necessary in the present grave national emergency. Lord Kitchener is confident that this appeal will be at once responded to by all those who have the safety of the Empire at heart.' The *Sheffield Daily Telegraph* carried an advertisement for temporary commissions in His Majesty's Army. Two thousand junior officers, unmarried and aged between seventeen and thirty, were immediately required, to remain in the army for the duration of the war, or - though this was not mentioned in the advertisement - until they were killed or maimed. Volunteers would receive an allowance of £20 for uniform and £5 15s for equipment, but details of what regular pay they might receive were omitted. They were encouraged to apply in person to the commanding officer of the nearest army depot.

But was Sheffield likely to be a plentiful source of recruits? That depended on how strongly its citizens supported the war. The same newspaper believed they could be relied upon, writing:

Sheffield has approved of the war, demonstrated its loyalty, and kept its balance. If the spirit at present displayed is continued, the worst will be faced with cheerfulness and equanimity. In the sober way in which we have accepted this unprecedented situation, we have proved ourselves sane, thoughtful citizens. Sheffield has refused to catch either war panic or war fever. It did suffer a little from the food panic in the early days of last week, and there were great runs on the grocers' shops by people anxious to lay in stores. But that was before the Government had taken action to prevent the increase of prices. With regard to money, Sheffield kept its head splendidly. When the banks opened on Friday, after their four days' holiday, there was no rush to take money out. On the contrary, the volume of business was no more than might have been expected in view of the long suspension, and the fact that people paid money into the banks was eloquent testimony to their confidence in the financial stability of the country. Sheffield is

59

united in its support of the war. The city is in agreement that the war was forced on us, and the note struck in many pulpits last Sunday that it is a righteous war finds a response in hundreds of thousands of hearts.

As much as this article attempted to convince readers that Sheffield was indeed a city of 'business as usual', the public was still digesting the reality and enormity of what was happening, realising that life would not be the same for the foreseeable future. But what many hoped would not change was that they would have some football to watch, and perhaps for a short time take their minds off what was happening across the English Channel. They did not have to wait too long to find out. After ten days or so of training, Sheffield United arranged two practice matches for the late afternoons of August 19 and August 24. The gate proceeds were to be given to the Prince of Wales's War Relief Fund, which nationally had reached a sum of £1,200,000 by the middle of August. As the players prepared for the new season by regaining some of the fitness they might have lost over the summer, the British Expeditionary Force of advance troops began to land in France. They advanced to the Belgian border, where they first encountered the German First Army at Mons in southern Belgium. The day before Sheffield United's second public practice match, the Battle of Mons commenced and the British army suffered its first casualties of the war.

Sheffield United were luckier than some clubs in that they could at least continue to use their own ground; Newcastle United's St James's Park was in the hands of the military. Civilians were not permitted to enter the stadium, except for the players, who were allowed to train there but were denied use of the club's gymnasium and baths. The pitch was said to be 'churned up and unfit for football' and club officials were reported to be 'in a quandary'. Liverpool, Everton, Nottingham Forest, Manchester United and Manchester City were also affected – more than three hundred horses were stabled at City's Hyde Road - but all were confident of their early games going ahead as scheduled. The clubs said that arrangements could be made for stable accommodation to be provided under or near the stands, presumably for the army horses that might still be present, and not for players, spectators or even directors. It was further thought that grounds near the coast would be particularly attractive to the military men, in which case they would be gladly given up, despite there being no reports of any such venues being commandeered. But just a few days later it turned out that the news from the north east was not so bad after all. Newcastle's directors had regained control of St James's Park and all its facilities after the army vacated, having been there for a fortnight. Only a few soldiers remained to tidy up the premises, and they must have done a wonderful job on the pitch as it was now apparently in good condition.

These army 'groundsmen', however, were no match for Sheffield United's pitch curator, a Mr Murtay, as United held their first public practice match on an area of turf described as 'perfection'. As well as the greensward, there were ground improvements to gaze upon in awe, as the Shoreham Street earth mound had been concreted over and terraced, and tip-up seats installed in the John Street stand. Spectators were also keen to greet the new players and welcome back the old, but some of the latter were missing through injury or illness. Centre half Fred Hawley was held back as it was felt the hard ground would be injurious to his sensitive knee, whilst that 'tough specimen' of a goalkeeper, Harold Gough, was surprisingly laid up at home in bed with stomach trouble. A new goalkeeper, Ernest Blackwell, was tried in his place and Harold Pantling, a new signing from Watford, played at right half. Also on show were a new back, Holmes, and inside left Wally Masterman, signed from Gainsborough Trinity. Earlier in the week the reserves had beaten the first team in a private practice match, so the regulars were determined not to be embarrassed again in front of the paying public, but the youngsters kept them out until just before half time. The new men impressed, especially Pantling, described as 'a dark-skinned youth of spare athletic build'. Holmes 'showed a lot of speed' but Masterman, 'a powerfully built youth' who seemed 'disinclined to use his strength on friends', had few opportunities. When the real thing started United's fortunes would depend much on 'silky' inside right William Gillespie, who, as usual, was reported to have passed the ball with remarkable accuracy.

The possibility of football being a fine source of income for the various war charities was now becoming widely recognised. The Football Association, the Football League and the Southern League met to formalise the arrangements for donations, recommending that clubs make direct grants where possible. It was decided to let the clubs use their own discretion as to which funds they would donate to, and they were encouraged to play more practice matches before the official September 1 start date to raise more money, with all profits from such games going to the various funds. The only concession was that the railway fares of the visiting team should be paid out of the gate receipts. Sunderland FC and Chelsea FC had pre-empted the decision by earlier announcing they would give to relief funds a proportion of their gate receipts from every match played until the end of the war. Several fund-raising practice matches had already been played, from which the approximate receipts were £200 at Chelsea, £165 at Liverpool, £70 at Clapton Orient and £54 at Blackburn Rovers.

However, some were aware that money was short, and that working men might find it difficult even to attend matches, never mind donate to war relief funds. An unidentified 'well-known northern sporting official' proposed that clubs should consider lowering admission charges to help those whose income might be reduced in the current conditions. He argued: 'This would be much better for the clubs to have big crowds at threepence a head than small ones at sixpence; and they would be rendering good service by enabling thousands of people to take relief from the anxieties of the war in watching their favourite game.' His idea fell on deaf ears. For a start there was a Football League rule setting the minimum entry charge for League matches at sixpence, and rules were rules. Charles Clegg,[13] a Sheffield man and chairman of the Football Association, was asked his opinion. He replied: 'I think it is hardly called for yet. Nothing has been said about it. If there is any idea of raising money for relief funds through League gates, it would be better to do it by giving a percentage of the takings. Once the charge for admission had been lowered, it would be hard work to get it up again.'

Clegg was becoming an increasingly busy man, taking the chair at a conference of the major football organisations. He stressed in his speech that it was important that everyone should do everything possible to assist in any way the provision of funds for the relief of sufferers through the war. England could not avoid the horror of war any more than other countries involved, he said, but every man could do something to meet the call on the nation's sympathy and resources. There

---

[13] Sir John Charles Clegg, better known as Charles, was a football icon. He played at international level, refereed Cup finals, was fundamental in the founding of Sheffield United FC and served on the boards of Sheffield Wednesday FC and the Sheffield United Cricket and Football Club. He was the first person to be both chairman and president of the Football Association, earning the nickname 'The Napoleon of Football'. He was teetotal, a non-smoker and is generally regarded as the first man to be knighted for services to football.

was a universal wish to assist relief work and he was convinced that footballers would do their share in the present national emergency. He added that he and his fellow officials should do everything within their power to avoid causing panic amongst the public, and he believed that calling football off would be inconsistent with this conviction. In his words, it would be a mistake for him and his colleagues to entertain any idea of cancelling the season. One important point of detail was agreed at the conference, at the request of the Army Football Association: that any professional footballer who joined up would be permitted to play for his unit. Current Football Association rules prevented that; perhaps rules were not rules after all.

Strictly, the rules also did not permit clubs to sign players from the army or navy. This rule was intended to retain in the military men who might be good footballers but Barnsley FC secretary/manager Mr W. P. Lewis asked for this interpretation to be clarified. His club had lost a player, Newton, who had enlisted in the Barnsley Battalion (12th Battalion York and Lancaster Regiment), so Lewis wondered if he would be able to re-sign for Barnsley after the war. In normal circumstances the answer would have been in the negative, but these were not normal circumstances. The Football Association ruled that a football soldier could play for his battalion (on home service) and also, where possible, continue to play for his club while actually a member of the forces. On the restoration of peace professional footballers who returned from war service would be eligible immediately to take up their former club positions.

There was then a plea for footballs (old and new) to be sent to commanding officers for the use of soldiers in their hours of recreation. Footballs for the troops had been in short supply during the Boer War, and, it was reported, may be again. Footballs were not all that 'Tommy Atkins' wanted at the front. It was revealed that soldiers liked to discuss the fortunes of their football teams whenever the chance arose, and to that end their families back home were constantly being asked to send newspapers; in the case of Sheffield men they wanted the Saturday evening sports paper *Sports Special Green 'Un*, which was said to be as important to them as their daily rations. Harry Allwood, a referee from Birmingham serving in France in the Coldstream Guards, wrote in a letter home: 'If football does not appeal to the imagination of certain gentry at home, it has great fascination for the gallant fellows at the front; they do not want it stopped.' Surely if the men on the front line were so interested in the football back home, that was another good reason for it to continue? Their morale would suffer if they had no football news to talk about. Indeed, they were so enthusiastic about the game that they challenged their French allies to a match, but there was no report as to its outcome.

The *Sheffield Daily Telegraph's* sports columnist 'Looker-On' agreed with Charles Clegg, writing: 'His remarks were applied to football, but they fit most other games and means of recreation as well [and] should be taken to heart by the folks who are, as we think, much too hurriedly announcing the abandonment of this and that sporting function. "Business as usual" is a sound motto, and for the present, at any rate, "Games as before" should go with it.' Clegg's words were most certainly taken to heart by the people of Sheffield. A crowd of almost 16,000 was present at Hillsborough for Wednesday's only public practice match. Admission was a mere penny, but still £83 4s 10d could be donated to the Prince of Wales's Relief Fund. Sheffield United's second public practice match took place a few days later in front of 4,328 paying spectators. Harold Gough, recovered from his illness, was back in goal and, along with several of his veteran colleagues, impressed more than any of the newcomers.

Particular attention was paid to Wally Masterman's performance; a lot was expected of him as he had been the subject of good reports at Gainsborough. He 'gave a few excellent passes, and made one great raid upon the goal, which suggested possibilities'. Still, there was nothing to suggest that United's regular line-up for the coming season would be much different to that of the previous campaign. Left back Jack English was again not risked, and Hall, on trial, was given a second game at half back. Then, to take the United players' minds away from the concerns of preparing for a new League season, some relaxation was found in a twelve-a-side cricket game at Thrybergh against a local team. United won by 115 runs, with Jimmy Simmons top scoring in United's innings with 69. They then bowled out Thrybergh for just 51, as Jack Elms (a member of United's training staff) took five wickets, George Utley four and Bill Brelsford two.

As the season fast approached, United's prospects were looked upon as favourable. In the 1913/14 season the defence had played well, and it had been reinforced by the addition of promising younger players. However, promise was one thing, and it had yet to be put to good effect on the pitch in League matches, but observers who had seen the practice games believed the new men were 'made of the right kind of stuff'. United boasted versatility too: Albert Sturgess and Harold Pantling could both operate at half back or full back. Looking back at United's short history, they had always done best when they had a sturdy half-back line, so it was vital that this part of the team should have strength in depth, and it did. As well as Sturgess and Pantling, there were George Utley, Bill Brelsford and Fred Hawley to call upon. Good things were expected of centre forward Joe Kitchen, who liked to take any opportunity to shoot at goal, right winger Jimmy Simmons was recognised as one of the most skilful in the league, they had the mercurial Irishman William Gillespie at inside right, and if inside left

Stanley Fazackerley could rediscover his form of the previous season United would have a formidable front line. Only the left wing position was not settled, with Jimmy Revill and Bob Evans competing for it. Revill got the nod for the first league game at Sunderland.

United's visit to Sunderland was not until September 2, but elsewhere the season started the previous day, in unprecedented and, since then, unrepeated circumstances. Some who called themselves patriots said it was morally wrong to be playing football during war. Other equally patriotic people opined that it was about much more than morality. They realised that a great many footballers were ordinary working men with families to support and without football they would have no means of doing that; married men were not yet being asked to volunteer for the military. They also pointed out that footballers were performers, just like actors and music hall artists, and no one was yet suggesting that theatres should be shut down. Like the thespians and singers, footballers were providing a form of public service in troublesome times. Relaxation was as important as recruitment.

On the eve of the season the Football Association came out in unfettered support of its game. After a meeting at its Russell Square headquarters, it issued a statement. First, it appealed for those who could do so to render service to the army and the navy, and for those who could not, to give generously to the relief funds. Indeed, the Football Association had already donated £1,000 to the Prince of Wales's Fund and £250 to the Belgian Relief Fund, expressing sympathy to that nation for its sufferings. Now it got down to the nitty-gritty: the Football Association considered that total suspension of football would be 'mischievous rather than beneficial'. However, it urged all clubs to 'give every possible assistance by releasing players during the war'. A resolution that 'clubs having professional players are urged to give every facility for their temporary release' was passed, and four officials were appointed to confer with the War Office as to the best way of putting this resolution into practice. The War Office, the F.A. said, was opposed to the closing down of football and added that the two organisations would work together to induce all who were interested - players and spectators - to volunteer for active service. The F.A. then produced some figures. It stressed that there were about a million football players in the country, of whom only around seven thousand were professionals. Of these only 2,500 were full-time professionals, the remainder also holding other jobs. It was the duty of all these players to respond in a patriotic manner to any appeal made to them.

The Football League immediately followed suit, expressing similar sentiments to those of the Football Association. It confirmed that the new season was to go ahead as scheduled. Chairman John McKenna made the following tub-thumping statement:

> *Thousands upon thousands of the flower of British youth and manhood, who, upon and around the playing fields of this country, have acquired and developed the splendid characteristics of the fearless and undaunted warrior, are, at the peril of their lives, fighting the battle of honour and uprightness against military despotism in the greatest struggle the world has ever known. In considering the course to be adopted with reference to our great winter game, we are not unmindful of the days of deep sorrow now with us, and yet to come, days when the dark clouds that surround us will oppress and appal us. To sit and mourn is to aggravate the nation's sorrow. At home our clubs were in a helpless*

position, as their contracts entered into with all the formality of legal contracts must be performed as far as possible. We feel that the advice offered by politicians, press, and commercial authorities that 'business should be carried on as usual' is sound, well considered, and well reasoned advice. We, therefore, without the slightest reservations, appeal to the clubs, the press, and the public, that the great winter game should pursue its usual course. Especially do we appeal to the press that the same prominence and publicity should be given to the reports of the games as of old. Sacrifices will be necessary; let them be made cheerfully and let every club remember that football must discharge to the full its duties and obligations to this war, those engaged therein, and those who will suffer therefrom. Every club should do all in its power to assist war funds. Every player should specially train to be of national service, at least in national defence. Whilst we unreservedly authorise the due fulfilment of the League programme, we must all accept to the full every obligation that we can individually and collectively discharge for our beloved country and our comrades in arms, who, in this fight for righteousness and justice, at the risk of their lives, have answered to duty's call.

The League also voted for a sum of £250 to be given to the Prince of Wales's War Relief Fund and commended several clubs and players that had already agreed to make weekly contributions from gate receipts and wages respectively. It recommended that clubs should arrange for their players to undergo military drill and set up miniature rifle ranges at their grounds for shooting practice, presumably using something other than a football. Crystal Palace FC offered the suggestion that players of all London professional clubs should be placed at the disposal of the War Office for two days each week for drill practice at Hyde Park, Clapham Common or other suitable area, and that on two afternoons they should be released from football training to practise rifle shooting under instructors provided by the War Office. In this manner at least 250 men could be drilled together and, if successful, the scheme could be extended across the country. Middlesbrough FC pointed out that their players had already begun military training under the supervision of the club's directors. The directors of Sheffield United FC offered the use of Bramall Lane to the newly formed Sheffield City Battalion, the 12th (Service) Battalion York and Lancaster Regiment, commonly known as the 'Sheffield Pals' Battalion', for the drilling of new recruits. Training for these men began on the Bramall Lane pitch at 9am on September 15 and continued for six hours, with a two-hour break at midday. Unfortunately, the turf soon felt the effect of men pounding up and down in file, so the United directors asked that they be moved to a different area of the ground (perhaps the cricket outfield). Their request did not cause a problem as the men were now divided into smaller groups, undertaking different activities, and it was not long before the recruits moved to other open areas of the city, such as Norfolk Park, to train. Amongst their number was a former Sheffield United reserve player, P. Doncaster, now Regimental Quartermaster and the battalion's authority on physical training.

Clubs were also warned by the Football League to make early travel arrangements for away matches in view of the possibility of the military using regular rail services for the transportation of troops. Nottingham Forest FC, depleted by the loss of three players - John Bell, William Fiske and Robert

Firth - who were army reservists, asked for permission to borrow two or three players, which was granted. Other clubs in the same position would be treated similarly. The *Sheffield Daily Telegraph's* 'Looker-On' was glad that the Football Association and the Football League had 'kept their heads' and were 'determined to make the best of a bad job'. An abandonment, he believed, would have been nothing short of a 'panicky' measure. The same writer could see one possible silver lining in the clouds of war. He hoped that an era of parsimony would put an end once and for all to the 'fancy' transfer fees that were now commonplace. Referring to the large fee paid by Sheffield United to Barnsley for George Utley in November 1913, he wrote: 'We may take it pretty well for granted that no more cheques for £2,000 and more will change hands over the heads of professional players for a long time to come, and it must be pretty doubtful whether that state of affairs will ever be reached again.'[14] Clubs were being forced to pay over the odds when they urgently needed players, sometimes beyond what they could afford, in an effort to remain competitive. Just before the start of the season was normally when a number of big transfers went through, but now all was quiet as clubs chose to continue with the players they already had. 'Looker-On' trusted that there would be three big pluses to this enforced course of action: one, that it would lead to a great improvement in the coaching of players; two, that clubs would ensure they got the best out of youngsters they picked up for little or nothing; and, three, that more attention might be paid to the cultivation of real skill in

---

[14] At the time the record British transfer fee was the £2,500 paid by Blackburn Rovers to Heart of Midlothian for striker Percy Dawson in February 1914. For three months Sheffield United held the record at £2,000, when they bought George Utley from Barnsley. Dawson's record stood until February 1922, when Scottish club Falkirk paid £5,000 to West Ham United for Syd Puddefoot.

the game. Almost one hundred years later Sir Trevor Brooking and others are still saying the same things.

But that was a discussion for another time. Now that the decision to go ahead was official, concentration could be turned to the teams, the players and the fixture list. For Sheffield United, a visit to Roker Park, Sunderland, awaited.

CHAPTER FIVE

THE PLUCKIEST AND BEST HEARTED

The 1914/15 English football season opened on September 1 as the Secretary of State for War, Lord Kitchener, arrived in France to confer with Field Marshal Sir John French, the Commander-in-Chief of the British Expeditionary Force. The same day the Battle of Néry took place in northern France. The engagement saw one of the last occasions in which British forces used a classic cavalry charge to successfully alter the course of a battle; three combatants were awarded the Victoria Cross. The following day German troops advanced to within thirty miles of Paris, forcing the French Government to flee to Bordeaux, and Sheffield United's League season commenced at Sunderland. It was not an auspicious start for United; they were beaten 3-2 and, worse, lost William Gillespie, described by the *Sheffield Daily Telegraph* as 'the pluckiest and best hearted of Sheffield's prominent footballers', for the season to a broken leg. They were also missing injured centre forward Joe Kitchen, and although stand-in David Davies was reported by to have been 'a thorough trier', he could not get the better of Sunderland defender Charlie Gladwin, who gave his Welsh opponent somewhat of a 'knocking about'. The defeat was bad enough, but the loss of Gillespie, who in modern terms might be described as the team's major 'playmaker', was a severe blow. The match report in the *Telegraph* explained how the unhappy incident occurred:

> *A most unfortunate and regrettable occurrence, in the form of a serious accident, marred last evening's First League match at Roker Park, where Sheffield United and Sunderland commenced the season. The victim was William Gillespie, United's brilliant International inside right, who broke his left leg in the last minute of the game. It was done in a daring raid, which was absolutely typical of the plucky, light-hearted Irishman. United were a goal to the bad, and he set off at full speed to try and level the score. As he ran, Gillespie was challenged by the Sunderland captain, Thomson. They were shoulder to shoulder for a short distance, and then Gillespie flew ahead. The next thing that happened was that the United man spun clean over in the air and came heavily to earth. At the same time there was an ominous snap, and the referee almost immediately called for the ambulance men, and after a long delay Gillespie was hoisted on to a stretcher and taken into the dressing room, afterwards being removed to the hospital. Under these circumstances a hard fought and interesting game ended in a general gloom.*

Sunderland scored early when a rare mistake by goalkeeper Harold Gough handed them a goal, and a second soon followed. Jimmy Simmons pulled one back with a goal that drew comparisons with modern-day football. First there was an unsuccessful appeal for offside against outside left Jimmy

Revill, then a further shout that the ball had gone over the line before he crossed it to Simmons. The score then became 3-1 to Sunderland at half time and in the second half David Davies scored with an effort that certainly would not have been allowed today. Sunderland goalkeeper Scott saved a shot from George Utley but 'clung [on to it] too long. While he was trying to dispose of the ball, Davies raced in and kicked it clean out of his hands into the net.' It was in going hard for the equaliser that Gillespie suffered his terrible injury. He remained in Sunderland Royal Hospital, where upon initial examination it was believed to be a clean break. However, a recent discovery called X-rays revealed his leg to be broken in two places. He underwent surgery, having a silver plate inserted and riveted to the bones to hold them together. Clearly even in war-affected 1914 football clubs could afford to make sure that their players received the best possible medical treatment.

It was important that United soon found a way to replace Gillespie, as their first home game a few days later was against city rivals Wednesday. The committee's plan was to move Stanley Fazackerley to inside right and give a first opportunity to new signing Wally Masterman at inside left. The game would also give the club the ideal opportunity to gauge the feeling of the city's public towards football and the war effort. A relief fund collection was to be made, led by a band comprising fifty members of the Boys' Brigade, and compensation paid to the band that was normally engaged to play at Bramall Lane because their own usual collection would have to be cancelled. In addition, the club committee stated it would not stand in the way of any players who wished to enlist, and in an effort to attract volunteers from what was expected to be a large attendance, permission was given for Mr G. H. Bibbings to speak to the Bramall Lane crowd. Bibbings was a former organiser of the Independent Labour

Party who advocated voluntary enlistment. The Independent Labour Party was opposed to militarism and therefore to the war, causing some of its prominent members, who saw themselves as patriots, to resign. Presumably Bibbings was one of these men.

The loud-voiced Bibbings was to make an address from the Bramall Lane end at 3.15pm and at the Shoreham Street end at half time. Hatless, he stood on a portable wooden platform three steps high and just large enough to take one man, to make his speeches. A recruitment poster hung over the front of the platform while several men wearing fedoras stood around it holding flags affixed to tall staffs. A man boasting a fulsome white beard held a Union Flag. The spectators, almost all wearing the large flat caps fashionable at the time, and a number of policemen, listened apparently attentively. Small boys peered between the railings at the front of the enclosure. Behind them was a smattering of women. Even if the eligible men heard Bibbings's message, they may not have heeded it. Recruitment drives had taken place during the opening games of the season at Sunderland and Leeds City, with Roker Park hosting a marching band headed by a recruiting sergeant and two men carrying hoardings displaying enlistment notices. They were cheered all the way around the ground but the success or otherwise of their mission was not known. Spectators at the Barnsley v Grimsby match at Oakwell also had to strain their ears to hear of recruitment opportunities. They were addressed by the Mayor of Barnsley, an honorary Colonel and an acting Colonel of the Barnsley Battalion of the York and Lancaster Regiment. They all appealed for people to enlist in the new unit.

The game against Wednesday was the first chance that probably all of the Sheffield United followers had to see their team in meaningful action. Those that travelled to Sunderland would have been few or none, given that it was played late afternoon on a working day. But this was now Saturday afternoon, the proper time for a working man's entertainment. And professional football was decidedly popular; attendances had seen a steady rise since its inception. The first dozen or so years of the twentieth century proved to be a boom time for the game: new terraces and grandstands were being built at grounds all over the country to cope with the increasing demand, and sometimes not even they could cope with the numbers wanting to come and watch. Sheffield United's average attendance had risen every season except one since 1905/06, with a great leap between 1911/12 (14,549) and 1913/14 (21,503). The first Saturday of the season would go a long way towards testing the public's current appetite for football.

For United, Joe Kitchen, who tore a thigh muscle in the final practice match, and Fred Hawley were still absent, as well as the unfortunate Gillespie. David Davies would deputise for Kitchen once more, but he was considered not such a complete player who did not bring his wingers into the game as much as Kitchen did. United's rearguard was seen to be a match for that of Wednesday, but without Kitchen and Gillespie in United's forward line, Wednesday were stronger in this area. The visitors from Hillsborough were favoured to win, and win they did, 1-0 in front of a healthy crowd of around 30,000 spectators, proving that despite the arguments put forward against it, football had retained its popularity amongst working men. It was a match of 'delightful entertainment' in which United failed to take any of their superior number of scoring opportunities. Some of the vocabulary of the *Sheffield Daily Telegraph* match report appears amusing and innocent compared to today's style:

> *[Wednesday] were pretty obviously staggered by the alacrity with which they were assailed. Rush*

followed rush. Davies, who led United's forwards,
is not the equal of Kitchen in tactics, but he is a
magnificently built little chap with no end of
pluck and all the fervour which the Welsh are
famed for. He went charging through again and
again, once knocking Davison flying as the latter
held on to a dropping ball, an incident that led to
a rare skirmish near Wednesday's goal. Out on
the right wing Simmons was a box of tricks,
passing the understanding of McSkimming, and
too smart at times even for Spoors, upon whom he
did not hesitate to use such weight as he has.

But the efforts of Davies and Simmons were to no avail. United had lost both of their first two games, but more importantly, on a national scale football was back and for the moment showed little sign of allowing its opponents to get their way. Across the English Channel there were hopeful signs of a change in fortune for British troops, who had suffered heavy casualties as the German army advanced on Paris, pushing back the British and French. At his meeting with Field Marshal Sir John French, Lord Kitchener ordered that French's army should not retreat any further, as French wished to do to rest and re-organise. As Sheffield's football rivals battled it out at Bramall Lane, so began the First Battle of the Marne. The German march on Paris was halted in one of the most important single events of the war. Some 1,700 British soldiers were killed over the seven days of the battle, but the French army fared much worse, losing 80,000 men. It ended German hopes of a quick victory, but resulted in four years of virtual stalemate along the Western Front. The same day, off the Berwickshire coast, the scout cruiser HMS Pathfinder was sunk by a German U-boat, costing the lives of 259 men.

CHAPTER SIX

A SMALL CLIQUE OF VIRULENT SNOBS

Football was back, but its critics had not gone away. One of the leading anti-football campaigners of the time was Frederick Charrington, an eccentric philanthropist, East End temperance worker and member of the wealthy brewing family, who had disinherited himself from that business in order to devote himself to the advancement of Christianity and temperance. In the late nineteenth century he conducted a campaign against music halls, which he believed encouraged drunkenness, lost working days and corruption of morals. Whilst a member of the London County Council he voted against all applications for liquor licences. He now directed his attention to football. After writing in the *Morning Post* that it would be a national shame and disgrace 'if we have our best athletes charging one another on the football field, instead of charging the Germans on the battlefield', he next wrote a letter that was published in leading newspapers, in which he branded footballers and the football authorities 'unpatriotic':

The unpatriotic decision of the Football Association has filled me, and doubtless tens of thousands of Britishers, with shame and indignation. It is in direct opposition to Lord

Roberts' magnificent protest[15] against football being continued during the war. What an appalling contrast it is to the fact that three well-known International Belgian footballers have already given their lives for their country; and Huysmans, the Antwerp player, has been wounded at the front; and Carpentier, the French champion boxer, has sacrificed thousands of pounds to go to the front and fight for his country. If the policy of the Football Association is still adhered to and persisted in, the words of Kipling, of 'Flannelled Fools and Muddied Oafs' will indeed be true. The walls of Ripon have already been placarded with the words, 'Wanted, petticoats for all able-bodied youths who have not yet joined the Army.' These words are still more applicable to our athletes and I suggested that the thickest flannel petticoats should now be provided for our cricketers and footballers. I contend that it is simply a question of gate money with the Football Association, and their paltry contribution of £1,250 will deceive nobody.

After next verbally attacking the players of West Ham United for being 'effeminate and cowardly' in playing football while others of their age were fighting, Charrington carried on his protest in person at a Fulham FC match at Craven Cottage. It ended in his allegation of assault against two officials of the

---

[15] Field Marshall Lord Roberts, speaking at the formation of a 1,600-strong battalion of Royal Fusiliers by businessmen from the City of London on August 29, 1914, said: 'My feeling towards you is one of intense admiration. How very different is your action to that of the men who can still go on with their cricket and football, as if the very existence of the country were not at stake! This is not the time to play games, wholesome as they are in days of piping peace. We are engaged in a life and death struggle, and you are showing your determination to do your duty as soldiers.'

club. Fulham had given Charrington permission to encourage recruitment amongst footballers and spectators, providing he did not speak against football. At half time Charrington rose from his seat to address the estimated 12,000 young men in attendance, beginning: 'I come here to protest against this football.....' Fulham chairman W. G. Allen, seated close by, asked him to stop but he simply repeated what he had already said. At this point, according to Charrington's version of events, he was dragged roughly along the gangway by the two men, who then nearly threw him down the steps using 'grossly unnecessary violence'. Charrington protested that he had paid for his seat and he had not been asked to leave the premises before the men seized him. West London Police Court granted his assault proceedings against the two Fulham officials. The case, at which Football Association secretary Frederick Wall and Fulham secretary/manager Phil Kelso were amongst those to give evidence, was heard two weeks later. After the court was told that Charrington's 'tall silk hat remained on his head, he did not lose possession of his cigar, and he never lost his foothold', the two officials were found not guilty of assaulting him. The judge also awarded costs of two guineas against Charrington. It was a bloody nose for the man nicknamed 'Crusader'.

Undeterred, Charrington continued his campaign. He had already taken it to the highest possible level - King George V, no less - by means of a telegram to His Majesty, so being thrown out of Craven Cottage was a minor setback. The King was patron of the Football Association; Charrington politely enquired whether he intended to remain so:

> *May it please your Majesty to remember that Lord Roberts recently said it would be disgraceful if football was continued during the war. The Football Association have now decided to*

continue their matches despite all protests. Your Majesty has set an example to the nation in sending two noble sons to the front. Millions of your Majesty's loyal subjects will be anxious to know if your Majesty's name will still be used as patron of the Football Association.

The King must have read his telegram - or perhaps it was intercepted before it reached him - as it was deemed worthy of reply, a task carried out by the King's Private Secretary, Lord Stamfordham, who wrote back:

The question raised in your telegram to the King has received the careful consideration and respect which is due to anyone speaking with your great experience and authority. I gather that the Football Association are in direct communication with the War Office, and that a general desire has been expressed by the Association to assist in obtaining recruits for the army. I understand that there may be difficulties in giving up all the matches of professional football clubs, in view of contracts which have been made with the players, but the doings of the Association will be carefully followed, having regard to the King's position as patron.

Unhappy with this response, Charrington wrote again. This time Lord Stamfordham's reply was abrupt and to the point: 'Many thanks for your letter of the 14th September. I am afraid that it will not be possible for the King to take any action with regard to the affairs of the Football Association.' Charrington persisted. He telegraphed Football Association president Lord Kinnaird asking if he intended to resign his position because of the organisation's 'unpatriotic decision' to continue the football season. Kinnaird replied by writing: 'Giving up football entirely is not so simple as you think. Contracts have been made which can be enforced in a Court of Law, and you could not advocate the breaking of contracts.' He then added: 'The reasons for continuing some football are too long for a letter.' Such reasons were to be elaborated upon later.

In response to Charrington's antics, another letter writer 'A. G. D. B.' disagreed with his crusade, insisting that football was good as it kept players fit and healthy, for war if it came to that. He wrote in the *Sheffield Daily Telegraph*: 'Shall we eliminate sport, and leave young men with nothing better to do than loaf around, and stand disseminating news at street corners, whereby they will but tend to lose their alertness and vim? Rather let them play football and play hard. Keep vigorous, fit and keen; and the nation shall be the stronger and the purer, and its developing manhood readier for the stern call which is yet almost certain to come.' An unnamed former professional player, now said to be in an 'official position', concurred. He was quoted as saying: 'Seventy-five per cent of the players are married men, many with children. If football is stopped, will they go to war? Not until the thousands of men upon whom the country has a prior call have gone, because they must think of their responsibilities. Stop football, and you merely add to the distress caused by the war.'

Charrington found an ally in author Sir Arthur Conan Doyle, who declared: 'There was a time for all things in the world. There was a time for games, there was a time for business, and there was a time for domestic life. There was a time for everything, but there is only time for one thing now, and that thing is war. If the cricketer had a straight eye let him look along the barrel of a rifle. If a footballer had strength of limb let them serve and march in the field of battle.' Conan

Doyle published a pamphlet entitled *To Arms,* to which Frederick Smith, Conservative MP for Liverpool Walton and the man in charge of the Government's Press Bureau, contributed. Smith expressed surprise that any appeal for recruits should be necessary and wondered how any healthy young man, unhampered by private obligations, could read newspaper reports of the war without doing all in his power to join the small British force in France. He picked out the 'thousands of able-bodied, unattached young men' who unconcernedly loafed about in Hyde Park and other open spaces, before turning his wrath on 'the great northern, midland, and western cities which send tens of thousands to cheer their representatives on the football field, but are unmoved by the terrible experiences of our men on the field of battle'. Finally, he demanded that every qualified man answer the appeal for volunteers 'in the only way that will save his honour, his freedom, and his country'. A similar pamphlet issued by Charrington, designed to shock, showed a photograph of a large football crowd in which not one man was wearing khaki. What Charrington unscrupulously failed to disclose was that the photograph was taken months before the start of the war.

John Watts Ditchfield, the Bishop of Chelmsford, joined the argument, saying he believed the call for football to be stopped was right. He could not understand men who had any feeling, any respect for their country, men in the prime of life, taking large salaries at a time like this for 'kicking a ball about'. It seemed to him something incongruous and unworthy. Another member of the clergy, a Rochdale vicar, was of a similar view, writing: 'The spectacle that may be seen any Saturday pm of thousands of men playing football while their country is in the death-grapple for its very existence is more than pathetic. Our men must respond to the call.' A correspondent to the *Newcastle Daily Chronicle* wrote: 'I noted your report that 30,000 had witnessed the Newcastle United football match. The duty of every man capable of bearing arms is to fight, not to play games. I maintain that the clubs should enable every player to go to the front.' *The Times* then published a letter from historian Professor Albert Frederick Pollard of University College, London, criticising football players and watchers:

> *Football is an excellent thing, even in time of war. Armies and navies can only be maintained so long as the community fulfils its function of producing means for their support; and healthy recreation is essential for efficient production. A man may be doing his duty in other fields than the front. But there is no excuse in diverting from the front thousands of athletes in order to feast the eyes of crowds of inactive spectators, who are either unfit to fight or else unfit to be fought for. Every club who employs a professional player is bribing a needed recruit to refrain from enlistment, and every spectator who pays his gate money is contributing so much towards a German victory.*

A number of further letters opposing football were published in *The Times*. 'An Old Blue' wrote: 'Are games and sport the only things that now stir the blood of our youth? Here are our football clubs arranging their fixtures as usual! What we want to see is not our athletes kicking footballs about to amuse a crowd of idlers, but doing their best to learn how to kick the German army out of France and Belgium,' and a Mr Meath from Bray in Ireland declared:

There must of course be some who are needed to carry on the ordinary work of the country but let these determine that any leisure time which may be at their disposal shall be spent in learning to drill, to shoot, and to march, rather than in amusing themselves in the ordinary manner. They can keep themselves just as physically fit in this way as by playing games, and far more so than by looking on at cricket or football matches or races.

The Times, an avid opponent of football, began running mock advertisements for 'Petticoats for Footballers'. It then reported that people in France, forced to seek refuge away from the fighting wherever they could find it, could not believe that Englishmen were playing cricket and football while these poor women and children were suffering great misery and losing everything they owned to the German invaders. The *London Evening News* followed the lead of *The Times*, announcing that it would not publish its usual Saturday evening football edition for the duration of the war: 'Our football edition has an enormous sale. It caters for the lovers of a great British game, for the most popular of all British games. This is no time for football editions. This is no time for football. This nation, this Empire, has got to occupy itself with more serious business. The young men who play football and the young men who look on have better work to do. The trumpet calls them, their country calls them, the heroes in the trenches call them. They are summoned to leave their sport, and to play their part in the great game. That game is war; for life or death. Then, when we have won the greater game, it will be time to go back to the lesser. Football will be played again and the football edition of the *Evening News* will reappear.'

Such verbal and written demonstrations caused the football authorities to re-visit the subject and the Football League held another meeting, this time in Bolton, to consider the advisability of continuing the season. It unanimously and, judging by its tone, adamantly, carried the following, if brief, resolution:

> *In view of the request from certain people to stop football, the management committee have taken counsel with their clubs, and the committee are even more decidedly of the opinion that in the interests of the people of this country football ought to be continued.*

The statement was welcomed in football circles. It was only two games into the season, but it was noticeable that match attendances around England had not been up to the levels of the previous season, a fact much exaggerated, according to some, by football's critics. Two Monday afternoon games in Lancashire, at Burnden Park and Turf Moor, had drawn 25,000 and 20,000 respectively, figures that stood up well with Saturday afternoon gates elsewhere. In an attempt to appease those who were vehemently protesting against football, the Football Association decreed that recruiting stations were to be set up on or adjacent to grounds and recruitment posters and notices put up around grounds and printed in match programmes and the local press. The posters were to display slogans such as: 'Up till now you have looked on at our games. We now call upon you to play it. Forwards wanted, no backs. Play up.' Arrangements were to be made for prominent figures to address players and spectators, urging those who were physically fit to enlist at once. The Football Association received a letter from the War Office thanking it for its efforts towards recruiting. The letter added that it was unlikely that local recruiting officers would have the facilities to arrange for the opening of temporary recruiting stations at grounds and suggested that it might be possible for clubs to ferry would-be recruits from the ground to the local recruiting offices in motor cars or other forms of transport. This proposal seemed as unlikely to occur as the setting up of temporary recruiting stations.

The dissenters were not assuaged by anything the Football Association or Football League said. Another Charrington backer was the Very Reverend Dr Thomas Charles Fry, the Dean of Lincoln. He stopped short of demanding wholesale cessation of football, but he wanted several strict measures introduced, including the cancellation of all professional football contracts, the stopping of football betting coupons and the banning of anyone under the age of forty from attending matches. Correspondence ensued between Fry and Frederick Wall, secretary of the Football Association. Fry believed that the apathy of spectators (towards the war, not towards football) was preventing sufficient protest being raised against the game. According to him, this apathy was exacerbated by the evil of organised and unorganised betting, which, he said, was 'the ruin of true sport'. He claimed he had been told by footballers, whom he declined to identify, that if clubs banded together in unison they could force the abandonment of football. He then demanded an end to further communication. Fry had written about 'the men who have money invested in football gambling', causing consternation in the ranks of the Football Association, which wondered if he meant that he believed the F.A. was benefiting from betting. Ignoring Fry's wish to end correspondence, the F.A. called for an explanation of his comments, to which Fry did not respond. Wall wrote:

> *Reverend Sir, I note that you decline further correspondence. The matter therefore stands that*

you have adduced no evidence in support of your
statement that 'The continuance of professional
football was due not merely to the apathy of the
onlookers but to the bookmakers and the betters,
and the men who have money invested in football
gambling.' The statement is false in fact and a
slander upon those who have charge of the game.
Although made in ignorance it affords no
justification for its non-withdrawal by you. You
may possibly be prepared to get somebody to deal
more effectively with the evil. If so you may rely
upon the support of The Football Association.
Believe me, Yours truly, F. J. WALL

That the Football Association should have to defend itself against the Dean of Lincoln and others was, some claimed, due to the conduct of certain members of the F.A. Consultative Committee who had been expressing opinions in the negative when it came to the continuation of football. If there was a split behind the closed doors of the F.A., publicly it stood as one, taking a more belligerent stance than had been apparent in previous statements, when it pointed out the iniquity of the attacks on football when other forms of recreation and entertainment were escaping unscathed. The Association also hinted at what might be termed the 'snobbery' of some of the critics when it remarked: 'Football, which is essentially the pastime of the masses, is the only sport which is being attacked. It is producing more men for the army, and money for relief, than all the others. Other sports, and places of entertainment, are being carried on as usual.'

Sporting newspaper *Athletic News* angrily defended the working man's rights, rounding on men such as Charrington, Conan Doyle and Fry, stating: 'The whole agitation is nothing less than an attempt by the ruling classes to stop the recreation on one day in the week of the masses. What do they care for the poor man's sport? The poor are giving their lives for this country in thousands. In many cases they have nothing else. There are those who could bear arms, but who have to stay at home and work for the army's requirements, and the country's needs. These should, according to a small clique of virulent snobs, be deprived of the one distraction that they have had for over thirty years.' Another writer wrote similarly, stating that those who opposed football no doubt spent their evenings in a private box at the theatre and their days playing golf, or in other ways adding to their own personal pleasure. Perhaps unexpected backing for football came in a letter from Lance Corporal Lionel Hayburn, serving in the 31st Signal Company of the Indian Army. He wrote: 'Why is it only soccer that is attacked? Why not golf, hockey and other outdoor sports? What about closing music halls, theatres and dancing rooms?'

But however much football matches could be used for recruitment and fund raising, or, as Reverend Fry said, for the money that could be made from gambling, the real reason for the desire to carry on was the professional nature of the game. Football's weekly turnover was said to be in the region of £250,000, which could not be suspended without financially harming a great many people, a point made by F.A. secretary Frederick Wall when he said that the footballers put out of work might then become dependent upon the relief funds they were now helping to swell by their playing. Opponents hoped, of course, that the footballers would instead volunteer for active service. A further consideration was that amateur clubs, in whichever sport, could go into hibernation as they had not made such a capital outlay in terms of buying players, awarding them contracts and making ground improvements, on which returns had to be made.

There was a widely-held opinion that the agitators against football were prejudiced, falsely believing that the game in general and its principal employees – the fit and able-bodied players – were unpatriotic in earning money playing sport when the country was in a state of crisis. In reality, footballers were signing up in large numbers all over Britain, albeit that few, if any, were well-known names from the bigger professional clubs. The Northern Alliance, a north-east based professional league, stated that overall two-thirds of its players had enlisted. The Durham Football Association reported a similar position. One star player from a top club who did want to join up was Sunderland's England international Charles Buchan, who in the 1950s became famous once more for his self-edited magazine *Charles Buchan's Football Monthly*. In later life he wrote that the Sunderland directors as good as threatened to sue him for breach of contract if he enlisted, so he did not volunteer until after the end of the football season.

But the Football Association remained concerned by the measure of opposition to football and sought further talks with the War Office. The F.A. informed the War Office that it was prepared to request that all its members stop playing matches if it would assist the War Office in its duties, and sent to all affiliated clubs additional recruitment posters to be displayed at grounds, this time with more serious wording that did not resort to plays on football words. The posters soberly stated: 'Recruits for the army are at the moment most urgently needed. Players and spectators who are physically fit, and otherwise able, are urged to join the army at once.' The Scottish Football Association also consulted with the War Office and as a result confirmed its intention to continue its season. The Southern League, at the time almost equal to the Football League in prestige, followed suit and vowed to continue playing. The League also decided to give fifty guineas to the Prince of Wales's War Relief Fund.

The War Office left the decision whether or not to cancel the football season in the hands of the governing body, and indeed implied that the War Office appreciated the efforts made to recruit at football grounds: 'The question of whether the playing of matches should be entirely stopped is more a matter for the discretion of the Association, but the [Army] Council quite realise the difficulties involved in taking such a step, and they would deprecate anything being done which does not appear to be called for by the present situation. Should your Association decide to continue the playing of matches, the [Army] Council trust that arrangements will be made so as not to interfere with the facilities at present afforded to the recruiting authorities.'

In mid September the *Sheffield Daily Telegraph* columnist 'Looker-On' believed – mistakenly as it proved – that the opposition to football was on the wane. 'There is every reason for saying that the greatly magnified volume of protest against the continuance of football during the progress of the war has now reached the vanishing point,' he wrote. He added that although the sentiments of those who opposed the sport could be appreciated, there were overwhelming arguments in favour of its continuation. According to him, football was being 'viciously attacked', and unfairly. If all unmarried professional footballers enlisted there would not be enough of them to form one battalion and stopping the game would destroy one of the best recruiting vehicles in the country. He concluded by saying: 'All this is now being realised and sport is now being continued very largely as usual. That there are thousands who wish for it is seen in the attendances at all the important matches.' In addition, all over the country football grounds were being given over to the military for much of the week so that rifle and drill training could be given to players and members of the public. Indeed, the Sheffield United players were taking part in some of the military instruction at the Bramall Lane, an occupation they found a relief from the monotony of football training.

As the arguments raged, Sheffield United, despite still being hampered by injuries to important players, picked up their form after their two opening defeats. They collected their first point with a deserved 1-1 draw against West Bromwich Albion at the Hawthorns on September 12. Like United, Albion had upgraded their ground, adding more covered accommodation, but in heavy rain even this inducement was not enough to produce a big crowd, which was estimated at just 7,000. United suffered more injuries, to left back Jack English, who hurt his foot and was limping for the rest of the game, whilst Jimmy Revill, Stanley Fazackerley and Bill Brelsford all received bruising, adding to United's already six-strong injury list. Fazackerley scored first, but Albion levelled when Harold Gough let slip a low shot that was 'more difficult to hold than an eel'. But Albion too were hard hit as Jesse Pennington was limping, then goalkeeper Hubert Pearson had to leave the field, severely cutting his eye as he landed on David Davies's knee. The home crowd 'hooted and booed' at Davies but Pearson later said the collision was accidental. United were sorely missing William Gillespie and there was scepticism expressed about the movement of Fazackerley from inside left to inside right to replace him. Fazackerley had enjoyed a good understanding with left winger Revill, which the newcomer Wally Masterman had failed up to now to reproduce. Again Davies worked hard but he was not as good a leader of the forward line as was Joe Kitchen.

With Everton due at Bramall Lane the following Saturday, the United committee decided to address their forward problems by rearranging the line. Davies was to move from the centre to inside right, Fazackerley went back to his best position of inside left and Masterman was tried at centre forward. United gained their first win, 1-0, with a goal from Davies, though Everton played the better football. Masterman worked hard in his new position, but the experiment was deemed not to be a success, even before he had to retire with an injury. English, too, limped through much of the game again. The goal came after Davies had switched back to centre forward. United won, but overall it was not a satisfactory performance. United's primary problem was the number of injuries sustained. Every week trainer George Waller complained of seven or eight leading players being unable to play and others playing whilst hurt. When the committee met to select the team to go to Stamford Bridge to face Chelsea more changes to the forward line were necessary as Masterman was likely to be out for a few weeks. Thankfully the defence was not badly affected, although English had received a few knocks. The forward problem was solved by moving Davies to the centre again, with Simmons going to inside right and Jack Thompson drafted in from the reserves to take the right wing position. The promising Thompson, signed from Scunthorpe, had given a good display in a recent Midland League match and had shown decent form for the reserves all season. It had been hoped that the youngster's introduction so soon would not have been necessary, but Kitchen's performance in the same reserve match proved he was not yet healthy enough to play in the first team. But the directors' plans were disrupted when Revill withdrew ill, so the team took the field with two different wingers, Bob Evans coming in on the left. In a game 'fast and full of sparkle' United played well and secured a draw thanks to another goal from Davies. Thompson, on his first appearance, 'quickly found his form and responded well to the repeated passes with which he was plied' and Evans also did well, so United could be relieved at finding two new candidates for the forward line. As newspaper readers digested reports of the match, on other pages they could also read about the latest horrendous losses suffered by the Royal Navy. On September 22 three armoured cruisers, the Aboukir, the Hogue and the Cressy, were sunk in the North Sea by a single U-boat, costing the lives of 1,459 men. Unlucky fifteen-year-old cadet Kit Wykeham-Musgrave was aboard all three ships as they were torpedoed. He was initially on the Aboukir but as it was going down he swam to the Hogue, which was struck as he was climbing on board. From the sinking Hogue he swam to the Cressy, where he was able to enjoy a cup of cocoa before it too was hit. Wykeham-Musgrave jumped off and clung to a plank of wood, being rescued three hours later by a Dutch trawler.

As United prepared for their last game of the month at home to Bradford City, they could look back on mixed efforts so far. They had been unfortunate to get nothing against Sunderland and Wednesday, took a deserved point at West Bromwich, were lucky to beat Everton and brought another point home from Chelsea in a game that could have gone either way. With Bradford reportedly 'at sixes and sevens' United had an excellent chance of their second victory. The (yet again) re-vamped forward line had done as well at Chelsea as any combination that preceded it, and Thompson's debut performance pleased everybody. Evans showed signs of a return to previous form and Davies was filling in assiduously for Kitchen. With the half-back line and defence in full working order, it was hoped United could continue without undue discomfort until the injured men returned. But the meeting with Bradford City produced only a disappointing 1-1 draw, though United had enough chances to win easily. It took a Fazackerley equaliser after City scored first to take the point. Right back Bill Cook, Fazackerley and Davies were United's best performers, but the two wingers did not shine as they had done at Chelsea. United had won one, drawn three and lost two of their first six matches, but at least were unbeaten in the last four.

As important to United as the points total were the attendance figures, which had held up well at Bramall Lane, but other clubs were not so fortunate. As directors throughout the country fretted that there would not be enough money to pay their professionals and contribute gate money to the relief funds, as they were expected to do, a radical proposal was suggested. It was one that would not go down well with the players.

CHAPTER SEVEN

CHARITY COVERED A MULTITUDE OF SINS

At the end of September the management committees of the Football League and the Southern League met in London to consider the financial situation created by the war. What they resolved to do made unhappy reading for the players:

> *This conference, after carefully considering the returns supplied by the clubs of members' subscriptions and gate receipts during the first month of the season, and comparing the same with the corresponding period of previous seasons, is unanimously of the opinion that to continue the game throughout this season and retain the services of all the professional players engaged by the clubs, it is imperative that players' wages should be reduced.*

Moreover, a sub-committee had already been appointed to formulate a plan to bring the resolution into action. The next move was to consult the Players' Union, which the Leagues' representatives were to meet in Birmingham a few days later. The immediate financial problem was with the Second Division clubs: the First Division attendances, though not as high as usual, were mostly enough to keep clubs operating. However, some Lancashire and north-eastern First Division clubs had also felt the effect of falling gates.

Three weeks earlier the whole of the Bolton Wanderers playing squad had unanimously agreed a voluntary contribution of five per cent of their wages to the National War Relief Fund for the duration of hostilities, resulting in a total weekly donation of about £6. Now their other professionals may have to do something similar to help their fellow players, and if they did not do so voluntarily, legislation might have to be introduced to force them. The proposed levy, on both players and clubs, would go into a fund that would be used to help players and clubs in difficulty. The Players' Union, growing in strength since a threatened strike a few years earlier, had to be brought on board or the plan would never work. An additional part of the proposal was to give visiting clubs a further ten per cent of gate receipts, thus reducing the financial gap between those clubs that attracted large attendances and those that had to survive on smaller crowds. It was a principle of mutual assistance that had never before been seen in the Football League. It was hoped that, if agreed, the charitable scheme would not be in operation for a long period as gates were optimistically expected to improve, and that few clubs would need to ask for assistance. One point that had not been discussed so far was the question of what would happen to any balance in the fund once the situation had reached such a state of improvement that would render it unnecessary.

There were more significant reasons other than disinterest, some argued, for the decline in gates. One was that that there had been few all-local games as yet. The attendance when Wednesday played at Bramall Lane was some way higher than for United's other two home matches, as was Aston Villa's when West Bromwich Albion visited, and the same would no doubt be true when Newcastle went to Sunderland. Many clubs had their more attractive fixtures still to come and until more games had been played a true picture of attendance levels could not be reached. Moreover, the falling off of gates over the first month was not as great as might have been expected given that a state close to panic hung over the country.

The *Sheffield Daily Telegraph* produced some statistics, albeit estimated ones as attendances given in the newspapers were usually guesswork; the official figures were not calculated until later, and then not divulged to the press. The numbers were telling: fifty-two matches in the opening month of the 1913/14 season attracted 1,381,000 people, whereas fifty-four matches in September 1914 produced a total of 835,000, a decrease of 546,000. On the face of it this was a very large decline but, according to the newspaper, 'it cannot be attributed with surety to either lack of interest through sentiment or to an inability to find the necessary admission money'. It was added that both causes had to be taken into consideration, but there was another, which should not be overlooked: the absence of tens of thousands of former spectators, now wearing the uniform of His Majesty's army or navy. These three causes could be fairly accepted as contributory, and in nearly equal proportions, to the reduction in the size of crowds. More attendance figures were then given, which, in the opinion of the writer, were not as serious as might appear at first glance. The aggregate attendance on the first Saturday of the season was 192,000, on the second Saturday 102,000, on the third 183,000, and on the last Saturday of September 174,000, fluctuations largely explained by the attractiveness or otherwise of the fixtures. It was noted that there were attractive games to come in October that might surmount anything seen so far in the season.

The Football League management committee and the Players' Union, represented by chairman Colin Veitch of Newcastle United, secretary Harry Newbould, an ex-player with Derby County and former manager of Derby and Manchester City, and Oldham Athletic captain Charles Roberts, sat down together in early October to discuss the League's wage deduction proposal. The Union delegates heard that the scheme consisted of four points:

1. Contributions to the Relief Fund by players are to keep the game going, and no violation of principle is entailed.
2. The scheme to be suspended as soon as possible.
3. The surplus money to be returned to the players, commensurate with the amount of the players' contributions.
4. Clubs to be asked to contribute an equal amount, commensurate with the contributions of players, to assist clubs in difficulties, such contributions to be put to the Relief Fund.

A further Football League meeting was held in Manchester to fine tune the details of the wage deduction scheme and the contributions from clubs and to hear the response of the Players' Union. The twofold scheme in which the players would help the players and the clubs would help the clubs was, first, to allow for the deduction from players' wages on a graduated scale according to their level of pay. These amounts were to be used for the purpose of assisting other players whose wages had been reduced by their clubs. Second, clubs were to pay a minimum of two-and-a-half per cent of their gross gate receipts to a common fund, from which clubs in financial difficulty would receive assistance. Clubs subject to such monetary relief would not be permitted to sign a player without the consent of the Football League committee. At the time of the meeting around a dozen clubs had applied for relief but not all had yet received any monies. Those that did receive payment would class it as a trading debt. Overall, there had been a drop of some fifty per cent in the takings from season tickets, and thirty per cent in match receipts.

The conference was adjourned to allow clubs time to consider the proposals. When they re-convened, Football League secretary Charles Sutcliffe informed those present what each club's contribution would be, and explained that the contributions from players would range from fifteen per cent down to five per cent, in direct proportion to the wages received. It was estimated that the scheme would raise a sum of around £8,000 by December 31, at which time it was hoped to be able to terminate it, as it would have served its purpose. The club delegates agreed to the proposition without dissent. Furthermore, the League was to ask the Football Association to forego its five per cent surcharge on English Cup tie gates, which amounted to a sum of £4,000 the previous season. If the F.A. assented to this request, the League would donate this additional amount to the Relief Scheme. The F.A. referred the matter to its finance committee for consideration. Indeed, the F.A. still had to decide whether its cup competition would proceed. Preliminary rounds had already been played, but the professional clubs were not due to enter until the first round proper in January.

The players were a different matter. The meeting learned that the players of six clubs had objected to their wages being docked. Several of Wednesday's players had objections, but as yet there was no definite pronouncement from Sheffield United. Only ten out of twenty-nine Tottenham Hotspur players were in favour, those of Bradford City were against, and Newcastle United's men were reserving their opinion for the time being. Managers of several clubs had met prior to the conference and decided to contribute to a special fund for the benefit of the managers and staffs of needy clubs, on the same basis as the players. If fully accepted, it would be a far-reaching and novel plan. The time-honoured system of 'every club for itself' was to be cast aside. Clubs would have to open their books to inspection by the Football League management committee, undermining the system of control the clubs had always enjoyed since the foundation of the League. They would lose their independence and liberty, some thought for the better. It would be interesting to see how they would cope with their change of circumstance.

Meanwhile, Sheffield United's programme continued with a charity game against Wednesday at Hillsborough, followed by a League visit to Burnley. The attendance at the charity match was a disappointing 5,000, who watched 'one of the lamest games imaginable'. Referring to the poor quality on show, one observer commented: 'Charity covered a multitude of sins.' Wednesday won 2-0. United then gained their first away League victory at Turf Moor, mainly due to brilliant goalkeeping by Harold Gough in a game in which Burnley captain Tom Boyle admitted that United were 'just a bit the better team'. United's right-side attacking pairing of Jimmy Simmons and Jack Thompson was prominent, whereas inside left Stanley Fazackerley 'was too prone to cease his efforts when threatened with a tackle', leaving left winger Bob Evans with little sight of the ball. It was a heated match, with Fazackerley heading in when Simmons quickly took a disputed corner before the protesting Burnley players were in position to defend it, then Joe Kitchen, making a welcome return, scored a second before Burnley pulled one back with a shot that needed a deflection to beat the immaculate Gough. After the corner award that produced the first goal, the referee was 'roundly abused for precipitancy', the Burnley players were 'very demonstrative' and the home crowd was 'one of the least tolerable for many years'. United half back George Utley 'was subject to running comments, mostly of a far from complimentary nature' and Evans was the recipient of a handful of clinker collected by one spectator from the side of the pitch. More modern-day visitors to Turf Moor, especially in the 1970s, 80s and early 90s, will understand the temper of the locals and that not much changed over the next several decades. The 1914 Sheffield United team was delighted to leave Lancashire with maximum points and no further injuries.

Tottenham Hotspur were the next visitors to Bramall Lane, on October 17. Even though Spurs were not the force of old, they still retained the glamour of being the first London club (and at the time a Southern League club) to win the Cup, in 1901 – when they beat Sheffield United 3-1 in a replay at Burnden Park. A crowd of around 22,000 witnessed a 1-1 draw, a disappointing result for United after their victory at Burnley. Fazackerley, suffering from a cold, was out, so the versatile Davies played his third position of the season. The Welshman was a great trier wherever he played, but he did not possess the skill of Fazackerley, who was 'much missed'. Both goalkeepers excelled but Gough was lucky when Jimmy Cantrell hit the post with 'a rasper, when Gough was out of distance'. The goals came just minutes apart in the second half, Thompson's opener for United being described as 'rather a gift'. The result was blamed squarely on the 'adoption of wrong tactics', according to the *Sheffield Daily Telegraph*, in that United did not efficiently utilise their superior attacking unit. Managers were obviously tactically naïve a century ago too.

On October 24 United travelled north east for the second time in six weeks, on this occasion to St James's Park, where a dramatic match ensued, resulting in a 4-3 win for the home side. United's preparation had been hampered by a disrupted journey on Saturday morning, when their train was held up behind two troop trains between Sunderland and Gateshead. The players arrived in Newcastle just twelve minutes before the scheduled 3pm kick-off, in which time they had to rush to the ground and change. They did so with remarkable alacrity, as the game was delayed by only six minutes, a crowd of 28,000, including around three thousand soldiers (who were given free entry at all grounds), waiting patiently. The United team was reported to have been full of understandable anxiety as they waited on the delayed train, wondering if they were going to arrive in time, and began the match 'in a very natural state of flurry'. Not surprisingly, the home players were fresher as United struggled to come to terms with their hurried arrival, and Newcastle took the lead when Curtis Booth scored in the first few minutes. United were then dependent on goalkeeper Harold Gough, who 'rose to heights unknown even of him', one save in particular standing out when he charged down a shot from Booth and received a knee to the head for his trouble. He then made another splendid save from Tommy Goodwill[16] and watched Angus Douglas hit the rebound over the bar. United gradually regained their composure and after Joe Kitchen had unaccountably missed an open goal, the centre forward played a good pass from a difficult position to set up Jimmy Simmons for the equaliser. Simmons's shot was 'a beauty, from about eighteen yards' range, rising all the way to goal'.

Newcastle regained the lead early in the second half with a deflected shot and increased their advantage to 3-1 with twenty-two minutes remaining. At this point David Davies, who suffered a bad ankle injury in the first half, was forced to leave the field, but United reduced the deficit when Albert

---

[16] Private Tommy Goodwill was killed in action on July 1, 1916 serving with the Northumberland Fusiliers. Service No. 28/159, Memorial Reference Pier and Face 10 B, 11 B and 12 B, Thiepval Memorial.

Sturgess found the net with 'a capital shot' from an opening created by a deft back-heel from Jack Thompson. Three minutes later Thompson levelled the scores following a fine solo run. United seemed to have done enough to get some reward for their perseverance, especially so considering their travel problems and the loss of Davies, as Newcastle's attacks were bravely beaten back by a valiant defence. George Utley, having moved into the forward line when Davies was injured, reverted to his normal half-back position to help his defence. United escaped one penalty appeal when the referee missed a clear case of handling, but in the last minute another handball was given against Jack English. The United full back raised his hands to protect his face from a shot but 'the visiting players who were nearest aver that the ball struck him in the stomach, and was never near his hands'. A 'wild scene' followed, as United's players harassed referee Mr Chadwick to try to persuade him to consult his linesman, whom, they contended, had flagged for a goal kick. Mr Chadwick's handling of the situation was weak; his whistle had apparently not sounded at the instant of the alleged handball, but a penalty was still the outcome. Frank Hudspeth beat Gough from the spot to tip what was reported to be the best game seen at Newcastle all season in the home team's favour. Simmons had been the best forward on display, the half backs faced 'a very pertinacious foe' and the backs, despite occasionally kicking erratically, were very good. The *Sheffield Daily Telegraph's* report finished with effusive praise of Gough, described as 'the great man of the day'. United could take heart from their dogged display in difficult circumstances, but it left them with just eight points from their first nine games and languishing in thirteenth place in the League table. As the Sheffield public contemplated United's poor start to the season, they might also have read that soon after United's defeat at Newcastle, the sentences of the three Sarajevo conspirators, whose actions instigated the current Europe-wide conflict, were announced in the Bosnian capital. The man who fired the fatal shots, Gavrilo Princip, escaped execution as he was under twenty-one, as did Nedeljko Čabrinović. Both were sentenced to twenty years in prison. Muhamed Mehmedbašić had escaped to Montenegro after the June 28 attack, from where he found refuge in Serbia. Three other members of the dissident group, Danilo Ilić, Veljko Čubrilović and Mihaijlo Jovanović, received death sentences.

CHAPTER EIGHT

STOP THIS SCANDAL

The football season was now well underway and the period from October to early December 1914 saw renewed and vigorous opposition against its continuation. The popular satirical magazine *Punch* threw its weight behind the anti-football campaign, issuing a small handbill and a larger poster promoting recruitment amongst football players and spectators. The handbill showed a hand-drawn figure of Mr Punch telling a striped-shirted footballer as he was about to go and play: 'No doubt you can make money in this field, my friend, but there's only one field today where you can get honour.' Below was written the statement in smaller print: 'The Council of the Football Association apparently proposes to carry out the full programme of the Cup Competition, just as if the country did not need the services of all its athletes for the serious business of War.' The reverse of the handbill featured a quotation from a leading article in *The Times*. The handbill and poster were both freely available to callers at the London offices of *Punch*.

The Times picked up the theme in earnest, printing numerous letters and leader articles denouncing football and its poor recruitment record. Mr William A. Beckett of St James's Square, London, suggested that footballers might be able to enlist and continue playing for their clubs on

Saturdays, undertaking military training at their closest large population centre during the week. Perhaps a 'football brigade' could be formed, he opined. His letter was prescient: he realised that soldier-footballers would not be required to go on active service until at least the end of the season, thus it was practical to form a brigade of the manner suggested. His idea became reality a few weeks later. Academic and former politician Roper Lethbridge of Devon wrote: 'Will you permit me, as a lifelong supporter of the noble and manly game of football, respectfully to point out to the Football Association that at this moment, by the strangest irony of fate, one of the worst enemies of recruiting is football! Our flow of recruits of the best and most athletic type would be immensely accelerated if only the Football Association would show some patriotic spirit regardless of gate money. But so long as the football authorities insist on keeping the great Cup matches and similar allurements going - alluring the players from their duty by fat wages, and the spectators by selfish pleasure - so long will many of the best of our young athletes conclude that the need for more fighting men cannot possibly be so urgent.'

An innovative idea was put forward by Mr William Boosey, managing director of music publishing company Chappell & Co. of New Bond Street, London. He proposed that instead of football competitions, there should be published 'recruitment results', in which the success or otherwise of towns and counties would be displayed as a sort of league table. 'The imperishable distinction of those towns and counties coming out at the head of their list,' he wrote, 'will be something very different from the transient glory of a season's success at cricket or football.' Public figures and politicians were also getting, or remaining, involved. The irrepressible Frederick Charrington sent a telegram to Admiral Sir John Jellicoe, Commander-in-Chief of Britain's Grand Fleet (effectively the head of the Royal Navy) asking him to join his campaign against football. However, the Admiral replied that he considered it undesirable that officers on active service should express opinions on matters of public controversy. Charrington also wrote to every Field Marshal in the British Army. Next, the Poet Laureate, Robert Bridges, went public with his opinion:

> *I certainly voice the feeling of the country in declaring that it is high time that professional football should be discontinued. I have heard that at the beginning of the war those persons who are responsible for the arrangement of professional football felt doubts and sought advice of the War Office, when, not receiving precise instructions, they resolved to continue their matches as usual. They must now perceive that this decision was a mistake, and they should remedy it as soon as possible. It is high time that our footballers let the world see what they are really made of and that they do not deserve the execration that is falling upon them.*

Discussion and argument about football proliferated in the press, but it took a surprisingly long time for the matter to reach the formal attention of the House of Commons. Equally surprisingly, it was the Liberal Unionist MP for Orkney and Shetland, Cathcart Wason, who in mid November raised the subject during a debate about income tax. He remarked:

> *[The Football Association] protest their entire desire and willingness to stop these matches, provided the War Office recommends that it should be done. Only the other day the Right Honourable Gentleman the Under-Secretary of*

State for War said he looked upon attendance at these football matches as exceedingly undesirable and very harmful; so that in that way I hope we will see something done almost immediately. What I contend is that we ought to have a tax of at least a half of the gate monies imposed upon these great matches. It is high time professional football should be discontinued. If the Chancellor of the Exchequer could adopt the suggestion I make of imposing the taxation of one half the gate money where these professionals are employed, not only would be gained a very large revenue, but he would have the further advantage of getting a very large number of the very best possible fighters into the ranks.

Wason was not to be satisfied, as Edwin Montagu, the Financial Secretary to the Treasury, replied, saying: 'I fear I cannot see my way to adopt my Honourable Friend's proposal.' However, if certain MPs had their way, spectators at football matches would soon be paying more for their pleasure. During a debate on professional football on November 23, William Bridgeman, Unionist MP for Oswestry, called for the railway companies to discontinue their practice of selling tickets at below the normal price to people travelling to matches. He wanted them to be charged double, with some of the additional receipts being given to war relief funds. Walter Runciman, Liberal MP for Dewsbury and President of the Board of Trade, advised that he understood that the railway companies had no intention of changing their policy. Bridgeman responded by asking that now the railways were under the control of the Government, couldn't something be done? Runciman's reply was that the subject could be re-considered, but it would not be right to restrict any such policy to one sport alone. On the suggestion that the Government could do what it wanted as it had 'commandeered' the railways, Runciman stated that this was not the correct term and the Government had taken control not to influence the rates the companies charged for normal travel but to ensure that sufficient transportation for troops was available.

The debate continued three days later, when Unionist MP for Mid-Armagh, Sir John Lonsdale, asked Prime Minister Asquith if he was aware that recruitment efforts amongst spectators at football matches had produced disappointing results, and whether he would introduce legislative powers to cancel all professional football matches during the war. Asquith replied: 'Communications are taking place with those who are responsible for the organisation of football matches from which I hope for good results. I do not consider that a case exists for such legislation as the Honourable Member suggests.' Lonsdale continued the theme by stating that the previous Saturday just one man had enlisted out of the many thousands in attendance at a number of football grounds. Asquith said he had seen that report, but was pleased to say there had been a much better response in Scotland. Lonsdale would not let up, virtually demanding that the Prime Minister 'stop this scandal' by bringing in legislation to commandeer all football grounds for military purposes. But Asquith would not be drawn on the subject, stating he would rather 'trust to the progress of the communications which have taken place, and appeal to the general good sense of all football players'.

In mid November the Football Association secretary Frederick Wall made a public appeal 'to good sportsmen' in an attempt to encourage football players and supporters to volunteer for duty. He said:

> *The need for more recruits for our army is very urgent. Appeals should not be necessary. Every*

man must know his duty to himself and to his country. There are approximately three millions of men with no family responsibilities. I ask these to show that they are good sportsmen and to enlist now and help the other good sportsmen who are so bravely fighting England's battles against the world's enemy. As a result of a recent meeting of the Council of the Football Association, the Association offered to put their grounds, with the exception of one day a week, at the disposal of the military authorities, and, further, stated that they were prepared to request all their members to cease playing matches if the War Office were of opinion that such a course would assist them. The Army Council having replied that the question of the stoppage of football matches was one for the discretion of the Association, the Council of the latter expressed the opinion that its members should continue to play matches, 'where, by so doing they could assist, and did not hinder the authorities in recruiting.'

Wall realised that he and the Football Association needed to be seen to be doing something positive to aid recruitment at matches. The Association reiterated that prominent gentlemen would speak during the half-time interval of matches, and that, at the end of each match, a band would march to the nearest recruiting depot, hopefully taking with them, Pied-Piper-like, those amongst the spectators who wished to enlist. This wasn't much, and it was unlikely to appease the dissenters. Immediately after Wall's plea, *The Times* reported that a major recruitment effort had been made at Highbury during an Arsenal match but that very few of the crowd had volunteered. What the writer mischievously, and probably deliberately, failed to mention was that the game in question involved the reserve teams of Arsenal and Chelsea, so the attendance was very small. Other reporters put the blame for the lack of recruits amongst young men squarely at the door of the Government, which, by censoring the newspapers, made the situation on the front lines seem not as bad as it was in reality. But things really must have been bad, because now it was reported that the soldiers at the front were asking far less about football. Indeed, newspaper accounts of football matches even moved some officers to what was termed 'righteous wrath'.

Renewed recruiting efforts were instigated at football matches towards the end of November but they were reported to be 'grievously disappointing'. *The Times* believed there was something about the spectator of professional football that made a recruiting appeal doomed to failure. Recruitment sergeants were present at Stamford Bridge for Chelsea's match but not a single person could be persuaded to enlist. Other football grounds suffered similarly. A match at Arsenal was a comparative success – there, one man volunteered. Critics pointed out that this position contrasted with the number of volunteers from other sports, such as rugby, cricket and rowing, which had all contributed great numbers of men to the service. Such criticism was disingenuous, as football had also provided tens of thousands of volunteers, but relatively few from the ranks of professional players and the people who watched them.

The half-time recruitment speech at Stamford Bridge when Chelsea played Notts County was made by Colonel Charles Burn, Conservative MP for Torquay, who said: 'I want you to understand that I am a sportsman as well as a soldier. I believe in football. I believe in your games being carried on as usual. I have come here to ask if there is any young man who has no encumbrances to join the forces. I don't say come. I say, "Come, for God's sake. You are wanted." I have given my son.

He enlisted at the start of the war. He is now dead. I have given my house up as a shelter for the care of wounded officers. I say to you young men that if I had twelve sons I would give them all, as well as my own life, for my country and my King.' A large number of the spectators were dressed in khaki. 'I have no need to speak to you young men in uniform,' added Colonel Burn. 'I raise my hat to you.' It did no good. It was claimed in the press that the attendance at this game was around 30,000, whereas the Football Association stated it was below 15,000. To back up its figure, the F.A. gave exact numbers of people at the match who were ineligible for recruitment: 6,702 military men, 783 boys and a small number of ladies. There would also have been a large number of men too old to enlist, but these could not be counted precisely. Frederick Charrington predictably remarked that the paucity of recruits at football matches was 'a slap in the face of the War Office'.

That football had failed to provide recruits was clearly indicated in a published list showing how several clubs had performed. In Birmingham there had been a disappointing response from the local professional footballers, yet some of the smaller clubs had disbanded, as the majority of their players had enlisted. Mr Campbell Orr, secretary of the Birmingham County Football Association, issued a circular to local clubs suggesting that meetings be held to impress upon members and their friends the absolute necessity for every young man who was physically fit and sufficiently free from domestic responsibilities to give his services to the nation without delay. In Brighton, not a single young man had volunteered at the previous Saturday's match, although thousands of able-bodied men were present. 'Such a crowd,' said one of the recruiting officials, 'is a disgrace to the country at such a time as the present. All they seem to care about is football and home comforts, while our brave soldiers are experiencing so much discomfort and hardship to protect the country.' In Nottingham, the reserve battalion of the Robin Hood Rifles marched to Forest's City Ground in the hope of encouraging recruitment. At half time they marched around the ground and were greeted enthusiastically, but that was the only result achieved. At another Forest match, motor cars stood outside the ground displaying signs reading: 'If you want to enlist, jump in.' The number of new passengers was not revealed. In Cardiff, six recruits were gained at the home team's game against Bristol Rovers. It was better at Everton, where scores of recruits joined up at the match, after which a band marched through the local streets with a banner appealing for further recruits. However, some blame was directed towards the military authorities themselves for the lack of success in recruiting at football matches as they were not making the best use of the opportunities handed to them. For instance, it was suggested that the various city battalions should march at their local ground every Saturday, instead of being drilled in apparent secrecy.

Some believed that the continuation of professional football was in itself a deterrent to the young men who attended matches. 'It has a moral effect,' said one recruiting officer. 'These professional footballers of England are the pick of the country for fitness. Nobody has a right to say that any body of men are not doing their duty, and there may be excellent domestic reasons why every one of these thousands of players does not enlist. But when the young men week after week see the finest physical manhood of the country expending its efforts in kicking a ball about, they can't possibly realise that there is a call for every fit man at the front.' Others involved with recruitment agreed that the game contradicted recruitment appeals.

Critical letters continued to pour in, supported by equally critical newspaper articles, especially in *The Times*. But 'The

Thunderer' could also be balanced in its views, at the same time placing some of the blame at the door of the censors. The press, it said, had sometimes been treated with scornful contempt, and had even received threats, when in fact it was cooperating eagerly with the authorities 'within judicious limits'. Reproachful letters from the public criticising 'the snug armchair brigade' and its disregard of 'the thin (very, very thin in some places) khaki line in the trenches' were, according to *The Times*, 'unjust'. As the newspaper said: 'The nation cannot see what it is not permitted to know.' Correspondents were invited to pay attention to the last official statement made on behalf of the Government on the subject of recruiting. It was uttered by Lord Kitchener at the Guildhall Banquet on November 9. The Secretary of State for War said: 'I have no complaint whatever to make about the response to my appeals for "men." The statement may not square with the advertisements which have since been issued, nor with the miserable result of the appeals at Saturday's football matches in London, but it is all we have to go upon, and must stand as the Government view. So long as it stands it silences criticism, but it is not the view taken by the nation, any more than by the army in the field, and we fear it will prove to be but one more instance of the way in which the Government have failed either to understand or to trust the country.' Kitchener astutely realised that the Government had made mistakes and that some of the responsibility must lay at their door for any shortage of volunteers that may exist.

When it came to criticism of football and its players, however, *The Times* was unequivocal, writing:

> *We are glad to think that public opinion is setting steadily and rapidly against the continuance of professional football at this time of national danger. The question, indeed, is not quite so*

simple as it sounds. For good or ill, and whether we like it or not, the great League championships have become in normal times an absorbing interest and recreation to millions of people for whom other interests and recreation are far to seek. They form the weekly holiday for countless workers in this country, especially in the north, whose happiness and contentment are none the less important for the strain imposed by the war. Many of these football enthusiasts are too old to fight. A large number of them are rendering services, only less valuable than those of the fighting line, in the great factories now working night and day to provide arms and equipment for the troops. They cannot fairly be barred from an occasional hour's amusement, and it will be something of a problem to provide them with a substitute for their traditional Saturday afternoon. With the professional champions themselves there can, of course, be no sympathy whatever. From the very nature of their trade they are in the prime of manhood, more than qualified to pass any test of age and health, and physically the flower of our potential recruits. Their own conscience, and the opinion of their fellows, must be their judge. Still less can there be any sympathy with the managers who are virtually bribing them away from their country's service. From every point of view - and chiefly that of our strenuous allies and our own soldiers, whose old interest in the fortunes of their favourite teams is plainly turning to disgust - it is high time that there should be an end of what is becoming a national scandal. The more football the better for those who need such recreation; but let it be a game and not a business.

The newspaper printed a poem, written by a Mr Lochhead, imploring players to 'leave the lure of the football field' and 'take your place in a greater game, where worthier deeds are done'. The poem ended, somewhat melodramatically: 'The God of Right will watch the fight, and referee the game.' A writer who called himself 'An Old Player,' wanted to know who was to blame for football's poor record of recruiting. 'Is it the professional footballer,' he asked, 'who, by playing, diverts the minds of the manhood of this country from the sterner things across the Channel, or is it the director of the football club, registered as a limited liability company? If the clubs were run for the game only the present high rate of wages would not be paid to retain the most skilful players.'

Walter N. Landor, JP, of Rugeley in Staffordshire, placed the blame squarely with the football authorities, who should stop the game forthwith, he said. If they wouldn't do it, the Government should: 'Many thousands of our young men still seem to be far more interested in the result of these matches than in the deeds and sufferings of our soldiers, and the sudden stoppage of these matches would deprive them of their usual topics of conversation and might make them take the war far more seriously than they now do. If the football authorities should be recalcitrant or plead that they are unable to break their contracts with their players without the authority of an Act of Parliament, such an Act might be passed in the present session, which would make all payment of gate money illegal during the King's pleasure.' 'An Old Soccer Back' agreed, writing:

The worst foe to recruiting is the professional footballer. Every Saturday dozens of fit, active young men go forth to a spectacular combat for money. Hundreds of young men also fit and well pay to look on. They are absolutely obsessed all the week with these matches. It would be stopped but for two reasons: (1) The pretended one - sanctity of contract. This is, of course, all nonsense; if the players and the Association agree to cancel their contracts of course they are cancelled. I hope that absurd reason will never again be put forward by anyone. (2) Money.

John Ross of Dublin called for the introduction of conscription, as voluntary recruitment was not working, as did Evelyn Hubbard, the chairman of Guardian Assurance and a former director of the Bank of England, who wrote: '[There is] a strong feeling of dissatisfaction at the present working of the voluntary system. An undue proportion of married men are leaving their wives and families in response to Lord Kitchener's appeal and coming forward to fill the places at the fighting line which ought to be filled by the thousands of able-bodied lads and single men whose devotion to football has overpowered their patriotism. The pitiable result of Colonel Burn's appeal at Stamford Bridge is nothing short of national disgrace. Surely it is time that further League and Cup football matches be stopped and that military service be at once made compulsory for all bachelors between the ages of nineteen and thirty-eight who come up to the necessary standard.'

Almeric Paget, Conservative MP for Cambridge, concurred with both men, writing: 'The evidence accumulates from many parts of the country that the country does not as a whole yet realise that we are fighting for our very existence both as a nation and as an Empire. Nor will this be fully realised till the Government calls upon all those who are eligible in the military sense to take their share. At the same time letters are reaching this country both from officers and privates which show that the men at the front are beginning to feel that the strain upon them is well-nigh intolerable and that they are beginning to ask why their numbers should be so deplorably few in relation to the whole people and why the khaki line is so very, very thin. One may refer to the disgusted amazement with which Canadians and Australians and others who have come thousands of miles to fight find so large a number of able-bodied men wholly absorbed in football. I believe that there are hundreds of thousands of men in the country who would be prepared to do their share if they knew that their neighbours would all be equally compelled to do theirs also. I am aware that there are many conscientious objectors to any form of what they call conscription, and there is much truth in the contention that men compelled to serve against their will are a source of weakness and not of strength in any army. I myself believe heartily in the value as well as the necessity at the present time of compulsory military training for all citizens, and I contend that this is not conscription.'

The Times made sure the subject remained in the public's consciousness, but in its next critical piece it proved it did not understand the affinity a football follower has with his local team:

> *Public opinion against professional football grows stronger and more definite week by week. We have already expressed our agreement in its condemnation of a national scandal. It is monstrous that at a moment when the country is calling upon her young men to fight for her, numbers who are physically best fitted to fight should be bribed to spend their manhood in play. We have refused, however, to impute indiscriminate blame to the thousands of*

spectators who make the great football matches their weekly recreation. Some, no doubt, are mere loafers who ought to be at the front or on the drill ground, but many others work throughout the week in our mines and our mills and our factories, doing their duty as citizens, by helping to provide us with the sinews and the very instruments of war. The weekly football match is their habitual amusement and they earn, and are entitled to, amusement. We may not approve of the particular sport that fascinates them. But there it is. They have the football habit, and we cannot break them of it. Can nothing be done to direct it to a different channel? Our soldiers love football too. Would not a series of matches between the different county regiments now under training, culminating, it might be, with a contest between 'North and South', create a fine spirit of emulation amongst the several corps, and be as attractive to their friends as any matches played by 'mercenaries'? If the crowds came from their own counties and boroughs, as they would largely do, were such contests to become the fashion, the bonds between the regiments and their districts would be strengthened, and many who came to see their local corps win goals, might stay, to help them in winning hostile trenches.

E.V. Speller, assistant secretary of the Amateur Football Association, stressed that his organisation had abandoned its programme as soon as war was declared after it issued a circular to all clubs informing them that, in the opinion of the A.F.A., it was 'right and proper' that clubs should cancel their fixtures, advice that was universally followed. He added that some three-quarters of all members of the Association had enlisted. He concluded his letter by stating: 'I consider it an everlasting disgrace to the sport of Association Football in this country that it should be carried on as if nothing unusual was occurring when dozens of our relatives and friends have died or are enduring the agony of wounds in the knowledge that they have done their share in contesting the right of our country to exist.' Mr Speller's superior, the secretary of the A.F.A. Mr H. Hughes-Onslow, felt obliged to correct a misconception on the part of his assistant: it was not three-quarters of the members of the Association who had signed up – it was all of them (of those who were eligible).

An opposing view was put forward by an unidentified director of a professional football club. He said: 'The club which I help to manage is one of those clubs which are either struggling to maintain a position in the First Division or fighting to get out of the Second. Like the majority of the League clubs it is heavily in debt, and the great difficulty facing its directors is that although the club is a limited liability company its assets are of such a nature that they have had to pledge their personal credit at their bank for an overdraft of thousands. The only asset against this is the transfer values of the players. The poorer clubs have existed for years solely on the credit of these transfer values. We have not carried football on for profit. It may be said - with justice I agree - that we ought to release our players for service, stop football, and take our chance of our bank's mercy until we can recover our players after the war. Our difficulty is that we are under legal liability to pay wages until the end of April, and in some cases for two years beyond, and unless the men choose to release us we are bound to go on paying. It is not fair to ask us to do this. Of course, if the men would join the Army, the difficulty would be solved, but I doubt whether the majority can be expected to do so. Over three-quarters of the better-paid professionals are married men with children dependent; further, it must be confessed, they are somewhat spoiled by public favour. They have given up the trades to which they were trained, for a brief - if well paid - career, in the expectation of being ultimately established in business later by a benefit, and their whole future depends not merely upon safety, but upon absolute perfection of limb power. Allow me a word as to spectators. I see that the whole League gates last Saturday were under 200,000. Out of these a large percentage are actual soldiers. Only a certain proportion of the rest are of eligible age, and out of these many are engaged on railways, transport work, and industrial manufactures, the maintenance of which is just as essential to the war as a supply of troops. It would be very safe to say that not ten per cent of this total gate - i.e. 20,000 - are eligible for service. It is obvious from the figures that the critics of football have greatly exaggerated their case, when they attempt to prove that football is responsible for slow recruiting.'

The anonymous director was backed by George Wagstaffe-Simmons, the honorary secretary of the Hertfordshire Football Association, who also believed that football was doing all it could:

> *The campaign against the playing of professional football is based upon a complete misconception of the facts. The assumption that it is a foe to recruiting is not borne out by facts, and the demand that football should cease is remarkable in view of the claim we so persistently make as a nation that we are not given to panics. In England 4,392 professionals have been registered with the Football Association this season, this being a much less number than usual, as so many have joined the colours. Many of the 4,392 have*

enlisted since they were registered. The total number of players who obtain their living by playing football is under 2,000, and of this number more than two-thirds are married. There are less than six hundred players who are not married or who are not responsible for the maintenance of homes, and those six hundred ought to enlist. Their measure of responsibility is the same as that of the 2,300,000 single men in England and Wales who have not yet enlisted. Is there anything approaching fair play in the persistent attempt to hound down and deprive of their living if they do not enlist the six hundred I have mentioned, and at the same time to allow the other 2,300,000 to escape? Those who play and watch football cannot understand why this sport should have been singled out, bearing in mind that it has contributed more men to the colours and more money to war funds than all other sports combined. Over 100,000 amateur football players have responded to the call to arms, and others are joining every, day. The contracts into which professional players have entered are sneered at as an excuse for them not enlisting. There is not a club that will refuse to release any player from his engagement if he wishes to join the forces, but a club has no power to determine an agreement without the consent of the player. They are commercial agreements in law, and if they were broken otherwise than by mutual consent the aggrieved party would obtain damages.

But an 'Old Soccer Back' claimed that the football director's letter had served simply to support the opposite view to that he wished to get across, as he had confirmed that it really was just a question of money. *The Times* agreed:

> *The correspondence on this subject in our columns has elicited that the chief objection felt by the promoters of professional football to its abandonment during the war is a financial one. With every allowance for men who, like many others, have been faced by the war with an unexpected financial predicament, it cannot be admitted that this objection is a good one. The difficulty confronting professional football clubs is not greater than has been met by many other commercial undertakings, and with a good will to face it, it can be faced.*

Regardless of the opinions of *The Times* and its contributors, the *Sheffield Daily Telegraph's* 'Looker-On' believed that Frederick Charrington's crusade had 'entirely failed' because he did not have the support of the general public, a statement apparently contradicted by the number of letters in the national press. 'Looker-On' accused Charrington of attempting to secure for himself 'a little cheap advertisement' after issuing a pamphlet in which he claimed that football carried on for the sake of those who gambled on the outcome of its matches and for the clubs to make profits. Such a statement proved how out of touch Charrington was with reality, as most clubs were struggling to make ends meet in the current circumstances. Charrington believed that thousands of young men would not enlist because if they did they would be deprived of their chance of 'shouting at football matches', a claim strongly refuted by 'Looker-On'. How foolish of Charrington – they would have plenty of chance to 'shout' in the trenches.

In late October there was much interest in a meeting of the Football League, at which an amended scheme to aid clubs and players hit by the football financial crisis was to be discussed and, it was optimistically hoped, adopted. There had not been unanimous acceptance by players of the wage deduction plan previously proposed. Manchester United's players had received criticism for their rejection of the scheme but had since withdrawn their objections, and Tottenham Hotspur's were requesting special dispensation on the grounds that the cost of living was higher in London. Their request was unlikely to be met. Prior to the meeting there had been a leak of information to a Manchester newspaper, which reported that the players of the two Sheffield clubs had refused to ally themselves with the wage deduction scheme, whilst Aston Villa indignantly denied that their players were amongst the 'malcontents'. Many players were worried that a precedent would be set if legally binding contracts ended up being set aside. What would happen to players who refused to agree to wage reductions was not known. There was a suggestion that they would not receive any wages the following season until they had paid up, but this seemed an excessively drastic solution. Eventually all the dissenting players fell in line. Wednesday's players had been incorrectly reported as being the last to agree to the scheme, as other clubs were adopting the same position until the last moment. The Players' Union was criticised in the press for having 'an unfortunate tendency to do the wrong thing' when doing the right thing might put it in a stronger position and increase its popularity and membership. The Union was accused of displaying a lack of unity, allowing the players of every club to act on their own, until finally it saw the folly of continuing to defy the Football League and agreed to its contributory assistance scheme. It had failed to rise to the challenge and, it was suggested, the current season might witness its end. How could a union of players exist when so many of its members acted in their own selfish interests? The Players' Union did not meet its demise, whilst the wage deduction plan was discontinued in mid January, after thirteen weeks, and the club contributory scheme terminated after each club had played eleven home matches under its regulations.

Away from the politics of contracts and wages, Sheffield United were due to meet Middlesbrough at Bramall Lane on the last day of October. Stanley Fazackerley returned to replace the injured David Davies as United were expected to maintain their recent good home record against the Teessiders. However, it did not turn out that way as United fell to another defeat, this time 1-0 in a game in which they suffered yet more misfortune. They were hampered from the start as influential captain George Utley was absent, hurt in the annual Sheffield v Glasgow match a few days earlier. Morning rain made for a heavy pitch and a poor crowd witnessed a first half almost devoid of excitement, the closest to a goal coming when goalkeeper Harold Gough elected to kick instead of handling and made little distance with the wet ball. He was forced to scurry back to his goal to concede a corner. Midway through the first half a heavy midfield collision put Jack Thompson, who up to that point had been United's cleverest player, out of the game, the second consecutive time United had suffered such a handicap. Ten minutes into the second half United were given a penalty when Weir's attempted clearance hit his teammate Jackson and rebounded on to the former's hand. Despite their being 'no earthly intention about the handling', according to the *Sheffield Daily Telegraph*, the penalty decision was instantaneous, but United spurned the opportunity as Joe Kitchen struck the ball straight at goalkeeper Davies and put the rebound well wide.

Middlesbrough's winner came with twenty minutes remaining as Storey's dribble and pass presented Elliot with a good chance, which he took. Before Thompson's injury United had shaped quite promisingly, but once he had departed Kitchen and Jimmy Simmons were 'easily kept at bay by the Middlesbrough heavyweights near goal'. Down to only four forwards, United's efforts flagged towards the end of what was another luckless defeat.

United's attendance against Middlesbrough, around 10,000, was their lowest of the season, but elsewhere, despite bad weather that 'combine[d] a shower bath and a trip to Iceland', the picture was better. Aston Villa had their best crowd of the season for the visit of Newcastle United, and throughout the country over 200,000 people spent their Saturday afternoon watching football. How, it was asked, would those 200,000 occupy their time if there was no football? Even army recruits were given Saturday afternoon off and needed something to keep them entertained. This was of no consolation to Sheffield United, who were 'being blown about by pretty near every adverse element'. Seldom a match went by without one of their players being injured, but the *Sheffield Daily Telegraph's* 'Looker-On' was optimistic: 'The season is still comparatively young, and if only United can shake off the ill fortune which has so far dogged them, we believe they will not finish up so badly.' Wise words, which would ultimately prove to be accurate.

Morale-boosting news for United came in the form of the return to Sheffield of William Gillespie after two months in a Sunderland hospital. He would not be able to play for an indefinite period, but his personality would certainly lighten the dark mood that surrounded Bramall Lane due to the team's poor run that had so far brought two wins, four draws and five defeats. Drastic, even desperate, measures were now to be tried in a bid to reverse United's fortunes. For the forthcoming visit to unbeaten Manchester City, Joe Kitchen and Stanley Fazackerley were dropped and captain and leader of the half-back line, George Utley, described as a 'brainy man', was to be given a run at centre forward. Other changes included Jimmy Revill, normally a left winger, on the right wing, and Jimmy Simmons, usually a right winger, at inside right, with the returning Fred Hawley taking Utley's place in the half-back line. To an extent the changes worked, as United came away from Hyde Road with a well-earned point from a goalless draw after a 'gallant struggle'. The early exchanges did not bode well for United, as '[the backs] did nearly everything they should not have done, and many things we had never seen them do before', such as Jack English being knocked up in the air by one of Fred Howard's bull-like charges. Utley showed excellent conception of his new position, and his additional weight was useful against the City centre half Ted Hanney. He proved to be a tremendous leader of both the forward line and the team. United enjoyed a stroke of luck when a terrific shot from Howard struck English's foot and then the crossbar, then Howard and Billy Gaughan missed ridiculously easy chances. United, though having less possession, were playing the better football and had their fair share of efforts on goal. However, Harold Gough was one again the leading figure, and, unusually, some of his saves produced applause and cheers from the home crowd. He also had to crash through his own full backs, who were crowding in on him, in order to clear the ball. The *Sheffield Daily Telegraph* match report heaped praise on Gough. 'Too much cannot be said for Gough,' it wrote. 'Gough takes such performances as a matter of course, and there is no fear of his getting inflated ideas of his ability.' *The Times* agreed, calling Gough 'a brilliant goalkeeper', adding that 'the skill of this player was not altogether responsible for the failure of the home team to score. The Manchester forwards are on the light side, and on the heavy ground they were not so effective.' All in all, it had been an encouraging display by United.

Despite the relative success of the result against Manchester City, more alterations to the line-up were in store. It was noticed that Fred Hawley, on his return from injury, was not yet at full effectiveness, and Utley was too important to the half-back line to leave him at centre forward. So, Hawley was left out of the team to play Aston Villa, and Stanley Fazackerley came in at centre forward, where, it was hoped, he would 'redeem himself by an exhibition of resolution, which has been lacking somewhat'. The changes did not have the desired effect, as United were beaten 1-0 at Villa Park. They survived a missed penalty, struck against the post by Andy Ducat, but a rare slip by Gough, when he moved too late, allowed the same player to score the winner. United suffered yet another injury, when Bob Evans was kicked in the face and required stitches over his right eye when he returned to Sheffield. It was not an exciting game, as the *Sheffield Daily Telegraph* amusingly explained: 'There were times when one would have been better employed in sleeping.' Fazackerley was not a success at centre forward, showing 'a precipitancy to get rid of the ball at all costs' but, on a good note, the defence played 'in splendid harmony'. If only the forwards could raise their standards: the 'goals for' column in the league table showed United were being poorly served by their front line. Numerous formations had been tried in this department, but each one made little difference. United had now gone three games without a goal.

United's scoring problems did not concern Mr Edwin Sorby, of Broom Road, Rotherham, who wrote to the *Sheffield Daily Telegraph* to complain about the stance taken by its columnist 'Looker-On':

In spite of Mr Punch's cartoons, and in spite of the plain hint from Parliament, I see in to-day's paper that ['Looker-On'] is still allowed to go on whining about the necessity of playing such games, and he even pulls out the pathetic stop and talks about the players being turned adrift. The only place they could drift to and should drift to is the army. Can anyone doubt that if the leading professionals of say, the Sheffield Wednesday team, announced that on a certain Saturday they would march to the recruiting office, that they would be followed by thousands of their supporters?

A few days later Mr Sorby wrote again: 'In your columns on November 19, under the heading "War Office and F.A.," the following appears: "No meetings can compare with football gatherings in the attendance of men and youths eligible for the army." This frank admission by the F.A. at once disposes of all attempts on the part of yourself or "Looker-On" to shelter football behind any other form of entertainment, either on the stage of off it. The total cessation of football is, for many reasons, not to be desired, nor would it be fair to the companies concerned, but many of the minor leagues and competitions might well cease, and the men so set at liberty could arrange amongst themselves either to join the army or be drafted into the First League teams. The directors and shareholders of these companies cannot be allowed to control the actions of these men in war time as they have done in peace time.' Sorby was supported by a writer calling himself 'Once A Player':

The football professional continues on the primrose path content to draw his wages and attract his thousands of young spectators week by week, and the Council of the Football Association allows him to do so. 'Oh! But we have printed an appeal to our professionals and spectators to enlist and we have allowed recruiting speeches to be made at our matches.' This reply leaves one cold, as does the plaint about the difficulty of breaking contracts. Read the accounts in to-day's papers of the miserable response made on Saturday to the appeals at various League matches. Nothing more humiliating has occurred since the war began. There is one simple fact that the Council of the Football Association knows better than anyone else. So long as there is a League or Cup match to see on Saturday afternoon, so long will the thousands of young men who are now attending them refuse to enlist. These matches are literally the be-all and end-all of their existence. Knock off the matches and you will find the recruiting figures will go up at once.

Next Mr Douglas Sladen wrote, supporting a tax on gate money, and suggesting that the Government should issue an order stating that no one of military age could play sport in any place to which the general public had admission, unless he was a member of the regular or reserve forces. Although sounding highly impractical, at least Mr Sladen did not restrict his idea to football, but perhaps golf could be excluded as so few men of military age played, he said. Perhaps Mr Sladen was a regular golfer. Mr George Swift of Matlock was next to put pen to paper, and perhaps unexpectedly, criticised the position of Mr Sladen and others. Swift expressed disgust at the efforts to stop football, and said that spectators of the game had as much right to watch as had golfers to play and hunters to hunt. He believed that if the Government came to the conclusion that it wanted more men, it would take not only footballers and their followers, but all kinds of sportsmen. Swift was a rare voice in the pages of the press, and 'Looker-On' hit out at the remainder, asking why such tirades were directed almost entirely at the sport of football. Football, he wrote, was a spectacle beloved of the democracy and should be closed down when all other forms of sport and entertainment were closed down. If the War Office was happy for the game to go on, so should everybody be. Only when the Government declared that the continuation of football was undesirable would his newspaper advocate closure. 'Until then we see no reason for doing so,' he concluded. 'Looker-On' received probably unexpected backing from the ranks of the clergy. Canon Goodall, the Vicar of Rotherham, praised the *Sheffield Daily Telegraph* for its 'consistently patriotic common sense view' of the situation. No newspaper had been more prominent in its support of the game, he added, continuously adopting a tone of 'plain and lofty warning'.

Returning to events on the field, it was now reported that Sheffield United were to abandon the experiment of trying various players in the centre forward position and were to bring back Joe Kitchen, who was 'showing more of his old dash with the reserves'. Meanwhile, William Gillespie had dispensed with his crutches and was undergoing treatment at the Edgar Allen Institute, a physiotherapy clinic founded by the local steel magnate of the same name. If only the skilful Gillespie had been available, surely the forward line would not have struggled so badly. Liverpool, just a couple of places above United in the table, were the latest visitors to Bramall Lane on November 21, and United put an end to their five-game winless run by beating them 2-1. Prior to this match United's home record was awful, bringing only four points and three goals from five matches, so the victory was much needed. The visitors were hopelessly beaten and had goalkeeper Kenneth Campbell to thank for keeping the score down, as for a change there was life and eagerness in the United attack. The first goal came after sixteen minutes, when Jimmy Simmons 'raced across to the inside-left position to get the ball, got it, and as promptly seemed to lose it, but in some remarkable fashion regained it, and beat Campbell with a very fast shot from an extraordinary angle'. Liverpool levelled after thirty-five minutes but George Utley prompted his forwards again and again until the over-active Simmons scored his second just before the interval. Simmons was at the heart of everything, seeming like a magnet to the ball. He hit the post from twenty-five yards, before putting the ball the wrong side of the post from just three yards out. All three of United's half backs performed well, but Simmons was the undoubted star, his cleverness on the ball being compared by the *Sheffield Daily Telegraph* to that of Sunderland's international player Charles Buchan.

For once United would be able to name an unchanged team for the following week's trip to Bradford Park Avenue, on the last Saturday in November. After the fine display against Liverpool, a rare away victory was anticipated. But it did not transpire as United lost 2-0. They did not play badly, but could not get the fullest value out of their play. Joe Kitchen, recently restored to the team, was still not on top form, resulting in a lot of fine wing play coming to nothing. After the game the United management was called upon to persist with the present forward combination, as repeated alterations had produced little reward. However, this might not be possible as Jimmy Revill was 'severely damaged' just before half time. As for the players, they were urged to put more 'boot' behind their shooting, and shoot more often! They took the advice: a week later United recorded by some distance their best victory of a so far disappointing season. They met Oldham Athletic, the league leaders, judged by many to be the strongest and best-balanced side in the First Division. More changes to the United team were required; Revill was now injured, so Joe Kitchen moved to outside right, with David Davies at centre forward and Wally Masterman at inside left. Perhaps more significantly for United's prospects, captain George Utley was also missing. In attempt to cope with the loss of their captain, United adopted a change of tactics that surprised the visitors, whose half backs appeared not to know what to do about it. The new formula was described as a 'long-passing game' that was 'thoroughly appreciated by the 8,000 people present', and produced three goals, from Simmons, Masterman and Davies. The long-ball game was clearly in existence almost a century ago.

On the last day in November the management committee of the Football League met in Manchester and reaffirmed its decision to continue the football season. It also advised clubs not to award benefits to players due to reduced gate income. Three days later the Football Association invited their counterparts from Scotland, Wales and Ireland to a conference at the Association's Russell Square offices. The meeting commenced at 12.30pm and lasted until 7pm, apart from an adjournment for refreshments in mid afternoon. Under the chairmanship of Sheffielder Charles Clegg, it was agreed, in consultation with the War Office, to cancel the four nations' international matches scheduled for the following spring. However, the current domestic seasons would continue. To this end, the Football Association released a statement to the press:

> *It was decided to recommend to each national association that the international matches for this season be abandoned. There is no evidence that the playing of football has hindered or is*

hindering recruiting. On the contrary there is good reason to conclude that football has encouraged and assisted recruiting. In these circumstances this meeting recommends that, except as regards the international matches, it is not right that football should be stopped or suspended. Further, the meeting is of opinion that to deprive the working people of our country of their Saturday afternoon recreation would be unfair and very mischievous.

The *Manchester Guardian* sympathised with the position of the Football Association, but not with football spectators:

There is a rather tragic contrast between the cry of the men in the trenches for every man to go out and do his part and the shouts of the crowds whom professional players entertain at home. We fancy that none of the other nations engaged in the war feels itself equally free to amuse itself. And the spectacle of a great part of the able-bodied manhood of England diverting itself with looking on at races and football while our men in France are taking part in a life-or-death struggle is one that brings searchings of conscience, in spite of the Football Association's business-like arguments for going on with their programme.

Clegg also spoke on the same subject at a 'football service' held at the Victoria Hall in the centre of Sheffield, where Sheffield United captain George Utley joined him on the platform. Clegg told the gathering: 'There is no doubt that more men are wanted, but every man will have to settle for himself what his duty is. I will say this for myself – I do not want to commit anybody else to it – that every capable man, who without good cause, refuses to help, is a coward and traitor to his country.' In response to those who believed football ought to be stopped, Clegg commented that such criticisms came only from people who had no connection with the game. He asked whether the critics would be prepared to give up their recreations, and why did they not extend their opposition to other sports and entertainment? Why should football be stopped in Britain when it was still being played in Belgium, France, Germany and Austria? He said the cessation of the game would hinder, not assist, the war effort, a view he claimed was supported by the War Office in its discussions with the Football Association. In fact the War Office was non-committal in its statements about football, consistently leaving important decisions to the game's authorities. Clegg concluded by dramatically calling on the Almighty to punish the German Emperor when he reached the afterlife, declaring: 'The Day of Judgement might be deferred, and although full punishment here might not be possible, it would be certain hereafter when the murderer of thousands stood before the God whose name he has so often blasphemed.' Also present at the Victoria Hall was Mr George Wagstaffe-Simmons, honorary secretary of the Hertfordshire Football Association, who said that already over 100,000 footballers had enlisted in the armed forces. He felt that the criticisms levelled at the young men who played football were unfair and unjust, and should be withdrawn. The meeting ended with Liberal Councillor Arthur Neal reading the lesson and Mr Robert Charlesworth singing 'Thanksgiving' and 'Come Unto Me'.

Soon afterwards the persistent Frederick Charrington wrote to Clegg asking for a one-to-one meeting. Clegg's reply noted that because Charrington had already petitioned the King and spoken to the War Office and Lord Kinnaird, the president of the Football Association, 'and in other ways acted in opposition to football, it was rather late, and would answer no useful purpose, to have an interview'. Charrington, in a second letter, expressed regret that Clegg would not agree to a meeting, and stated: 'My opposition is not against football in itself, but to professional football being played during the war. I think I have proved this by sending one guinea to Lord Roberts towards his football fund for the soldiers, for which I have received a letter of thanks from his lordship.'[17] Clegg did not respond.

The next important meeting on the national football agenda was to be held in early December, when the Football Association was to decide whether or not its Cup competition would proceed. It did not look promising. A proposal for abandonment was on the table, and there was the curious prospect of the final qualifying rounds being played, with the successful teams unable to enter the competition proper. The abandonment motion, put forward by Daniel Burley Woolfall, the first British president of F.I.F.A., the honorary treasurer of the Football Association and president of the Lancashire Football Association, read: 'That at the present time it is not desirable to proceed with the Cup competitions beyond the qualifying stages.' It had been assumed, erroneously, that because of Woolfall's office his motion was the official position of the Association but news leaked out that it would be hotly opposed. However, some southern-based members of the F.A. Council were believed to support Woolfall.

Pressure also came from the Scottish Football Association, which expressed a wish to abandon its own Cup competition, after discussions with Harold Tennant MP, Under-Secretary of State for War, who said:

---

[17] Charrington was also not averse to verging on bribery. He sent £5 to Tottenham player Arthur Grimsdell when he enlisted, in the hope that other players would be encouraged to follow.

I recognise the difficulties of the complete cessation of professional football, but, as I have stated previously,[18] I do not consider that, when so many homes are bereaved, and so many brave men are laying down their lives for our country, the full programme of amusement which we welcome in times of peace, is in accord with public sentiment, or with the cruel realities of this devastating war. I am glad to think that many thoughtful people share these views, as is demonstrated by numerous correspondents. I welcome the attitude of the Scottish Football Association, who have always been prepared to accept the view of the War Office, and who are now quite willing to adopt the view I have set forth, viz. the abandonment of both international matches and Cup ties.

If the English Cup was to be cancelled, the Football League would ask for permission to organise a competition of its own. The decision was made on December 7: the Cup was to go ahead. Once again the old arguments were put forward: cancelling the Cup would reduce recruitment opportunities, and many clubs were in financial trouble and needed the income the Cup would bring. It was also stated that there was little point in abandoning the Cup, as the Football League would then simply run its own competition, which would add up to the same thing. The Football Association's Finance

---

[18] Tennant's comment referred to a letter he wrote to Thomas Forsyth, the chairman of Airdrieonians FC, which found its way into the press: 'No objection is taken by the military authorities to occasional recreation. It is considered, however, that professional football does not come within that category, and that it can only be admitted on grounds of contract of employment. It is much more desirable that professional footballers should find employment in His Majesty's forces.'

Committee agreed to forego its five per cent cut from matches played from the first round proper, including the semi finals, which would please the Football League and its clubs.

On November 26 more than seven hundred British sailors had died when the battleship HMS Bulwark blew up in an accident on the River Medway, just west of Sheerness. Two days later, not many miles away from this disaster, an attendance of just 5,000 turned up for Arsenal's home game against Bristol City as extremely heavy rain in the south of England affected the already falling attendances at League games. Only one army recruiting officer was present at Highbury but the results of his efforts were not made public. The War Office optimistically sent handbills to the ground encouraging enlistment. They were distributed amongst the crowd, along with a printed version of the appeal made by Football Association secretary Frederick Wall earlier in the month. Wall also attended the match. Interviewed that day by *The Times*, Arsenal FC chairman Henry Norris claimed that the public outcry against football was damaging to the work of the recruiting agencies. 'Some players I have talked with,' he said, 'say they will not be bullied into enlisting. They are willing to take their part with the rest of the community. They would welcome conscription. Football has done splendid service to the War Office in assisting to secure men for the services. Only this week I was told by an officer in the army that football had proved the best recruiting agency of ail, and he viewed with alarm the threat of a stoppage of the game.' Norris, who was also chairman of the Fulham Voluntary Recruiting Committee, had spoken publicly to crowds at the Arsenal and Fulham grounds. He sagaciously continued: 'When you address a crowd you do not expect men to fall out suddenly and go to the recruiting office. They either go home to consult their fathers or other relatives, or interview their employers before coming to a decision that means so much to them. The fruits of the addresses at football matches and in other public places are seen on a Monday morning at the recruiting offices. It is unreasonable to expect men to walk away from a football match with a recruiting sergeant.'

Norris then went on to talk about the large reduction in gates at football matches. It was not because of a lack of interest or a lack of money, he said, but 'it is simply because the majority of [the absentees] have enlisted for the war'. However, at the Fulham v Barnsley match (Norris was also a director of Fulham) there were no efforts made to obtain recruits and, unlike at Highbury, no communication of any kind in regard to recruiting was sent by the War Office to the club. *The Times* then gave details of recruitment attempts at other games. At Bradford, where Sheffield United were the visitors, what had become the normal custom of a prominent dignitary addressing the crowd did not happen. No other form of recruiting effort was made amongst the 10,000 crowd. At the Manchester United v Newcastle United match, the number of spectators was a disappointing 10,000, an estimated one thousand of whom were men in uniform, chiefly that of the City Battalion of the Manchester Regiment. Of the remainder, many were either too old or too young to serve. Wounded British and Belgian soldiers also attended the match, but no meetings to promote recruiting were held, nor were any facilities provided for the enlistment of men. Reports from other grounds bore similar stories of abandoned efforts to obtain recruits, which hitherto had produced negligible response. No attempts were made in Sheffield, Birmingham and Sunderland. In Glasgow, printed appeals to the patriotism of football spectators were handed out, but otherwise nothing. At Blackburn, boy scouts distributed pamphlets inviting men to 'Fall in' but there were no facilities at the ground for those who wished to do so. A novel scheme was to be tried in Liverpool, where, with the approval of Lord Kitchener,

141

postcards were to be presented to eligible men attending matches. Recipients were requested to signify their desire to enlist or declare their reason for not doing so before returning the cards. Lord Derby, recruitment campaigner and former Lord Mayor of Liverpool, explained that by these means a census of football followers could be obtained.

Gates at professional matches were a cause for concern, not only for the cash-strapped clubs, but also for recruiting organisations, which had fewer men to persuade to join up. Attendance figures were published for several clubs' games in November, comparing them with the crowds on an equivalent Saturday a year earlier:

	21 Nov 1914	7 Nov 1914	17 Nov 1913
Chelsea	15000	25000	35000
Newcastle	8000	20000	25000
West Bromwich	10000	14000	35000
Grimsby	8000	7000	9000
Gillingham	3000	6000	6000
Crystal P	8000	7000	10000
Brighton	3000	5000	6000

At the smaller clubs, where crowds were generally lower anyway, the problem did not appear too severe, but the major clubs of London, the midlands and the north were suffering badly. The last Saturday in November saw a drop of 61,000 (from 234,000 to 173,000) in attendances at games in the Football League, Southern League and Scottish League compared to the previous Saturday. A portion of this fall might have been the fault of the awful weather and the earlier kick-offs that were necessary to conclude matches in daylight, but some proposed that it was due to the fact that football was incompatible with successful recruiting. The following week, with better weather, the numbers were up, but overall, compared to the previous season, crowds were well down. The *Sheffield Daily Telegraph* published comparative figures for the first Saturday in December. In the three main leagues (Football League Divisions One and Two and the Southern League), combined attendances had fallen from 342,600 in 1913 to just over 174,000 a year later. The average gate receipts for First Division matches, which were £735 in 1913/14, were now just £414.

One unidentified London football club official said that his club would welcome the compulsory abandonment of professional football, but Henry Norris believed such a drastic step was unnecessary. The letter writers to *The Times* continued to show that they were on the side of the unnamed official, not Mr Norris. A letter from a former player with Cambridge University and Corinthians Football Clubs (and therefore an amateur) was typical:

> *I venture to think, from what I know of the splendid type of character of our professional football players, that up to the present the large majority of them have not in any complete way yet grasped their country's need. Their minds would have been opened if they could have come round a hospital in France, full of our own wounded just brought down from the trenches. It is unthinkable that some of our finest athletes, men ready and equipped as far as physique is concerned, should not at once volunteer for hard military training if they really know their country's need. Surely [our great football clubs] will not only play 'the lesser game' until maybe they see their country invaded. Then it might be too late to have the honour of sharing in 'the*

greater game,' for though physically fit they would be untrained for war. I know that with them football is not merely a game, but also a profession. But how many professions have already been gladly given up for the time being, when the Empire's great need has been understood? There must be thousands of men in the crowds that still seem to go and watch these 'lesser games' who also might be training for 'the greater game.' They would soon follow when the players set the example. I would not for a moment give the impression that all football at home should stop. It has its own distinctive, cheering use, especially at this time. But let it not be the spectacular show carried on by men physically most fitted to serve their country in the greatest need of her whole history, and for idle crowds to watch. Let it be the school or club game of real recreation played by those too young or unable for genuine reasons to serve their country on the battlefield, or by those who play it as a game in between the hours of their military training.

Mr J. H. Farmer, of Mundesley, Norfolk, agreed. He believed that people were gradually coming to realise that the attraction of football was preventing men from volunteering. Watching football was a habit, he maintained, a suggestion proved by the fact that the cumulative attendances at matches so far had topped three million. Was this not proof of the insatiable, irresistible allure of the big match? 'Remove the cause and you destroy the effect,' he remarked. If the Football Association put a stop to competitive football, Mr Farmer felt that, deprived of his weekly stimulant and looking round for another, the football spectator might then be persuaded to 'take

144

part in the grandest game ever played on this earth and vindicate all that makes life endurable'.

Next to expound his point of view was the Right Reverend James Edward Cowell Welldon, the Dean of Manchester. He said: 'It may be fairly argued that men who might be serving their country at the front in her supreme hour of destiny cannot patriotically spend their time as players or spectators of football matches. But in reply it is possible to ask: what are men who are debarred from joining the colours to do in their leisure hours? Is not the football field a better place for them than the public house? Why should football-playing be regarded with less favour than horse-racing or theatre-going? It is perhaps a mistake to stigmatise a particular sport. If the sport is not wrong in itself, it can scarcely be wrong at the present time, except so far as it may conflict with public duty. Perhaps I may be allowed to add that the stage seems to differ from the turf or the football field, as the closing of the theatres would throw out of employment a large number of persons who, being women, could not in any circumstances serve as combatants.' So there were no male actors of eligible age?

From the front line came a more forthright letter from a Major in the medical service, who wrote: 'It makes me furious to think that we are all hanging on here to our positions, losing countless officers and men daily, while the British public will not enlist. More men are needed very badly, while they at home go on playing football, &c., as if we about here were not fighting to save an invasion of England. It is simply heartbreaking. It is a pity that the Germans do not land troops on our shores, just to wake England up to a true realisation of the position.' Mr George Pragnell, chairman of the Employers' Territorial Association and vice-president of the Amateur Football Association, argued that every man who was able to watch or play football on a Saturday afternoon would be better employed as a recruit in the Regular or Territorial

Army. Failing that, he could be trained in drilling for home defence as a member of a Volunteer Training Corps. Pragnell concluded: 'With a long experience of both athletics and recruiting, I have no hesitation in saying that at such a time as this the playing of professional (gate-money) football is a noxious drug, whilst the number of able-bodied men who look on is a national disgrace.'

Now, the Council of the Newspaper Proprietors' Federation decided that further, decisive action was required. Representing the London-based daily newspapers, the Federation decided that, with the exception of sporting newspapers, no daily paper would publish more than the bare results of football matches. It was merely a gesture, but it displayed their strength of feeling. But as one letter writer pointed out, such action was biased, as one newspaper refusing to promote professional football published 'three whole columns of racing news, half a column of amateur football and nearly a column of billiards'. *The Times* reiterated its opposition to professional football but denied that it was calling for its abolition 'because it amuses many thousands of spectators'. The newspaper conceded that there was a need for sporting entertainment for people who were performing valuable non-military services to the nation. It proposed that such entertainment could be provided by teams representing home-based regiments, playing matches outside their hours of military training. By these means, those who followed football could continue to do so without forgetting the war, as it would be permanently before their eyes in the form of soldiers playing the game. In the words of *The Times*: 'What has been something of a national scandal would take its proper place as a healthy part of the national life at a great national emergency.' The idea was quite rightly ignored by the football authorities.

Some members of the press were of the opinion that the football authorities were prepared to close down football if the War Office had wanted to do so, but the War Office officials consulted declined to commit themselves either way. Now, with many figures regarding recruitment being thrown around and exaggerated or underestimated to support each particular protagonist's case, *The Times* decided to carry out some real research by contacting clubs to obtain some accurate numbers, and in doing so defended the position of the clubs, possibly under pressure to do so from influential football people:

> *The nature of the communications passing between the recruiting agencies and those responsible for the control of football has not been disclosed, but that their cooperation has so far been imperfect is suggested by the statement of the secretary of a London club that recruiting at football matches has been entirely haphazard. It is claimed by members of the Council of the Football Association that upwards of 100,000 recruits for the army have been secured from the ranks of Association football, and that this total exceeds by far the combined recruits from all other branches of sport. All professional players of the leading clubs, in addition to the ordinary football training, undergo military drill on certain days of the week, and rifle ranges have been constructed on major grounds for daily practice. The fitness of this body of men for home defence or active service is unquestioned. The number of professional football players has been much exaggerated. A member of the Council of the Football Association states that the number of players registered with the Association this*

season is less than 5,000. Not less than 2,000 are serving in various branches of His Majesty's forces. There are in this country 2,000 players earning their living by the game. The number of first-class players is put at 1,500, more than two-thirds of whom are married. The total number of unmarried men who depend on the game for a livelihood is reckoned at six hundred. There are, roughly, 3,000,000 unmarried men of military age, of whom considerably over 2,000,000 have not undertaken service of any kind. People interested in football say they cannot understand why the six hundred football players who might enlist should be singled out for special condemnation. A football official in London believes that the professional clubs would welcome the compulsory stopping of football. The average decrease in drawings at matches throughout the country this season is fifty per cent, while the wages to be paid under contract, from which the clubs are unable to escape, amount to £272,000. Football must continue until it is prohibited by Act of Parliament. No football club has refused permission to any player who is desirous to enlist. The breaking of a contract is exclusively the right of the player.

The newspaper then published details of recruiting and fund raising that had been supplied by clubs. Most stated that recruiting was encouraged at every match and that players contributed between two-and-a-half per cent and twelve-and-a-half per cent of their wages to relief funds. Public collections were also made at most grounds.

West Bromwich Albion – Formed a 'West Bromwich Albion Company', attached to the 5th South Staffs Territorials, raised principally from club supporters. Eight players enlisted and a director joined the army as a Major. A total of £139 contributed to various war relief funds.

Preston North End – Three players joined the army and £285 contributed.

Lincoln City – All the sons of directors of military age, two sons of the secretary, all the sons of the working-men's committee and a director volunteered for service or enlisted. Three players joined the army, and £249 given to the war funds.

Manchester United – About three hundred recruits to the army, and about £300 contributed to war funds.

Liverpool – One player, one director, two sons of directors, and many shareholders enlisted. War fund donations and collections amounted to £554. Recruiting drives at every match.

Newcastle United – Three players enlisted; £196 contributed to relief funds. Public recruiting at every match.

Middlesbrough – Three club members enlisted and over 100 men signed their intention to enlist after one recruiting meeting. Contributed £140.

Bolton Wanderers – £130 contributed. No players joined.

Burnley – Two players and the assistant trainer serving. Special room reserved for recruiting officials; twelve enlisted at the last meeting. A sum of £177 raised for war funds.

Cardiff City – Hundreds of club supporters joined. Exclusive of collections, the club contributed £66. The majority of supporters of the club were engaged in coal and railway work, so were ineligible for enlistment.

Southampton – Twenty-three players enlisted. The secretary was quoted as saying: 'We are only a poor club, but doing all we can.' Exclusive of other collections, contributed

£58. The 5th Hampshire Regiment was making use of the ground for training on non-match days.

Swindon Town – Contributed £70. Nearly all supporters of the club were in the railway service, therefore were not permitted to enlist. Only two unmarried players in the team.

Nottingham Forest – Two players and scores of club members enlisted. £70 contributed. The club had been thanked for 'real assistance' given to recruiting officers.

Watford – Only six players unmarried; two enlisted. £46 contributed.

Brighton and Hove Albion – Three players joined the army, one of whom was killed. Harm had been done to recruiting by a message received from the recruiting office in October cancelling a meeting because 'sufficient men had enlisted'. Contributed £204.

Two days later *The Times* followed up by reporting that twenty players from Hull City FC, eleven from Plymouth Argyle FC and eight from Everton FC had signed up. None of the clubs mentioned were from London, which appeared to some to be less committed to recruitment than the provinces, a situation a group of clubs in the capital decided needed to be rectified.

Sheffield United's 1915
FA Cup winning line-up:
Back row - George
Waller (trainer), Jack
English, Harold Gough,
Bill Brelsford, Albert
Sturgess.
Middle row - Bill Cook,
Stanley Fazackerley,
George Utley (captain),
Wally Masterman, Bob
Evans.
Front row - Jimmy
Simmons, Joe Kitchen

*(photograph courtesy of
Denis Clarebrough)*

The front page of the
1915 FA Cup final
programme, produced
by Manchester United.
(left)

Jimmy Simmons, outside right and scorer of Sheffield United's first goal in the 1915 FA Cup final (left)

(photograph courtesy of Denis Clarebrough)

Stanley Fazackerley, inside right and scorer of Sheffield United's second goal in the 1915 FA Cup final (right)

(photograph courtesy of Denis Clarebrough)

Joe Kitchen, centre forward and scorer of Sheffield United's third goal in the 1915 FA Cup final (left)

(photograph courtesy of Denis Clarebrough)

George Utley, Sheffield United's captain and left half back in the 1915 FA Cup final (right)

(photograph courtesy of Denis Clarebrough)

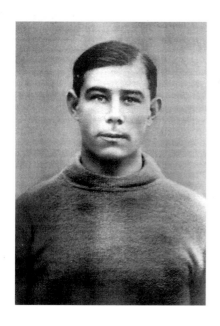

The men who made up Sheffield United's fabled defence:

Goalkeeper Harold Gough (above left)

Right back Bill Cook. (above right)

Left back Jack English (left)

(photographs courtesy of Denis Clarebrough)

Albert Sturgess, Sheffield United's right half back in the 1915 FA Cup final (left)

(photograph courtesy of Denis Clarebrough)

Bill Brelsford, Sheffield United's centre half back in the 1915 FA Cup final (right)

(photograph courtesy of Denis Clarebrough)

Two men who missed the final:
Inside forward William Gillespie, who broke his leg in the first league game and missed the rest of the season (left)

Half back and permanent first reserve, Fred Hawley (below right)

A Sheffield United season ticket for the 1914/15 season (below right)

(photographs courtesy of Denis Clarebrough)

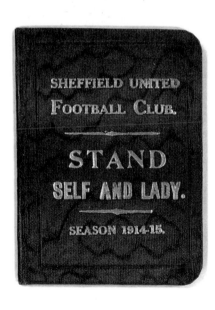

Jimmy Revill, (the
only Sheffield
United player to
lose his life in the
First World War
(right)

*(photograph
courtesy of Denis
Clarebrough)*

Charles Clegg:
player, referee,
administrator; a
Sheffield football
icon (left)

*(photograph
courtesy of Denis
Clarebrough)*

Mr G. H. Bibbings appeals for recruits to the forces at the Sheffield United v Sheffield Wednesday match at Bramall Lane, September 5, 1914
(photograph courtesy of the Local Studies Library, Sheffield City Libraries)

Lizzie the elephant, employed by Sheffield company Thomas Ward's for haulage, due to the shortage of horses, which had been taken by the army
(photograph courtesy of the Local Studies Library, Sheffield City Libraries)

CHAPTER NINE

THE CHARGE AT FOOTBALL IS GOOD, THAT WITH THE BAYONET FINER

The war was approaching four months old when, amid continued criticism from individuals and sections of the press about the continuation of League football, all the London-based Football League and Southern League clubs decided to confer to determine what measures they could take to assist with the efforts to attract recruits to the military services. Delegates at the meeting may have learned from newspaper reports that the intensity of the fighting near Ypres had ebbed and what was left of the British Expeditionary Force was holding a line in France from just south of St Eloi, past Armentières to Neuve Chapelle and Festubert, then to the La Bassée Canal at Givenchy. The regular British army had been virtually destroyed in Belgium and was now reliant on a regular supply of new recruits. The weather in northern France as December approached was terrible as continuous rain was replaced by snow; conditions in the trenches were particularly onerous.

Against this background the London clubs' representatives met in late November at Winchester House in the city. Their conference resulted in the following somewhat indignant resolution, which was issued to the press:

That this meeting of the representatives of the following London professional clubs; Chelsea, Tottenham Hotspur, Arsenal, Fulham, Clapton Orient, West Ham, Millwall, Queen's Park Rangers, Crystal Palace, Brentford, and Croydon Common, were strongly of opinion that the present agitation of a certain section of the daily London press is unscrupulous and unwarrantable and undignified and wholly opposed to English traditions and an abuse of the liberty given to the press, are nevertheless prepared to discontinue the game and close their grounds simultaneously with the closing of racecourses, golf links, theatres, music halls, picture palaces, and kindred entertainments.

As had been argued countless times before, why should football be the only form of professional entertainment to come under such close scrutiny and be under pressure to close down? There was little or no pressure on other sports to discontinue, and why had the theatrical arts escaped attention? After all, they too were enterprises reliant on paying audiences.

The London clubs' meeting led to another a few days later, organised by Football Association secretary Frederick Wall and attended by F.A. president Lord Kinnaird, Captain Thomas Whiffen, the army's Chief Recruiting Officer for London, the secretaries of all the London clubs, several southern-based clubs and a number of other interested parties, such as William Joynson-Hicks, Conservative MP for Brentford, and Arsenal FC chairman Henry Norris, the man responsible for relocating the former Woolwich Arsenal from south of the river to their new home at Highbury in 1913. At the same time he retained a seat on the board of Fulham FC and was also Mayor of the Borough of Fulham. Joynson-Hicks chaired the meeting, held at the offices of the Football Association, with the idea of promoting a Footballers' Battalion for the army. The meeting approved the idea, and Joynson-Hicks was instructed to confer with the War Office. Permission from the War Office for the new battalion was granted in mid December, resulting in a public meeting at Fulham Town Hall to formalise its formation. Its official name was to be the 17th (Service) Battalion (1st Football) Middlesex Regiment. When the season opened an attempt had been made to raise a footballers' battalion, but the response was so poor that the project had to be dropped, and the players who had volunteered were drafted into the various city battalions.

Around four hundred, a great number of them players, attended the Fulham meeting. The organisers desired to attract a full battalion of 1,350 men, comprising professional and amateur players and club supporters. *Athletic News* expressed a hope that there might be 'the Chelsea Company, the Tottenham Company, the Millwall Company, the Fulham Company, and so on'. As well as Norris, Joynson-Hicks, Kinnaird and Wall, sharing the main platform in the hall were Harry Bradshaw, secretary of the Southern League, William Hayes Fisher, Conservative MP for Fulham and president of Fulham FC, Captain Henry Wells-Holland, chairman of Clapton Orient FC, the Millwall chairman J. B. Skeggs, Colonel Charles Grantham and Captain Whiffen, representing the army, and representatives of Arsenal FC, Chelsea FC, Crystal Palace FC and Tottenham Hotspur FC.

The Sportsman newspaper carried a long account of proceedings. In his opening speech, Joynson-Hicks stated that most present were aware why they had gathered and of the attacks on football by a number of prominent people and newspapers, but this meeting was not the place to reply to such attacks. Recriminations could wait until Germany was defeated. The matter at hand, he said, was 'to ensure the successful formation of the Footballers' Battalion, or a Footballers' Brigade', or 'the Die Hards', as he nicknamed them. The appeals were being made 'from sportsmen to sportsmen'.

Before anything could happen in this respect, the clubs had to show favour, and the London clubs had already met to give their sanction, he informed the meeting. The clubs were prepared to pay the wages of those players who enlisted until the end of the season, and they would be permitted to live at their homes until called upon to bear arms. The directors of all the London professional clubs were unanimously in favour of the formation of the battalion, and had agreed not to stand in the way of any players who wished to enlist. Joynson-Hicks said that footballers, who were used to playing together on the football field, wanted to be together on the battlefield. Joynson-Hicks had requested from the War Office that any players who joined up would be given Saturday leave to play football and was pleased to announce that Lord Kitchener himself had granted that wish, until the end of the current season.

The Football Association placed its Russell Square offices at the disposal of the recruitment committee and already many applications had been received for officers and non-commissioned officers; Joynson-Hicks believed that it was better for men to be led into battle by those who had led them in football, so, if possible, the NCOs of the battalion would be footballers. Then, referring to the statement made by German Chancellor Theobald von Bethmann-Hollweg at the outbreak of war, Joynson-Hicks added that those who enlisted would be fighting not for a 'scrap of paper', not solely for Belgium, nor for the honour of Great Britain, but for their homes, their wives and their children, he added. People had to ask themselves: 'Can I live as an Englishman without doing something against the barbarians?' He then rallied the gathering by telling them that the game they had been playing was great but the game in Flanders would be greater; that the charge at football was good, but with the bayonet finer; that the cheers of the crowd were not to be compared with the sound of the bullet and the noise of the big guns.

To a 'hearty reception', Hayes Fisher rose to speak. He appealed to footballers and the friends of footballers to enlist, and believed they would easily raise the 1,350 men required for the battalion. He disagreed with the chairman that now was not the right time to respond to football's critics. There were about two thousand players paid exclusively to play football, he said, and some people mistakenly seemed to think that the moment these men enlisted they would be ready to fight, and 'if only they had crossed over, those two thousand could have driven the Germans out of France and Belgium'. He added that football was different to other professions in that if a clerk went to war and lost a leg he could return to his job afterwards, whereas a footballer obviously could not. He suggested that perhaps the insurance companies might be able to do something for footballers who found themselves in such an unfortunate position, and stated that the House of Commons was considering the question of pensions awarded in cases of disablement or death, remarking: 'I am perfectly certain [pensions] are going to be raised to a far better standard than ever before.' Hayes Fisher concluded by stating that players who signed up would be paid the full amount of their football contracts and would be reimbursed their expenses when travelling from the battalion's London base to play in Saturday games. Who would pay such expenses was a matter of some controversy several weeks later.

Lord Kinnaird endorsed the appeal that the footballers present set an example by being the first to join the new Footballers' Battalion. When Captain Whiffen, appealing as an 'old football player', asked for recruits to step forward, there was an immediate response. The first player to come forward was the Clapton Orient right winger Fred 'Spider' Parker, quickly followed by Frank Buckley of Bradford City and Archie Needham of Brighton and Hove Albion. As Buckley had previous army experience he was given the rank of Lieutenant, later to be promoted to Major. After what was described as a lull in proceedings, 'a few inspiring words' from Mr H. Glibbery, the father of a player in Essex, provided further impetus and eventually thirty-five signatures were secured, with the responses of the Clapton Orient and Croydon Common clubs being particularly gratifying. The complete list of volunteers was:

> *Arsenal - Tom Ratcliff*
> *Bradford City - Frank Buckley*
> *Brighton & Hove Albion - Archie Needham, Ralph Routledge, Frank Spencer, John Woodhouse*
> *Chelsea - William Krug, David Girdwood, Edward Foord*
> *Clapton Orient - Fred Parker, Jimmy Hugall, Nolan Evans, Harry Gibson, Richard Dalrymple, William Jonas,[19] Eddie King, Arthur Tilley, Richard McFadden,[20] Thomas Pearson*
> *Croydon Common - Ernie Williamson, Thomas Newton, Dick Upex, Cyril Smith, Albert Tomkins, Percy Barnfather*
> *Crystal Palace - James Bowler, William Middleton*

[19] Private W. Jonas, Service No. F/32, died July 27, 1916, Memorial Reference Pier and Face 12 D and 13 B, Thiepval Memorial

[20] Company Sergeant Major R. McFadden, Service No. F/162, died October 23, 1916, Grave Reference, III. B. 19., Couin British Cemetery

Luton Town - Hugh Roberts, Frank Lindley
Southend United - Frederick Robson
Tottenham Hotspur - George Bowler, William
Oliver
Watford - Reginald Williams, Alex Stewart, Joe
McLauchlan

Pointing to the thirty-five players, Joynson-Hicks said: 'This, gentlemen, is my thanks.' The proceedings concluded with a hearty rendition of the National Anthem.

Henry Norris had earlier expressed disappointment that not one player from Fulham had yet joined up. Nor were there any from Norris's other club, Arsenal, save their trainer Tom Ratcliff, who was one of the volunteers. Norris's disappointment was lessened on Christmas Day when Ernie Coquet became the first Fulham player to enlist in the Footballers' Battalion. But overall the take-up amongst footballers was slow: many years later Norris admitted that bribes were paid to the battalion's recruiting Sergeant for every man who signed up. He said that Joynson-Hicks contributed one shilling per man and Hayes Fisher and Norris sixpence each.

The Southern League immediately urged all its players to enlist in the new unit, but it was soon realised that the objective of 1,350 men was ambitious, especially as the battalion planned to restrict itself to recruiting from south of the River Trent. At the time professional football was dominated by clubs in the midlands, Yorkshire, Lancashire and the north east, with relatively few clubs in London and the south. In addition, for the first few months of the war recruitment was aimed at unmarried men, of which there were estimated to be only around six hundred employed as professional footballers. Even if they all joined up, the Footballers' Battalion would still be under fifty per cent subscribed. Nevertheless, various posters appeared encouraging enlistment, aimed at supporters of particular clubs. One such was headed 'Play the Game' and urged readers to 'sharpen up 'Spurs. Come forward now to help reach the goal of victory. Shoot! Shoot!! Shoot!! And stop this "foul play".' Another read: 'Do you want to be a Chelsea die-hard? If so join the 17th Battalion Middlesex Regiment and follow the lead given by your favourite football players.' Yet another called for the men of Millwall to 'let the enemy hear the Lion's roar'. A more general poster urged 'Young Men of Britain!!' to prove the German newspaper *Frankfurter Zeitung* wrong in its assertion that 'The young Britons prefer to exercise their long limbs on the football ground, rather than expose them to any sort of risk in the service of their country' and encouraged them to 'Give them [the Germans] the lie! Play the Greater Game and join the Football Battalion.'

Regular reports kept the public up to date with the progress of recruitment to the new battalion. By New Year's Day the total was one hundred; a week later it was two hundred. By mid January recruits were said to be coming in 'in fair numbers', but plenty of vacancies still existed. However, the recruits were by no means all footballers; many of them were supporters who wished to fight alongside the players of their clubs. A good number were followers of Chelsea, who wanted to serve with that club's famous amateur player and England international Vivian Woodward. By March 1915 the number of footballer recruits had reached 122 (twenty-eight of them non-commissioned officers), including the whole of the Clapton Orient team.

Eventually a figure of six hundred (mostly non-footballers) was reached. Colonel Charles Grantham, a former Rugby Union player for Munster in Ireland, was appointed Commanding Officer of the battalion, with Colonel Henry Fenwick as his second-in-command. The adjutant, Captain

Alexander Elphinstone, was a Cambridge 'double Blue', in Rugby Union and athletics. Commissioned officers, of course, had to be amateurs. Dr Russell Wakefield, the Bishop of Birmingham, who once was a footballer (for whom was not stated), was made Honorary Chaplain to the battalion. The Footballers' Battalion first paraded in public in the middle of January in London's Kingsway, where large crowds gathered to watch them. The unit was around two-hundred strong at that time and, after receiving their pay to date, they marched 'in swinging stride to their temporary quarters at the White City'. Three cheers from the onlookers resounded loudly as the battalion stepped out. It was reported that the spectators enjoyed pointing out players they recognised; one player easily spotted was a goalkeeper, unidentified in press reports, sporting a shield over an eye that was injured in a Cup tie the previous Saturday.[21] Despite the numbers of both enlisted players and the watching crowd, an officer of the battalion (probably Captain Henry Wells-Holland), was not happy, telling a newspaper reporter:

> *We want more players and we must have them. I am much disappointed, and not a little disgusted, and shall feel like ending my active connection with the game when the war is over. I have spoken to several [players] whom I thought I could influence, and they tell me they will wait until the end of the season and see.*

He received backing from William Joynson-Hicks and Lord Kinnaird, who jointly wrote to every professional player in England who had not yet volunteered for service: 'A large

---

[21] This goalkeeper was probably Millwall's Joe Orme, sent off the previous Saturday for fighting with Clapton Orient's William Jonas, who was also dismissed.

number of the finest players in the kingdom have already joined the battalion, but we do not see your name amongst them. Forgive us for pressing upon you the absolute necessity of rallying every available man to the colours. We do urge you as a patriot and a footballer to come to the help of the country in its hour of need.' The letter did not produce the desired reaction.

At the end of March, Colonel Grantham also had cause for complaint and wrote to the Football Association and the Football League, bemoaning the sluggishness of recruiting amongst professional footballers. For this, he did not blame the players, but football club management. Some players who wanted to enlist complained of active discouragement by club officials. Grantham wrote to the football authorities:

> As the officer commanding the Footballers' Battalion, it is my duty to bring the following facts to your notice. You are aware that some little time ago there was much controversy in the papers with regard to the manner in which the professional football player had failed in his duty by not coming forward to serve the country in its time of stress. The laxity of the football professionals, and their following, amounted to almost a public scandal. Mr Joynson-Hicks, MP, therefore raised the Football Battalion, and public opinion died down under the belief that most, if not all, of the available professionals had joined the Battalion. This is not the case, as only 122 professionals have joined. I understand that there are forty League clubs and twenty in the Southern League, with an average of some thirty players fit to join the colours, namely 1,800. These figures speak for themselves. I am also

aware, and have proof, that in many cases
directors have not only given no assistance in
getting these men to join, but have done their best
by their actions to prevent it. I am taking the
opportunity to ask you gentlemen if you and your
clubs have done everything within your power to
point out to the men what their duty is. Your King
and country call upon every man who is capable
of bearing arms to come forward, and upon those
who are unable to use their best endeavour to see
that those that can, do so. It is no use mincing
words. If men who are fit and capable of doing so
will not join, they and all those who try by their
words and actions to prevent them will have to
face the opinion of their fellow men publicly. I
will no longer be a party to shielding the want of
patriotism of these men by allowing the public to
think they have joined the Football Battalion.

Furthermore, a number who had enlisted claimed they had
been victimised, in some cases having their wages reduced
when they were not available to play or train. Some clubs were
said to have refused to select players for the first team because
they had joined the army. It was not club directors who were to
blame for this, but the paid employees, such as managers and
trainers, whose continued employment depended on the results
of their teams. Some in the Footballers' Battalion had also
been required to pay their own rail fares from London when
they had to travel to grounds outside the city. The fares should
have been reimbursed by their clubs, but the clubs saw this as
an unfair additional outgoing at a time when they were already
under financial pressure, and believed that it should have been
funded by the military authorities. They were giving up their
employees to the army, they were still paying their wages in

full and now they were expected to pay their expenses. Who could blame them for being upset? The Football Association declined to comment on the allegations of reduction of wages and non-payment of expenses, preferring to say that payment arrangements were a matter concerning players and their clubs. It could not interfere.

The Football League also voiced dissent at the contents of Colonel Grantham's letter, especially the accusation that the football authorities had failed to do everything within their power to encourage footballers to enlist. The League defended itself by stating it had issued a manifesto to clubs, which stated: 'This is the call of patriotism..... [we trust] that in the hour of England's need every young man would respond to the call.' The League then agreed a resolution, supported by most club representatives but opposed by Captain Henry Wells-Holland, chairman of Clapton Orient and an officer in the Footballers' Battalion, who concurred with the objections made by Colonel Grantham. Nevertheless, the following resolution was carried:

> *The general meeting of the clubs of the Football League heartily approves the declaration of the Management Committee, with reference to the importance of all professional football players who can do so joining the colours. They fully recognise the serious call of national and patriotic duty, and pledge themselves to continue to do everything in their power to support the Management Committee and other football authorities in encouraging recruiting in all phases of National Service.*

However, clubs had complaints of their own, protesting that military training robbed players of some of their ability on the football field, as the hard physical work, route marches and strenuous drilling caused them to lose some of their speed. Slower or not, the Footballers' Battalion was still able to play a match against members of the Sportsmen's Battalion (the 23rd Royal Fusiliers), who were said to include in their ranks 'many excellent players'. The venue was the picturesquely-situated ground of Fulham FC, at Craven Cottage, on the banks of the Thames. The Sportsmen's Battalion had a fair representation of cricketers, including England Test players Andrew Sandham of Surrey and Patsy Hendren of Middlesex.

By mid July the Footballers' Battalion was 1,100 strong, but William Joynson-Hicks felt it necessary to appeal for more men to come forward to form a second battalion. He wrote to various newspapers: 'The 1st battalion has been encamped for upwards of ten weeks in my park at Holmbury, and has improved out of all knowledge in appearance and in drill. They have now marched away for a few months' brigade training in Nottinghamshire, after which it is hoped they will go to the front and carry the fame of the Footballers' Battalion into Germany. It is, however, felt that there are still a large number, both of football players and football enthusiasts, who would like to join a similar regiment.' The second Footballers' Battalion (the 23rd Middlesex Regiment) was formed soon afterwards.

The men enlisted in the Footballers' Battalions did not see front-line service for some time, many experiencing their first combat at the Somme in the summer of 1916, a battle that cost Britain more casualties than any other in its illustrious history. The Footballers' Battalions suffered awful losses, whilst Frank Buckley and Vivian Woodward were wounded. Buckley received shrapnel injuries to his chest, puncturing his lungs, and was repatriated for emergency surgery; Woodward was hit in the thigh by a hand grenade. He too returned home to recuperate. Buckley maintained records of the fate suffered by the men he commanded in the Battalion, writing in the 1930s that more than five hundred of the original six hundred were dead, either killed in action or succumbing later from wounds received. Overall the Football Battalions lost over twelve hundred officers and men between July 1916 and April 1917. Andrew Riddoch and John Kemp give a comprehensive history in their book *When the Whistle Blows: The Story of the Footballers' Battalion in the Great War* (see Bibliography).

Thanks to Riddoch and Kemp and other Great War historians, the Footballers' Battalion is comparatively well known, but in fact it was preceded by a few weeks by a largely forgotten battalion that included in its ranks a large number of Heart of Midlothian FC players. In late November 1914, Sir George McCrae, a textile manufacturer and trader and former Liberal MP for East Edinburgh, was given permission to raise the 16th (Service) Battalion of the Royal Scots, the oldest infantry regiment in the army and nicknamed 'Pontius Pilate's Bodyguard', in his home city. McCrae announced that he would have sufficient volunteers 'within seven days'. His confidence was well founded, as five days later eleven professional players from Hearts became his first enlisted men. The next day two more players followed their teammates.[22] At the time Hearts led the Scottish League and were recognised – even in England – as one of the most attractive teams in Britain. The example shown by the Hearts players and an appeal by the club's manager, John McCartney, provided a lead to other professional players, sportsmen and football supporters. Within another six days McCrae had a full complement of 1347 officers and men, including hundreds of Hearts followers and an estimated 150 supporters of Hearts' great rivals Hibernian FC.

---

[22] The thirteen players were Alfie Briggs, Duncan Currie, Tom Gracie, Jamie Low, Harry Wattie, Willie Wilson, Ernie Ellis, Norman Findlay, Jimmy Frew, Annan Ness, Bob Preston, Pat Crossan and Jimmy Boyd.

Hearts retained their top placing in the League past the turn of the year, but their players, fatigued by the rigours of military training, were understandably unable to maintain a level of football that had been described as 'dainty, dazzling'. A 2-0 defeat at Morton, when the players returned from night-time training just in time to catch the train to Greenock, was the turning point. They lost again the following week, whilst Celtic won twice, and the Glasgow club took the title. The *Edinburgh Evening News* bitterly remarked: 'Between them the two leading Glasgow clubs have not sent a single prominent player to the army. There is only one football champion in Scotland, and its colours are maroon and khaki.' After training in Edinburgh, Yorkshire and on Salisbury Plain, the battalion, commonly known as 'McCrae's Own', embarked for France in January 1916 and saw its first military engagement at the Somme the following July. Seven members of the Hearts first team were killed in action.[23]   Jack Alexander's book *McCrae's Battalion: The Story of the 16th Royal Scots* (see Bibliography) gives a detailed history of the battalion.

---

[23] Boyd, Currie, Ellis, Gracie and Wattie all died, as did John Allan and James Speedie, who served in other regiments.
Private J. Boyd, Service No. 18976, died August 3, 1916, Memorial Reference Pier and Face 6 D and 7 D, Thiepval Memorial
Sergeant D. Currie, Service No. 18999, died July 1, 1916, Memorial Reference Pier and Face 6 D and 7 D, Thiepval Memorial
Private E. E. Ellis, Service No. 19009, died July 1, 1916, Memorial Reference Pier and Face 6 D and 7 D, Thiepval Memorial
Private H. Wattie, Service No. 19112, died July 1, 1916, Memorial Reference Pier and Face 6 D and 7 D, Thiepval Memorial
Corporal T. Gracie, Service No. 19024, died of leukaemia, October 23, 1915, Grave Reference P. 107, Glasgow (Craigton) Cemetery
Lance Corporal J. Allan, Service No. 351268, died April 22, 1917, 9th Royal Scots, Memorial Reference Bay 1 and 2, Arras Memorial
Private J. H. Speedie, Service No. S/16102, died September 25, 1916, 21st Cameron Highlanders, Memorial Reference Panel 119 to 124, Loos Memorial

Many other English and Scottish footballers served in local 'Pals' battalions throughout the country. The exact figure of those who served may never be known, nor may the number who lost their lives. One famous player who died in action was Evelyn Lintott,[24] former amateur player and England international, who played for Plymouth Argyle, Queens Park Rangers, Bradford City and Leeds City. Whilst at QPR Lintott signed a professional contract so that he could be sold to Bradford City for £1,000, a sum that helped Rangers climb out of financial trouble. When war broke out he joined the army and became a Lieutenant in the West Yorkshire Regiment, thus being the first professional footballer to receive a commission. He was killed on the first day of the Somme, July 1, 1916. A letter in the *Yorkshire Post* told of how he met his death: 'Lieutenant Lintott's end was particularly gallant. He led his men with great dash and when hit the first time declined to take the count. Instead he drew his revolver and called for further effort, again he was hit but struggled on but a third shot finally bowled him over.'

Former Welsh international goalkeeper Leigh Roose was another to fall. A player for a number of clubs between 1901 and 1912, Roose was renowned for his bravery and eccentricity. He was a large man for the age – over six feet tall and weighing thirteen stones – a size he put to good use both inside and outside his penalty area. He was not averse to rushing outside the area and shoulder charging opponents. In his first international game he bundled an Irish winger over the touchline, knocking him unconscious. His throwing, kicking and punching covered prodigious distances, he had a reputation for saving penalties and he enjoyed entertaining the crowd. Once he sat on the crossbar while play was at the other

---

[24] Lieutenant E. H. Lintott, 33rd West Yorkshire Regiment (Prince of Wales's Own), died July 1, 1916, Memorial Reference Pier and Face 2 A, 2 C and 2 D, Thiepval Memorial

end of the pitch. In 1916 Roose enlisted as a private in the Royal Welsh Fusiliers. Serving on the Western Front it was said that his throwing abilities made him an ideal man for propelling hand grenades. His first action resulted in his being awarded the Military Medal for bravery, as the regimental history explains: 'Private Leigh Roose, who had never visited the trenches before, was in the sap when the *flammenwerfer* attack began. He managed to get back along the trench and, though nearly choked with fumes with his clothes burnt, refused to go to the dressing station. He continued to throw bombs until his arm gave out, and then, joining the covering party, used his rifle with great effect.' He was promoted to Lance Corporal but was killed towards the end of the Battle of the Somme. His body was never found.[25] Roose's story is told by Spencer Vignes in his book *Lost in France: The Remarkable Life and Death of Leigh Richmond Roose, Football's First Play Boy* (see Bibliography).

The sole Sheffield United player to lose his life was left winger Jimmy Revill, who played in ten League games and one Cup game during the 1914/15 season but was not selected for the Cup final. Serving as a Lance Corporal in the 104th Field Company, Royal Engineers, he died from wounds sustained at the Battle of the Scarpe on the first day of the Arras offensive on April 9, 1917. He is buried along with 3,003 other First World War victims (eleven of them unidentified) at Bethune, Pas de Calais, twenty-nine kilometres north of Arras.[26] United staged a benefit match for his widow and family in January 1918, from which they received £130, a sum worth over £7,500 today. The *Sheffield*

[25] Lance Corporal L. Rouse, Service No. PS/10898, died October 7, 1916, Thiepval Memorial (his name is spelled incorrectly on the memorial)

[26] Lance Corporal J. W. Revill, Service No. 108670, Grave Reference VI. C. 80., Bethune Town Cemetery.

Daily Telegraph and the *Sheffield Independent* both reported his death on April 16, 1917. The *Telegraph* wrote:

> *News was received in Sheffield on Saturday, with very great and general regret, of the death of Jimmy Revill, who for some seasons prior to the war had been a particularly useful and very speedy forward in the United colours. He played with equal facility on the right wing or left, and had determination and pluck far beyond the ordinary. Short of stature, he nevertheless was an excellent footballer, and very popular. He has died in an English hospital as the result of wounds sustained at the front, and which necessitated the amputation of an arm and a leg. Revill was married, and joined up some fifteen or eighteen months ago, and had seen quite a lot of fighting.*

The *Independent's* report followed similar lines, but made no mention of the nature of Revill's injuries or the location of the hospital in which he died. Therein lies a mystery. If Revill died in an English hospital, would his body then have been transferred back to France for burial? It is possible that the *Telegraph* was mistaken and Revill died in a field hospital in France.

Several current and former footballers were decorated for bravery, three of them being awarded the Victoria Cross, two posthumously. One of the V.C. recipients was Bernard Vann,[27] who played sparingly for Northampton Town, Burton United and Derby County in 1906 and 1907. He was Acting Lieutenant Colonel in the 1/8th Battalion, The Sherwood

---

[27] Lieutenant Colonel B. W. Vann, died October 3, 1918, Grave Reference II. O. 1., Bellicourt British Cemetery

Foresters (The Nottinghamshire and Derbyshire Regiment) and was killed in October 1918. His posthumous V.C. citation read:

On the 29th September, 1918 Lieutenant Colonel Vann gave an example of most conspicuous bravery, leadership and devotion to duty during the attack at a Bellenglise and Lehaucourt, France. Under the cover of a thick fog, but also under a very heavy fire from machine and field guns, he displayed great skill in leading his men across the Canal du Nord. The attack was delayed by every description of enemy fire, coming from the front and right flank, as they reached the high ground above Bellenglise. Lieutenant Colonel Vann, realising that it was imperative that they advanced with the barrage, rushed forward to the firing line and with great gallantry led the advance. Because of his expedient action and his disregard for danger, his men, encouraged, continued forward reversing the whole situation. At a later time, single-handedly, he rushed a field gun, knocking out three of its crew. The fine leadership and gallantry of Lieutenant Colonel Vann was instrumental in making the day a success. It was during another attack, near Ramicourt on 3rd October 1918, that he was killed by a sniper's bullet through the heart.

Donald Bell,[28] a defender with Bradford Park Avenue, enlisted as a Private but by June 1915 he had a commission as

---

[28] Second Lieutenant D. S. Bell, died July 10, 1916, Grave Reference IV. A. 8., Gordon Dump Cemetery, Ovillers La Boiselle

Second Lieutenant in the 9th Battalion of the Yorkshire Regiment. He was awarded a posthumous Victoria Cross after being killed in July 1916. His citation read:

> *On 5th July, 1916 at Horse Shoe Trench, Somme, France, a very heavy enfilade fire was opened on the attacking company by an enemy gun. Second Lieutenant Bell immediately, on his own initiative, crept up a communication trench, and then, followed by a Corporal and a Private, rushed across the open under very heavy fire and attacked the machine gun, shooting the firer and destroying the gun and the personnel with bombs. This officer lost his life five days later performing a very similar act of bravery.*

William Angus played once for Glasgow Celtic and more regularly for junior club Wishaw Thistle before joining the 8th Battalion, Highland Light Infantry, in which he was a Lance Corporal. His V.C. citation read:

> *On 12th June 1915 at Givenchy, France, Lance Corporal Angus left his trench under very heavy bomb and rifle fire and rescued a wounded officer who was lying within a few yards of the enemy's position. The Lance Corporal had no chance of escaping the enemy's fire when undertaking this gallant deed, and in effecting the rescue he received about 40 wounds, some of them being very serious.*

Walter Tull,[29] who played for Tottenham Hotspur, Northampton Town and Glasgow Rangers, is honoured on both the Arras Memorial in France and at Northampton Town's Sixfields Stadium. He was an interesting character whose life is detailed in Phil Vasili's books *Colouring Over The White Line: The History of Black Footballers in Britain* and *Walter Tull (1888-1918), Officer, Footballer: All the Guns in France Couldn't Wake Me* (see Bibliography). Tull was a rarity in both football and the military of the time in that he was black. He enlisted in the Footballers' Battalion and was soon promoted to Sergeant. He survived the July 1916 Somme offensive, then was recommended for further promotion, receiving his commission in May 1917. Tull thus became the first black combat officer in the British army, despite regulations forbidding 'any negro or person of colour' taking such a position. Vasili explains further in *Colouring Over the White Line*: 'According to *The Manual of Military Law*, black soldiers of any rank were not desirable. During the First World War, military chiefs of staff, with Government approval, argued that white soldiers would not accept orders issued by men of colour and on no account should black soldiers serve on the front line.' But Tull did command and did serve on the front line, at the Somme and in Italy, before returning to France in March 1918 to take part in the attempt to break through the German lines on the Western Front. He led his troops in an attack at Favreuil but was struck by a bullet. Under heavy fire several of his men attempted to get him back to the British trenches but were unable to do so. Tull died soon after being shot; his body was never recovered. His commanding officer in the 23rd Battalion of the Middlesex Regiment (the 2nd Footballers' Battalion) wrote to Tull's brother Edward: 'He was popular throughout the battalion. He

---

[29] Second Lieutenant W. D. J. Tull, died March 25, 1918, Memorial Reference Bay 7, Arras Memorial

was brave and conscientious. The battalion and company had lost a faithful officer, and personally I have lost a friend.'

The formation of the two Footballers' Battalions was a formidable answer to people who, in the eyes of those involved in the game, unfairly singled out football for particular criticism. It showed that football and footballers did care about the war effort, enough to give their lives for it. Those who made the ultimate sacrifice were commemorated on a memorial unveiled in March 1924 by Charles Clegg, by which time he was president of the Football Association. Mounted on the wall of the F.A. offices in Russell Square, the tablet read simply:

> *IN REMEMBRANCE OF THOSE WHO TOOK PART IN THE NATIONAL GAME OF ASSOCIATION FOOTBALL AND GAVE THEIR LIVES IN THE CAUSE OF RIGHT AND JUSTICE IN THE GREAT WAR 1914-18*

Beneath was a quotation from *A Discourse of a Discoverie for a New Passage to Cataia* by Elizabethan soldier and explorer Sir Humphrey Gilbert: 'Give me leave to live and die in this opinion, that he is not worthy to live at all who for fear of danger of death, shunneth his country's service and his own honour.'

Eighty-six years later the Footballers' Battalions were remembered by the dedication of a memorial at Longueval on the former Somme battlefield. Supported by the Professional Footballers' Association, the Football Supporters' Federation and the Football League and partly funded by money raised by football supporters, it was unveiled on October 21, 2010. At its base are displayed the poignant words of Millwall player Private Jack Borthwick, who was wounded near the site of the memorial: 'This is worse than a whole season of cup ties.'

CHAPTER TEN

GOUGH WAS GOUGH - THAT IS ALL THAT NEED BE SAID

After their excellent win over league leaders Oldham Athletic on the first Saturday in December, Sheffield United next faced Manchester United at Old Trafford. Their cross-Pennine journey was successful, producing a 2-1 win. The forwards had not been in such energetic form since they beat Burnley at Turf Moor in October, and the victory was achieved despite their having to change the rearguard trio for the first time. Left back Jack English had a cold, so Albert Sturgess dropped back and George Utley resumed at left half. United's first goal resulted from a penalty, converted by Jimmy Simmons after a trip on David Davies as he looked certain to score. In the second half United's defence managed to 'emerge with success from a great scrimmage close to the goal, in which Brelsford and Cook came out with chief honours'. Midway through the second half, Wally Masterman, at last finding his old Gainsborough form, scored the second. Manchester pulled one back when Brelsford and Sturgess each waited for the other to kick clear, and the home side strove 'might and main' for the equaliser in deepening gloom, but failed to beat Gough, who received his usual fulsome praise from the *Sheffield Daily Telegraph*: 'Gough was Gough, and that is all that need be said.' It had been a rough game, refereed 'with a broad mind'.

173

Davies's shin bore 'a faithful imprint of [George] Stacey's studs' and Masterman received a 'hearty kick' above the knee, but neither seemed too badly hurt. In the lead up to the next game the trainer, George Waller, was able to happily declare that, apart from long-term casualty William Gillespie, for the first time this season he had no players on his 'sick list'. The management committee thus had some decisions to make; they opted to retain the same team for the forthcoming meeting with Bolton Wanderers. A worryingly small crowd of just 5,000 witnessed another good United win, their third in succession. Heavy sleet and very muddy ground greeted the teams, but the conditions did not hinder United. Joe Kitchen was performing better on the right wing than he had in the centre and Simmons continued his good form at inside right. Both scored, and Wally Masterman got his second in two games as United won 3-1.

United were able to cope with heavy sleet and muddy ground but on the Western Front similar conditions were proving a hindrance to the troops of both sides. Nevertheless, throughout December there were attempts by the British army, under pressure from the French, to take the initiative and end the stand-off that had developed along the front line. For example, on December 14 the 8th Brigade mounted an attack at Wijtschaete in Flanders but were turned back by heavy fire, leaving many casualties in No-Man's Land, tangled up on barbed wire defences. Four days later two further attacks were made at La Boutillerie in northern France, by the 22nd Brigade and the 20th Brigade. Both failed, resulting in great losses. The next day the 11th Brigade attacked east of Ploegsteert Wood in Flanders. Again they were repelled, on this occasion many lives being lost by what is today known as 'friendly fire': British heavy artillery barrages fell short of their intended target. At sea, on December 16 German warships loomed out of the North Sea mist and bombarded the towns of

Scarborough, Whitby and Hartlepool, killing over one hundred civilians and injuring some two hundred more.

As these onslaughts were taking place, the Football Association met to decide whether any special rules should be introduced for the Challenge Cup competition, and to make the draw for the first round proper. The F.A. stated that Manchester City FC had requested that there be no midweek replays, whereas Bury FC wanted the current replay system to continue. Wishing to avoid unnecessary midweek matches, the F.A. then announced the following resolutions regarding Cup ties:

- *In all matches after the first round, which are undecided at the end of ninety minutes' play, an extra half-hour must be played.*
- *No Cup tie should be played except on Saturday afternoon.*
- *In case of a drawn match, the competing clubs shall re-play the following Saturday.*
- *The season shall be extended one day to and including the 1st of May, to enable clubs to play postponed matches, and also for charity matches.*

At the same meeting it was announced that Crystal Palace FC had informed the F.A. that the Admiralty had commandeered their ground but that the Commanding Officer had notified the club that he had no objection to the Cup final being played there in April. However, the F.A. decided that in the current circumstances the final should be played outside London, a wise move as in February the Admiralty decreed that Crystal Palace could no longer be used by the public. The Cup draw then paired Sheffield United with Blackpool at Bloomfield Road. The mood was different in Scotland, as the Scottish Football Association decided by fourteen votes to thirteen to abandon its Cup competition. The motion was moved by Mr Tom Whyte of Glasgow Celtic FC, who pointed out that the Association had left itself in the hands of the War Office and once the Under-Secretary of State for War had expressed opposition to the Scottish Cup going ahead, there was no choice but to cancel it. Mr James Philip of Aberdeen FC unsuccessfully proposed an amendment that the Cup should go ahead as he was convinced that the public wanted football to carry on. If the Cup was cancelled, he believed, so should be all football. Mr Thomas Steel of Ayr United FC supported the abandonment motion, as he reminded delegates that Lord Kitchener himself had stated that international matches and Cup ties should be stopped.

Back to the business of English League football, Sheffield United entertained Blackburn Rovers on Boxing Day and suffered a 'grotesque result'. The attendance was a remarkable 28,000, more than five times higher than that for the Bolton game seven days earlier. Lesser games were suffering, but the appeal of matches over Christmas remained solid. Rovers' win was based on a stout defence and two goals from more than twenty yards' range, one low and true that gave Gough no chance, the other a high, looping shot that the goalkeeper misjudged, allowing the ball to slip from his hands, against the post, on to the line and, apparently, over it. United strongly protested against the goal being given but the referee was adamant. For most of the game the United forwards and half backs were 'hammering strongly at the Rovers' goal, yet only reduced it once', when Wally Masterman scored for the third game in succession. United 'retired very unluckily beaten'. Comfort could be taken, however, from the 'strong and enthusiastic' crowd and a collection of £14 16s 6d for the Prince of Wales's Fund. And it was the last time United would taste defeat until the first week in April, nineteen games later.

With no new injuries to report, United were once again able to name an unchanged line-up for the next game, at home to Notts County, two days later. A good crowd was present as Masterman and Kitchen sparkled in a 1-0 victory. The only goal came from a free kick taken by Bill Brelsford, headed on by Masterman and hit home by Simmons. A quick return meeting with Blackburn Rovers followed on New Year's Day, in which United gained revenge for their loss at Bramall Lane. A strong wind at Ewood Park made a high standard of football almost impossible but, after a welcome run of good fortune when it came to injuries, United lost a player hurt. However, so did Rovers, so for much of the game it was ten against ten. But United's loss was more pronounced, as their retiree was their outstanding goalkeeper Gough, who, after half an hour, dived at the feet of a Rovers forward and received bruising to his ribs and kidneys. His opponent in the collision, Danny Shea, sustained a seriously injured knee. United had the wind in their favour in the first half, their first goal being a somewhat of a gift, as it came from an unnecessary corner from which Fred Hawley scored. In the second half Rovers kept up an almost continuous bombardment of the United goal and they equalised when George Chapman drove home a free kick from twenty-five yards. United were dangerous when they managed to break away and gained their second goal, created by quick, clever forward work and finished well by Joe Kitchen. Rovers were criticised for adopting the wrong tactics in the second half for, with the wind behind them and full back Albert Sturgess in goal, they rarely tried a shot from long distance. United had a disorganised back division, but the half backs raised their game to compensate and Kitchen was 'a little too elusive' for his opponent. The deputy goalkeeper, Sturgess, described as 'The All-round Footballer', performed manfully. Earlier On New Year's Day 547 men had died when the battleship HMS Formidable was sunk off Portland Bill by two torpedoes fired from a German U-boat.

United promptly returned to Sheffield – but for an away game at Hillsborough on January 2, where the meeting of the city rivals and a welcome improvement in the weather attracted 28,000 people to the ground. The overhead conditions may have been better than had been seen lately, but underfoot things were different: 'from goal to goal was a sea of mud' that 'told heavily against scientific football'. The wing men of both teams shone, probably because their footing was more secure. United were forced to bring in Ted Hufton and Jimmy Revill for Harold Gough and Bob Evans, Hufton pulling off some 'sensational saves' and Revill putting in the cross for David Davies's equalising goal. In the final seconds of the first half United had been denied a goal when 'Kitchen finished a clean burst from the half way line by beating Davison and shooting into the net – hard luck…. the forty-five minutes had expired'. It was 1-0 to Wednesday with ten minutes left when United had an escape. Wednesday's George Robertson found himself alone with the ball and no United man close. He dribbled unopposed towards goal but hesitated; Hufton 'sprang at the ball and collared it, though only getting it away after a tremendous struggle'. The importance of Hufton's bravery was shown two minutes later, when Davies headed the goal that made it 1-1, which is how the exciting encounter finished.

After an unimpressive first part of the season, United's form was picking up just in time for the start of the Cup, and a journey to the seaside to play Second Division Blackpool.

CHAPTER ELEVEN

THE MASTERLY MASTERMAN

The build-up to the first round of the Cup on January 9 brought speculation in Lancashire that Sheffield United had offered Blackpool money to move the tie to Bramall Lane, which United denied. The reason for the story may have been that United were said to be unhappy about the close confines of Blackpool's pitch, with which they struggled to come to terms as the home team swung the ball around well. United were able to stem the tide and broke away to take the lead on fifteen minutes. George Utley was fouled, the free kick was played to Joe Kitchen on the right, he crossed with 'commendable accuracy' and Wally Masterman struck a 'studied shot' that gave goalkeeper Jimmy Kidd 'only a vision of some object hurtling into the net behind him. It was the ball, and Sheffield were a goal up.' But Blackpool were on level terms just a minute later when Peter Quinn hit the underside of the bar and the ball rebounded to Jack Sibbald, who easily beat Ted Hufton. The stand-in United goalkeeper then made a good save from Green, before United thought they had scored again when Kitchen's shot was punched out by Kidd. Many observers thought it was already over the line; later Kidd admitted as much.

In the second half came 'two episodes which gave the visitors and their numerous supporters considerable shocks', either side of another United goal. The first was when Sibbald shot over a yawning goal, but after this escape United regained the lead. There was a clever run by Kitchen, which he finished with a cross that found Masterman and Jimmy Revill waiting: 'The latter drew off and let his colleague take charge, and, making no mistake, the ex-Trinity man gave Kidd no chance of saving his drive.' United's second moment of fortune then arrived, when '[Joe] Lane got through the Sheffield defence and was presented with one of the gifts of a player's lifetime. He could have walked the ball past Hufton, but to the amazement of all he shot wide.' It was a great let-off, but perhaps United deserved their luck after Kitchen's 'goal' that was not seen, and an unrewarded trip on Revill in the penalty area. United had fewer chances but their finishing was far superior and they just deserved to win a game that was 'fast, exciting, clean and good'. The *Sheffield Daily Telegraph's* headline writer awarded the victory plaudits to United's double-goalscorer, 'The Masterly Masterman'. The second round draw gave United a difficult-looking home tie against Liverpool. After making the draw, the Football Association issued the gate figures from the previous weekend's ties. The attendance at Bloomfield Road was a healthy 9,462 but elsewhere the story was not so good. There was a large decrease in overall crowd numbers compared to the first round in January 1914, from 514,027 to 390,417. Gross receipts fell from £19,876 to £12,121.

The following week it was back to League action and, for Sheffield United, a home game against West Bromwich Albion. The good form continued with a 2-0 win. 'Very bright and enjoyable was the football served up on Saturday on Bramall Lane's present-day mud patch,' began the *Sheffield Daily Telegraph's* report. Harold Gough was back in goal for United, though Hufton had played well in his absence. George Utley was missing, so Albert Sturgess reverted to half back and Jack English returned after illness. 'There was dash all over the field' in the first half but no goals and United were criticised for appearing to 'have got into a habit of letting the other side cut out the opening work, which is not wise, and sometimes leads to disaster'. In this instance it did not, although Bill Brelsford cleared from between two forwards as they appeared certain to score, and Gough was almost beaten when English quickly put the ball back to him. He then appeared to be troubled by the sun as Crisp lobbed the ball under the bar before the goalkeeper punched it over 'at the last possible instant'. At the other end, Albion keeper Hubert Pearson was beaten by a shot from Sturgess but was reprieved by Jesse Pennington behind him, then United broke through three minutes into the second half. From a Jimmy Simmons corner, Masterman's shot was blocked and David Davies drove the ball home. Joe Kitchen forced Pearson to dive full length but the goalkeeper was rapidly up on his feet to clear Revill's follow-up. Masterman set Revill going, he sent in a high cross that Pearson should have helped over the bar, but instead he tried to catch it, failed, allowing Davies to score again. Albion played excellently, without reward, and any fortune fell United's way.

United were now going well after a poor start to the season and had an important Cup tie against Liverpool to look forward to. However, the tragedy of war was constant, despite the excitement generated by football. On January 19 a Zeppelin airship dropped bombs on the East Anglian towns of King's Lynn and Great Yarmouth, killing more than twenty civilians in their beds. *Sheffield Daily Telegraph* columnist 'Looker-On' reminded readers that the football they were enjoying at the moment may not be there forever, when in late January he thoughtfully wrote:

As the season steadily progresses we get nearer the time when the most serious position of football will have to be faced, and the situation viewed from the point of carrying on. The Leagues will come together to formulate their scheme..... for ascertaining the feelings of clubs and players, so that nothing need be done that is calculated to inflict unnecessary harm to the pastime. Everybody, however, is possessed of certain definite facts, and also that football cannot expect to proceed upon the same path and with the same methods and generous finance which obtained in normal times. With the Cup percentages, and the balance of the now terminating relief fund, it can be pretty well agreed that the clubs will be able to reach the end of the season without any actual stoppage or the non-fulfilment of a single League fixture. But to face another four months at the close of the season without a penny of income is a different proposition, and it is this situation that the Leagues will have to face and arrive at a common agreement upon. Obviously, the decision must be the one which will be possible for all the clubs to carry out, and the question of the payment of summer wages will be a vital matter for the League Board. What seems probable is that something in the nature of a general supervision of clubs and their operations with players up to a certain period, say August 1st, shall be observed. Then the position should be reviewed in the light of events. If there is no indication of hostilities being ended by then, we believe that football will have little chance of going on, for things will be

*begin to be getting degenerate. There will be a
demand, rather than a request, for men, and
public opinion may possibly have a greater
mandate for the suspension of all kinds of sport.*

Within a few days a meeting of the Football League, the
Scottish League and the Southern League was held in Preston,
to consider the present and future of football, especially the
depleted finances of clubs. However, no definite decisions
about the future were made at the meeting.

On January 23 Sheffield United stretched their unbeaten
run with a goalless draw at Everton in a game that the
Sheffield Daily Telegraph described as being 'hard, but
scientific' and in which 'several tempers were lost, and [were
not] recovered'. It had been 'some weeks since the wheels of
the United machine were so much out of gear' as they failed to
create much in attack. United's best effort came from Jimmy
Simmons, who 'nearly demolished the framework of the
Everton goal with a terrific shot', but the forwards were called
back to help in defence, a move that almost caused a goal
when Harold Gough had to save a very good but very
unintentional shot from teammate Bob Evans! The credit for
the point went to United's rearguard, 'the brothers Cook and
English', from whom 'a finer exposition of full-back tactics
has not been seen this season'. Cook 'kicked and cleared from
all kinds of seemingly impossible situations' and English
'showed some effectiveness, but with, apparently, less
expenditure of energy'.

The second round Cup tie at home to Liverpool was a week
away, and to help his players recover from the hard match at
Everton and prepare for their city rivals, trainer George Waller
sent fourteen of them (the eleven who faced Everton, plus
Utley, Revill and Fazackerley) on walks into the country, and
allowed them other breaks from their normal training routines.

The meeting with Liverpool was a tight affair, settled by a single, late, goal. United pressed for three-quarters of the game but their attacks were disjointed, for which Jimmy Simmons was handed the fault, displaying 'an inability to do himself justice' and indulging in 'extravagant wandering'. But players like Simmons were allowed some leeway, as it was admitted that 'his very unorthodoxy often makes him into a brilliant forward'. Liverpool's forwards were much smoother than United's, but were poor in front of goal, giving Gough a very quiet day. The nearest they came to scoring before half time was when 'with his backs squandered, Sturgess arrived in front of Gough just in time to head the ball away from [Fred] Pagnam', then in the second half Tom Miller, faced with an open goal, shot six yards wide, which 'must have provided Gough with a pleasant surprise'.

United's front line was not only individualistic, it also shot badly. Davies had no luck, committing a blunder when Simmons headed an Evans centre to his feet but he struck it wide, then Evans missed a chance when the ball cannoned to him off Simmons. Masterman 'could not find freedom on his feet', while Joe Kitchen kept trying to beat Bob Pursell on the outside when cutting inside might have been the better option. But with ten minutes to go United's forwards suddenly found their form. 'The work, its superb dash, its amazing cleverness, and the long sustained bombardment, reminded us irresistibly of that historic finish against the same club in the semi final, at Bolton, when United scored twice in the last eight minutes and forced a further replay.[30] It was a hurricane onslaught which

---

[30] This comment refers to the 1898/99 Cup semi final against Liverpool, which took four games to decide. The first game, played at Nottingham Forest, was a 2-2 draw. In the replay at Bolton, United were 4-2 down but Fred Priest scored twice in the last eight minutes. The third meeting, at Fallowfield in Manchester, was abandoned due to darkness with Liverpool leading 1-0, and United finally won 1-0 at Derby. They then beat Derby County 4-1 in the final.

could have but one ending,' wrote the *Sheffield Daily Telegraph*. The catalyst was the return to the field of English after a nasty knee twist. By this time Kitchen had moved to the centre, with Davies at outside right. Sturgess lobbed the ball gently towards goal, Masterman added a glancing touch to put it under the bar. It had almost crossed the line when goalkeeper Elisha Scott managed to turn it away for a corner, which resulted in the decisive goal. Simmons took the corner and the ball drifted to the far post, where Kitchen headed it in 'amid intense enthusiasm'. There were still five minutes to play and, realising that the best defence is a strong attack, United 'finished hammer and tongs' as Kitchen and Davies both nearly increased the lead. It had not been a comfortable game to watch from a United standpoint but they won – just – after 'a very memorable finishing dash'. The crowd of 26,734 included many visiting supporters, for whom special trains had been laid on, and also an 'extraordinarily large' number of soldiers. The *Sheffield Daily Telegraph* report ended with rare praise for the referee, who, in a match that required great firmness, 'got through his work very well'. The third round draw handed United a home game against Bradford Park Avenue, but the Football Association still declined to select a venue for the final, simply reiterating that it would be outside London.

Before the Cup game against Park Avenue, United prepared for a League visit to Bradford to play City. George Utley was out, so in came Harold Pantling for his debut. United went in to the half-time interval one goal down, and were lucky that the deficit was so small, Bill Cook and Jack English saving United from 'a total that would have taken a lot of reducing'. City scored when United were down to ten men, with Jimmy Simmons off the field following a charge from Bob Torrance. When he returned he was the recipient of a repeat by City's 'vigorous half back'. Poor Simmons was rendered ineffective for the remainder of the game. United drew level in the second half with a fine goal from Wally Masterman, after a move started by Fred Hawley and continued by Bob Evans. Masterman hit a shot that 'was rising as it sped for the net, and gave [Jock] Ewart very small chance of arresting its progress'. United then appealed for a penalty for handball by Torrance, causing 'a lot of heart burning both at the time and after the match'. Instead, the referee gave a free kick outside the penalty area. Even so, United only just failed to get what they thought was justice, as Joe Kitchen smashed the free kick against the bar. Pantling was praised for his assured first senior appearance, whilst half back partner Albert Sturgess found the ankle-deep mud a great handicap. The full backs were the best players; Cook, 'who rushes in where angels fear to tread and as often accomplishes the seemingly impossible', and English, 'the cool, calculating stylist'. The game left trainer George Waller with five patients in his 'infirmary', as Simmons and Davies joined Brelsford, Utley and reserve forward Box. Jack Thompson and Stanley Fazackerley were therefore recalled to face Burnley.

United extended their good run of results with a narrow win over the Cup holders from Turf Moor on February 13. However, the attendance was a pitiful 5,000 – it appeared that the public were saving their money for the big Cup matches to come – but heavy snow, followed by pelting rain, did not help. Burnley had a goal disallowed for offside but then United scored; Fazackerley's straight pass found Kitchen, who seemed to have lost possession but as goalkeeper Jerry Dawson and back Tom Bamford closed in he shot into the net. A splendid long shot by Sturgess was saved by Dawson, who then got his body in the way of a thirty-yard skidding shot from Kitchen. Without Utley, Brelsford, Simmons and Davies, it was a good win. All four were expected to be fit for the Cup tie against Bradford.

Meanwhile, Frederick Charrington's crusade against football was still going strong. The Cup was at its third round stage, and Charrington wished to know whether it was planned to continue the competition. His enquiry was raised in Parliament in early February. Charrington was active in the Mile End area of East London, whose MP was the Liberal Harry Lawson. The Honourable Member raised a question in the House of Commons, asking Prime Minister Asquith whether he had received a protest from Charrington in this respect. Charrington, said Lawson, had the support of many ministers of religion and the mayors of several boroughs, who all condemned the continuation of football and the playing of Cup ties and wanted to know whether the Government was going to take any action to stop it. Asquith answered the first part of the question in the affirmative, and informed the House that he was aware that negotiations had taken place between the War Office and the Football Association. As a result of these talks it had been decided to cancel the forthcoming international matches but the Cup ties would still go ahead.

A couple of months later Charrington took his protest into the House of Commons – literally – although it was not clear at the time whether or not his demonstration was actually football-related, as he was apprehended before he could make too much of a scene. Reports told of a tall, dark man wearing evening dress, an overcoat, and a silk shirt, who darted into the House through the doors leading to the members' lobby. He paused for a moment on the threshold, and then rushed up the floor of the House to the central table. He grasped the ceremonial mace and attempted to lift it from its position, at the same time shouting 'You have no right to.....' but before he could finish what he wanted to say he was arrested by the House of Commons police. It later emerged that Charrington was protesting against Members of Parliament partaking of alcoholic beverages in the members' lobby, but the episode showed the lengths to which this extraordinary man was prepared to go to make his point. He was by no means a single-issue 'Crusader'.

The Cup was to continue, but whether or not supporters would find it easy and affordable to travel to matches was another matter. The Railway Executive Committee announced a reduction of railway services in order to keep the lines as free as possible for military and naval traffic. Passenger trains were to be curtailed, and cheap fares on excursion trains for football matches, race meetings, public holidays and other special events were to be withdrawn from the beginning of March. Times were becoming tougher for football clubs too. When Chelsea FC made an application for a liquor licence for their Stamford Bridge ground, it was turned down by the magistrate, the Honourable John de Grey, who stated he would have nothing to do with football at a time of national emergency. He added that he did not want to give any facilities for entertainment at football matches. Chelsea defended the application by asserting that matches were conducive to recruiting, but the magistrate dissented, declaring that in his opinion football should be stopped. A valuable source of income, in this case for Chelsea, was denied.

With the start of the flat-racing season only a few weeks away, debate now surged about whether it should proceed, and inevitably football and racing became linked together, just as they had been the previous August and September. After all, as some argued, they were both unnecessary pleasures at a time of ongoing crisis. Lord Robert Cecil, Independent Conservative MP for Hitchin in Hertfordshire, speaking in the House of Commons, stated that football and horse racing were on exactly the same footing. Mr George Lambton, from the racing stronghold of Newmarket, in a letter to *The Times,* disagreed. According to Mr Lambton, racing and football were different because jockeys were small and footballers were big.

Although they could capably handle one-ton horses racing at high speed, jockeys were clearly too weak to hold a gun, because:

> *Football is played with a ball and twenty-two strong and sturdy young men. Racing is played with horses, ridden by small men, the majority under eight stone and never more than nine stone. To be a good football player you must be big, strong, courageous, active, and alert, all the qualities you look for in a soldier. To be a good jockey, you require these qualities, except that instead of being big, you must be small. Consequently they are not fit to be soldiers.*

Author and historian Sir John Holland Rose, of Christ's College, Cambridge, believed that jockeys being small was a good thing as 'it is conceivable that featherweight jockeys might render admirable service as scouts or messengers at the front'. Another letter writer, Mr R. J. Lawrence, of the Constitutional Club, Northumberland Avenue, London, was scathing in his criticism of footballers, stating: 'These men were the one class of the community who were in special training and condition when war was declared. There were enough of them to form three or four battalions. Yet months passed before there was any attempt to form one football battalion. League matches and Cup ties are in full swing. It is clear from the lists of players published in the papers which still boom football that very few of the regular players have joined.'

And so the opposition continued. 'That cry ['Business as Usual and no panic'] was..... a fraudulent one,' wrote academic Roper Lethbridge, of Exbourne Manor, Devon, in a letter to *The Times*, 'for it is put forward as if it were a recommendation from the authorities to the people at large that we should all stick to our pleasures of our money-grubbing, and let the other fellows do the fighting and the dying in the trenches; that we should still have the delirious joy of cheering in our thousands at the glorious exploits of the football athletes whom our gate money bribes to stay away from the war "as usual".' Mrs Bousted, of Westfield, Wimbledon Common, asked: 'Can anyone really pretend that racing and football are anything but a hindrance to that object [winning the war]?' From the front came a letter from an officer in a Canadian regiment, who wrote: 'When will the war end, you ask. God knows, but certainly not while untold thousands of slackers play football and race and strike in England. I suppose one has to be a hero in the midst of it to realise the tremendous gravity of the situation.' Reverend J. Bayfield Clark, of St Saviour's Vicarage, Herne Hill, London, warned, somewhat dramatically, that letting people go to football matches and race meetings was not only going to lose us the war, it was also 'the way to manufacture socialism'.

However, Lord Derby[31] was more considered in his judgement, stating: 'There is only one reason I see for stopping games, and that is if an employer in a certain district can say, "If you have this or that amusement you are going to induce men to stay away from their work on Government stores." Then I feel it would be perfectly right to stop in one place.' *The Times*, in one of its leader articles, was also balanced in its view, but still came out on the side of football and racing being discontinued:

---

[31] Edward George Villiers Stanley, 17th Earl of Derby, was twice Secretary of State for War and also served as British Ambassador to France. In August 1914 he organised one of the most successful recruitment campaigns to Kitchener's Army in Liverpool. He was Lord Mayor of Liverpool from 1911 to 1912 and served as honorary president of the Rugby Football League.

We find the playing of Association football defended on the grounds that working men must have some relaxation if they are to continue to supply the nation's needs at the high pressure existing at present. And as for racing, it is being carried on, we are told, not as a sport, but as an industry. Perhaps when the war is over we shall have come to regard sport as what it is - a struggle in which victory is of no intrinsic value.

The continued protests did no good. Football and racing went on, and for Sheffield United another big Cup tie was in prospect. Meanwhile, at the beginning of February 1915 it was estimated that there had been approximately 104,000 British army casualties on the Western Front.

CHAPTER TWELVE

WE HAVE NEVER DRAWN BREATH FROM THE MOMENT THE WAR STARTED

At the beginning of the twentieth century the city of Sheffield was almost exclusively a place of iron and steel manufacture, producing everything from the smallest teaspoon to the largest engineering casting. Its industrial heritage therefore contrasted markedly with the largely textile-based economies of neighbouring cities Manchester to the west, Leeds to the north and Nottingham and Derby to the south. Much of this distinction was due to topography - Sheffield's landscape of tightly packed wooded hills interwoven by its five rivers was the ideal environment to provide the water power that drove the forges and foundries and the fuel they consumed.

The city's primary trade following the Industrial Revolution was the manufacture of cutlery and small hand tools, but from around 1893 there came a steep climb in the production of heavier goods, in particular armaments and the associated tools of war. New technology and improved manufacturing methods enabled the design of deadlier and more massive weapons, and Sheffield led the way, so much so that one writer christened it 'The Arsenal of the World'. Meanwhile the city's light trades became stagnant: census figures showed that in 1891 32,100 people worked in these industries, compared to 34,800 in 1911, whereas the numbers employed in heavy industry shot up from 21,384 to 38,379 over the same twenty-year period. The number who described themselves in the census as engineers increased by some ninety per cent. By the start of the First World War, eight iron and steel companies in Sheffield employed over two thousand people; a further six had a workforce of more than one thousand. In 1910 the *British Association Handbook and Guide to Sheffield* described the city as 'at the present moment the greatest armoury the world has ever seen'. As an example, Government weapons contracts were responsible for half of Cammell's business prior to the war.

A further boost to the heavy industry of the city came with the introduction of the electric arc furnace, imported from the USA in 1910, thus increasing the efficiency of steel manufacture and the quality and types of steel produced; for the first time special alloys could be made in large quantities. The new technique proved to be a leap forward from the long-established method of crucible steel production, and by 1915 all the major steel producers in Sheffield had a reliable electricity supply to power their electric arc furnaces. Two years later there were thirty such devices in the city, including ten at Hadfield's, eight at Firth's, four each at Osborn's and Kayser Ellison and others at Balfour's, J. H. Andrew and Spear and Jackson. The war, and its concomitant requirements for all forms of munitions, vehicles and their attendant components, served to give further impetus to an already booming industry. The only drawback for ambitious and - some might say - greedy directors and shareholders was that after the introduction of the Munitions of War Act in August 1915 the Government maintained strict control of prices and profits, as well as of wages, working hours and employment conditions. A rapidly falling unemployment rate and a sharp increase in the quantity of weekly shifts worked in Sheffield's steel mills and engineering factories emphasised the surge in output and the numbers employed during the war years. [32]

A decade after the war, Dr William Herbert Hatfield, a Sheffield metallurgist, wrote (for an American readership): 'Metallurgical advances in themselves made possible a form and magnitude of warfare typical of the [First] World War. The modern battleship, destroyer, submarine, airplane and the armored tank, together with their armaments, were impossible but for the collaboration of the engineer and the metallurgist.' What Hatfield could have mentioned, had he not been so modest, was that much of that collaboration took place in his home city. Sheffield contributed enormously to the development and production of military hardware, from the manganese steel soldier's helmet to armour plate, rifle bullets, bayonets, the largest naval projectiles and even the army razor. In December 1914 the *Sheffield Independent* stressed how much of an impact the war had had on the industry of the city, writing: 'At no time in the history of Sheffield were so many firms engaged in the manufacture of materials for the purpose of carrying on war, and the output of material of that kind was never so large. It is fortunate that the requirements of the British Government and the [allied] Powers for which Sheffield firms work have increased in peace times to such an extent that the resources for the production of guns, armour, gun-shields, shells and other munitions of war were never so large as they are today.' A few weeks later the same newspaper reported: 'Wages are high, overtime is general in the East End and no skilled worker worth his salt is out of employment. After five months of war, the number of unemployed in the

---

[32] The UK's unemployment rate was 5.0% in 1914, 1.6% in 1915, 0.9% in 1916, 0.3% in 1917, 0.6% in 1918 and 4.2% in 1919. The average weekly shifts worked in Sheffield's heavy industries stood at 114,400 in 1914, climbing to 186,700 in 1918, before falling sharply to 144,200 in 1919.

city is only a thousand out of a population of about half a million.' On another occasion the *Independent* reported that demand for shells was so great that almost every company with the ability to melt steel was engaged in such work.

But there were problems, with both manpower and horsepower. Hordes of young men had enlisted in the armed forces so skilled labour was at a premium. Workers were therefore taken from the light trades industries (cutlery and hand tool manufacture), whilst Belgian and Dutch refugees, Canadian immigrants, people from outside the city and, from March 1915, women, were employed in their thousands to fill the vacancies. Until this time women might only have found work in the service of wealthy families, but now they could experience the freedom and wages that only men had previously enjoyed. Many former maids, cooks and nannies never returned to domestic service after the war. The armament factory women soon became known as 'munitionettes', risking their health on a daily basis as they handled dangerous substances without adequate protective clothing. Another name they acquired was 'canaries', due to the yellowing of the skin they suffered, caused by working with sulphur, an ingredient in explosives. Women were paid only around half of the wages received by men, a situation that persisted throughout the war despite a campaign for parity initiated by the Women's Trade Union League. Many such women were awarded certificates at the end of the war to thank them for their efforts. One was Ada Rodgers, who worked as a machinist at the National Projectile Factory, Templeborough, from March 1916 to December 1918. Her certificate is on display at the Imperial War Museum North at Salford Quays.

New accommodation was needed to house the influx of additional workers from outside the city, so in 1916 temporary huts were erected for them on Tyler Street and Petre Street,

195

overlooking the Don Valley, where many factories were situated. Another group of labour employed was that of prisoners of war, used as construction workers - under guard - at the Vickers factory. Companies that had employed a couple of thousand people before the war were now manned by huge numbers; for example, 11,000 at Vickers in 1916, and 6,868 (1,984 of them women) at Firth's in 1918, compared to 3,100 in 1914. From 1915 Firth's new National Projectile Factory at Templeborough employed a further 5,000. Hadfield's workforce was 5,690 in 1914 and 13,000 in 1918. In the era before the mass use of motor vehicles, companies still relied mainly on horses for haulage, but many working animals had been commandeered by the army. Some companies were so desperate that they employed highly innovative methods of moving stock: Thomas Oxley's had an elephant and two camels to pull its wagons, whilst Thomas Ward's used an elephant named Lizzie, which was said to do the work of three horses. Lizzie, leased along with its handler from a travelling circus named Sedgwick's Menagerie, entered local folklore. Anecdotes claim she once ate a schoolboy's cap, stole a pie by thrusting her trunk through an open kitchen window, and was so strong that she pushed clear a snowbound traction engine. In a 1931 obituary of her trainer Richard Sedgwick, Lizzie was said to have 'stuck her massive head behind it and moved it as if it was only a hand barrow'. She also became the object of a local insult; if a person was overweight they were said to be 'like Tommy Ward's elephant'. Oxley's animals were also supplied by Sedgwick, all apparently being returned to the circus after the war, none the worse for their labours, although it was reported that Sheffield's cobbled streets hurt Lizzie's feet.

By the middle of 1915 not only were existing facilities being used to their full capacity, but new workshops and factories were springing up out of necessity. In July Cammell

Laird's were commissioned by the Government to construct and manage a National Projectile Factory but suitable land was so scarce in Sheffield that the premises were erected in Nottingham. Firth's ran a similar facility at Templeborough, as did Hadfield's at its 225-acre Hecla site. In June 1915 the *Sheffield Independent* reported: 'Enormous new shops, tens of thousands of pounds' worth of new machinery, and thousands of extra workers have been provided and fully employed since war broke out. Further extensions are still to be carried out on a scale which would have made the directors of old stand aghast.' Septimus Bennett, a poet who in 1915 took work as a lathe operator at Vickers, did not look forward to his new job, colourfully writing: 'Belching furnaces, the rumbling noise of hidden machinery, the hissing of steam over black pools of water, the vast prison-like places employing seven, eight or even ten thousand hands, makes me shudder to think of having to work among such surroundings, not to mention living there'. Working conditions and the constant rush to achieve production targets meant that accidents were inevitable, though they were surprisingly few considering the amount of picric acid, cordite, ammatol, and other dangerous explosives that were in regular use. However, there were fatalities at Vickers' gun shop in September 1915 and at Cammell's in January 1917.

Other deaths occurred as an indirect result of the presence of the munitions factories in the East End of Sheffield. In late September 1916 a single Zeppelin airship mounted a night-time raid on the area, dropping some thirty-six incendiary bombs on a line from Burngreave, through Attercliffe to Darnall. It inflicted random damage; twenty-eight deaths were reported, with another nineteen injured. The victims were mainly residents in houses and cottages that were hit. Eighty-nine houses were seriously damaged, with many more receiving minor damage, along with a public house, the Baltic

Arms on Effingham Road. A Methodist chapel on Princess Street was destroyed. Remarkably, no munitions works were struck. The deadliest bomb landed on Corby Street, which ran parallel to Atlas Street, on which the Atlas Steel and Iron Works and the Norfolk Steel Works stood, but neither firm was touched. This particular bomb killed seven members of one family, five of them children, plus two other people living close by.

One report stated: 'The second or third bomb that dropped destroyed four small houses. It is known that two or three of the inmates were killed, one of them an elderly man. The other inmates, some of whom were blown down into lower rooms by the explosion, were rescued. A number of them were injured. The houses on the opposite side of the road were also damaged. One woman was saying goodnight to her sweetheart at the door when the bomb exploded, injuring him on the back and leg and knocking him down, and blowing the door down upon her. She was injured about the face. A soldier home on leave, who was in bed five houses away from the spot, was shot clean out of bed downstairs, where he arrived unhurt and smilingly went to look after his mother. In one street consisting of artisan dwellings, a row of houses was hit squarely by several high explosive bombs. Three houses were utterly wrecked at the top end, and the debris was piled up in indescribable confusion. Another dwelling was reduced to ruins, and it is believed a young married woman and her baby were buried.' One man likened the noise of the exploding bombs to 'that of a great rattle intensified a thousand times'. Another eyewitness remarked: 'The sound of the bombs dropping was like nothing so much as a clean shot from a gun which, preceded by a glare, seemed to indicate that the anti-aircraft guns had got to work. Each report was clear and well defined. The raid did not last more than four minutes. I heard eleven projectiles explode. To their credit folk seemed to take the business with characteristic British phlegm.'

Contemporary reports stated that the Zeppelin was chased away by anti-aircraft guns, but recent research throws doubts on the story, as the men of the local anti-aircraft defences were apparently attending a ball at the Grand Hotel in the centre of Sheffield. There were therefore no orders given to engage the airship, nor have any references been unearthed that Royal Flying Corps aeroplanes were sent to intercept it. Sheffield's air defences, later described as 'shambolic' and 'a fiasco' were subsequently improved, with the installation of additional searchlights and guns on the hills surrounding the city. As remarkable as the fact that no armaments works were hit was that the airship arrived anywhere near its target, as their captains rarely knew exactly where they were when flying over England at night. The captain of the German Naval Zeppelin L22 that hit Sheffield, *Kapitanleutnant* Martin Dietrich, admitted that he did not know whether he had bombed Sheffield or Lincoln, but was 'inclined to believe' it was the former! If the object of the raid was to inflict damage on vital arms factories, it failed, but if it was meant to spread fear and apprehension throughout the people of Sheffield, it certainly succeeded.

Unharmed and undeterred by such attacks, production continued unabated. Some of Sheffield's manufacturing statistics make staggering reading:

- *Seven million steel army helmets were made in the city, mainly by Hadfield's;*[33]

---

[33] Hadfield's manganese steel helmet weighed 25 ounces, some 12 ounces less than the German equivalent, but tests proved it to be far superior in its protection from bullets and shrapnel.

- Newton Chambers and Co. in Chapeltown, to the north of the city, manufactured two million shell casings;
- Baker and Bessemer Ltd in Rotherham produced over six million shells;
- Thomas Ward's, which specialised in ship breaking and steel recycling, handled 1,000 tons per day of scrap steel.
- Steel, Peech and Tozer's Templeborough Melting Shop, between Sheffield and Rotherham, was the largest of its type in Europe, containing fourteen open-hearth furnaces in which steel scrap was melted down for munitions production;
- Cammell's used a massive 12,000-ton-force armour plate bending press;
- Firth's supplied four million shells, 9,000 tons of gun forgings, 750 tons of torpedo components and 10,000 tons of marine driveshaft and turbine forgings;
- Hadfield's output, which later in the war was expanded to produce howitzers and trench mortars, increased from a value of £1.7 million in 1914 to nearly £10 million in 1918. The company's plant included almost three hundred heating furnaces, eighty presses, some of them with a 2000-tons capacity, and over twenty miles of railway track. It manufactured armour-piercing shells of 12 inches, 13.5 inches, 14 inches, 15 inches, and 18 inches calibre, the largest of which weighed one ton, was fired from a naval gun that weighed 150 tons, had a range of thirty miles, at which distance it could pierce one-foot thick steel plate. At fifteen miles' range it could perforate armour-plate 16 inches thick;

- Hadfield's National Projectile Factory was contracted to produce one thousand shells per week within nine months of opening, rising to four thousand per week after twelve months. It was so productive that its output at each stage was fifty per cent above contract.

But it was not merely a case of churning out huge amounts of variable standard goods. Quality was as vital as quantity. The precision required in the machining of gun barrels and some other components was considerable. The *Sheffield Daily Telegraph* described one such process: 'The particular gun made [at one factory] consists of two steel tubes, miles of ribbon wire, and a jacket. The exteriors [of the tubes] are to be turned and the interiors taper bored. And here a notable exception to ordinary standardised work occurs, for the outer and inner tubes must be mated, made in definite pairs, the one for the other. Any inner tube will not fit into any outer tube, even though to the ordinary eye they are all of precisely the same dimensions. In boring the outer tube, minute irregularities of surface occur and these have to be carefully ascertained by gauge tests and charted. The chart of an outer tube boring is then taken to a definite inner tube in the process of being tapered down, and the turner working to the chart reproduces on the surface of the tube every inequality or detail in the boring of the outer tube.'

At the end of the war, Sir Robert Hadfield, owner of the firm of the same name, commented that his company had been so busy that 'we have never drawn breath from the moment the War started until the armistice came'. However, it was not only the large companies making heavy armaments that profited. The machine tools and plant necessary for their production had to be manufactured somewhere too, and Sheffield companies such as Davy Brothers, Brown Bayley's,

Edgar Allen's, Jonas and Colver, Kayser Ellison, Samuel Fox, Beardshaw's, Marsh Bros, T. W. Pearson and Samuel Osborn benefited greatly. The work of Osborn's, which made drills, files, small castings, wheels, ball bearings, cutters and bomb casings, was reported thus: 'Practically the whole output was used directly or indirectly for war purposes. The company held War Office and Admiralty contracts for tool steels [for which] requirements doubled immediately; after the National Shell Factories opened, demand was terrific.' Its profits escalated from £35,000 in 1914 to £100,000 in 1918.

Osborn's products, and those of other smaller companies, were used to manufacture components for aircraft and naval equipment. However, normal carbon steel drills possessed insufficient strength to drill the small diameter holes necessary for precision components such as aircraft parts, so a new type of material, known as high-speed steel, was developed for the manufacture of twist drills, such as those manufactured by Osborn's. Tungsten powder was required for the production of high-speed steel, but unfortunately most of the world's tungsten ore refining took place in Germany. Britain had to find new sources and by 1916 had established two mines in Burma to supply the ore. The *Sheffield Independent* had earlier reported in 1915 that 'the demand for high-speed steel is enormous.' Another Sheffield-based advancement was that of a high-carbon, high-chromium dye steel used for toolmaking. Ironically, central to its development was a German-born metallurgist named Paul Kuehnrich, who moved to Sheffield in 1888 aged seventeen, before becoming a naturalised Briton. He worked for toolmakers Marsh Bros, and later purchased another tool steel company, Darwin and Milner.

There was a strong German influence in the Sheffield steel industry. As well as Kuehnrich, Charles Kayser, the owner of Kayser Ellison, and Sir Joseph Jonas, the owner of Jonas and Colver and a former Lord Mayor of Sheffield, were born in

Germany. Another well-established Sheffield company had a German name - Seebohm and Dieckstahl - but its majority shareholder was a local man, Arthur Balfour, who in 1915 wisely changed the firm's name to Arthur Balfour and Company. Other Germanic manufacturing companies did not fare so well, falling victim to anti-German hatred. Poldi, on Napier Street, was wound up as 'an alien business', whilst Bohler Bros, an Austro-German company, did not survive the war. In the circumstances, it was strange that none of Kuehnrich, Jonas or Kayser were interned, as hundreds more of their countrymen were, but they suffered in other ways. None was ever appointed to the position of Master Cutler,[34] which their achievements and pre-war standing might well have justified. Kayser Ellison was amongst the first companies in Sheffield to promote enlistment amongst its staff, so its owner escaped the worst of what can arguably be described as injustices. His named lived on for many years afterwards in the firm Sanderson Kayser Ltd.

Jonas and Kuehnrich were hounded throughout the war. In June 1918 Jonas, now aged seventy-three, was arrested and charged with passing information about armaments to the enemy. It was alleged in Bow Street Police Court, London, that he 'did obtain and communicate certain information prejudicial to the interests of the state and information useful to the enemy, and information relating to prohibited places and things therein.' When the case was heard at the Old Bailey in August and it was revealed that the 'offence' occurred in 1913 and took the form of discussions with a potential customer, he was found not guilty of committing a felony, but guilty of a misdemeanour. He was fined £2,000 and censured by the judge, Justice Lawrence. At the end of the month King George

---

[34] The Master Cutler is the head of the Company of Cutlers in Hallamshire, established in 1624. His role is to act as an ambassador of industry in Sheffield.

revoked Jonas's knighthood, then he was removed from the list of Sheffield Justices of the Peace and considered for deportation, but was permitted to remain. One writer bemoaned the 'speed and alacrity with which [Jonas] was stripped of his position in society' and called his treatment 'politically motivated'. Jonas died three years later.

Kuehnrich's name came up in Parliament in June 1915, one of nine people mentioned in a question regarding the internment of aliens. Sir John Simon, the Home Secretary, replied that three of the nine, including Kuehnrich, were naturalised British subjects and 'an Order-in-Council to cover such cases is being obtained'.[35] There were rumours in Sheffield that Kuehnrich was a friend of the German Kaiser, that he stockpiled arms at his Ecclesall home and that he drilled a secret army. He defended himself in a letter to the *Sheffield Independent* in April 1915, branding his accusers 'unscrupulous jesters' and offering to allow police to inspect his house. He was twice found guilty of criminal offences and fined: once for shining a powerful light at his home, then for possessing sixty-nine pounds of bacon. Luckily for him, another charge was dismissed - one of hoarding Bovril. Perhaps Kuehnrich should not be mentioned in the same breath as steel pioneers Benjamin Huntsman, Henry Bessemer and Harry Brearley, but his name and achievements in his field have been virtually forgotten in his adopted city. Whether that is due to his country of birth is open to debate.

There is no doubt that a great many Sheffield people made a great deal of money out of the war, yet for others, such as Sir Joseph Jonas, the owners of various German companies in the city, and the countless families who lost husbands and sons, it

---

[35] Orders-in-Council can be used to issue simple laws as a sort of decree. For example, in times of emergency, the Government may issue legislation directly through Orders-in-Council, foregoing the usual parliamentary procedure.

proved ruinous, either financially or domestically. It was a time of contrast; prodigious technological advances in methods of killing were mirrored by the primitive nature of early twentieth-century warfare, in which tens of thousands of men were sacrificed with hardly a moment's thought. Under pressure to produce ever more weapons in order to destroy ever greater numbers of the enemy, and anxious from constant worry over family members facing death and injury in the services, the workforce did not need a second invitation to escape the permanent travails of everyday life. Saturday afternoon leisure activities, particularly football, provided the men of Sheffield with just such an opportunity, if only for a few hours. For many of them in early 1915, that meant looking forward to watching Sheffield United making progress in the Cup.

CHAPTER THIRTEEN

ON PINS AND NEEDLES

As February 1915 drew to a close, the war on the Western Front had seen little progress for either the allies or the Germans since well before Christmas. It was an indecisive campaign of thrust and counter-thrust, small pockets of terrain being gained by one side, often before being soon reclaimed by the other. There seemed little likelihood at this stage of an outright victory for either side, a situation that persisted for much of the year. Elsewhere, losses of shipping and lives continued at sea. On February 24 the auxiliary cruiser HMS Clan McNaughton was declared missing, presumed mined, in the Atlantic Ocean, with 281 men on board.

Back home, Bradford Park Avenue visited Bramall Lane for the third round Cup tie against Sheffield United on February 20, and it proved to be an engrossing match, settled only in extra time. It was splendid weather for late February, the sun shining brilliantly on the 30,032 spectators, who were 'thoroughly interested from start to finish' as the action continually moved from one end to the other. A typically exciting incident came when 'English hesitated and United's goal seemed captured, until Cook dashed in and saved the situation'. 'It was simply amazing that the teams could sustain the pace so long,' wrote the *Sheffield Daily Telegraph*. United nearly scored when Bill Brelsford 'shot in, and Watson butted it on to Fazackerley with no one but [Ernie] Scattergood in front of him.' Fazackerley's shot lacked strength, and 'Scattergood got down to it right on the line'. There was a half-appeal for a goal, but Bradford heaved a sigh of relief. When extra time started, United's reputation as a well-trained team served them well. Somebody – possibly captain George Utley, as in this era the captain was solely responsible for on-field decisions once a game had started – decided that Joe Kitchen and Jimmy Simmons should swap positions, and it paid off. Fourteen minutes of extra time had passed and some of the Bradford players were showing signs of distress, when Kitchen, now on the right wing, sent the latest of several tempting centres into the goalmouth. It looked as though Scattergood would collect the ball, but defender Joe Crozier intervened and it deflected off him into the net. United's better stamina and their ability to raise a great effort when the game was still in the balance had seen them through to a deserved victory.

For the following week's League game against Newcastle United the United directors intended that Kitchen should retain the right-wing position, but the late withdrawal of Wally Masterman meant it was back to the centre for the player who created the decisive goal against Bradford. It was another successful day against the north-easterners, resulting in a 1-0 win, United's fourth in succession by this scoreline at home, in each case Kitchen being the match winner, a curious but welcome statistic. The match commenced with United secretary John Nicholson standing in for one of the linesmen, who had missed his rail connection. The only goal came in the first minute, when Stanley Fazackerley's low drive cannoned back to Kitchen, who sent the ball over the line. Albert Sturgess then hit the post but the strong wind made good football difficult.

Evidently not superstitious, the United directors selected thirteen players to travel to Oldham for the fourth round of the Cup on the first Saturday in March, and would decide the eleven later. There was an extra half back, Fred Hawley, and a sixth forward, Masterman. Oldham were challenging for the League championship but latterly had not been playing with the 'devil' that marked their early-season performances, drawing two and losing two of their last four. United, in good form themselves, had at least an even chance. The game was described as a 'great struggle', United repelling the best Oldham could offer in a 0-0 draw in which their defence held out against the home 'battering rams'. In two full hours on a mud-heap and in the face of a shifting wind, all the physical force came from Oldham; all the football came from United. Fazackerley's shot was turned around the post, Simmons shot over the bar, then David Davies and Fazackerley both missed a cross by inches. In the United goal, Harold Gough cleared from Albert Cashmore but the ball ran just a few yards to Ollie Tummon, who returned it much too high. United claimed a penalty on ninety minutes when Bob Evans went over the back of Jimmy Hodson but the referee was unmoved. In extra time a shot by Charles Roberts left its mark on Gough's crossbar before coming 'back up the field like a cannon ball'. Criticism was levelled at Oldham's tactics, 'chiefly in the obvious determination at times to play the man rather than the ball', their backs Billy Cook[36] and David Wilson being the principal offenders. The treatment of Kitchen by this pair 'was a very long way removed from fair play or sportsmanship'; Cook 'dashed into the winger time after time with only one object, and that was not to get the ball'. Davies and Evans also

---

[36] Oldham's Billy Cook was an abrasive and controversial character. Later in the season he was sent off against Middlesbrough for persistent fouling but refused to leave the field, forcing the referee to abandon the match. The Football Association suspended Cook for twelve months and fined his club £350.

suffered. Free kicks seemed insufficient punishment on several occasions 'when intentions and actions were very evident. We hope that there will be no repetition next Saturday, or there will be a lot of trouble for somebody,' wrote the *Sheffield Daily Telegraph*. When Davies and Kitchen exchanged places, the Welshman did not escape, 'as a marvellous collection of bruises testified'. Man of the match for United was left back Jack English, often 'in the wars', with United's own Bill Cook close behind. There was no doubt that United owed the hard-fought draw nearly all to their defence.

If they could overcome Oldham in the replay, United were to play Bolton Wanderers in the semi final at Ewood Park, Blackburn, to be refereed by Mr J. Talks of Lincoln, the man who took charge of the tie at Oldham and allowed so much rough play. The other semi final was Everton v Chelsea or Newcastle United at Villa Park. Both games were to kick off at 3.30pm on March 27. In the event of either of them finishing level after extra time, the Football Association's Emergency Committee was to 'make arrangements'. The selection of the venues received criticism in the *Sheffield Daily Telegraph*, which termed the choice of Villa Park as 'particularly unfortunate' if Newcastle had to travel to Birmingham, believing it would have been better for the winners of the Bramall Lane replay to go there. It was suggested that the Football Association might be expecting Oldham to win the replay, in which case Blackburn was the ideal location for Oldham v Bolton. Should Sheffield United prevail, it would be very unfair for them to have to play on the very doorstep of their opponents. In the *Telegraph's* opinion, there would have been very little to complain about had the venues been reversed. It was now up to United to 'open the eyes of the gentlemen who have presumed, we think, a little too much'.

There was to be little respite for United as just two days after their tough task at Oldham they played Chelsea in a rearranged League match, but Chelsea were in exactly the same position, having drawn 1-1 at home to Newcastle United in the Cup. As well as a Cup semi final place to fight for, the visitors were dangerously near the foot of the League table; United were looking to enter the top five. After their draws on Saturday, the teams had to be content with sharing the spoils again. Just 5,000 people watched a game 'containing a lot of very clever football, and not a few hard collisions, not all of which were pleasant to watch'. Joe Kitchen, perhaps still harbouring resentment at the treatment he received at Oldham, dished out some of his own, charging Chelsea's Danish amateur player Nils Middelboe in the back so heavily that he was given a sharp reprimand by the referee. There were four penalty appeals, three by United, two of them appearing reasonable - one for each team. First, Kitchen was tripped; later Chelsea's Harold Halse went down on the same square yard of ground. The referee, 'who seldom satisfied the crowd', denied the appeal each time. United's best player was Albert Sturgess, who was praised for the distance he kicked the ball, one hefty boot giving goalkeeper Jim Molyneux 'a rare teaser under the bar from more than half the length of the field'. It was as well that Sturgess was so effective filling in at left back, because his captain George Utley went lame, forcing him on to the left wing, with Bob Evans dropping back to left half. Bill Brelsford, normally a most combative centre half, 'amazed the crowd by his abilities in dribbling and accuracy of centres'.

One notable inclusion in the Chelsea team was the England international and well-known amateur Vivian Woodward, who was playing League football for the first time this season. He enlisted in the army almost as soon as war was declared, and although he had played a lot of 'company' football, he found the pace of the First Division rather different. He passed well, but missed a good chance. Chelsea took the lead after seventeen minutes, when Bob Thomson scored 'a very pretty goal' from fifteen yards, but Stanley Fazackerley levelled with a header from a free kick perfectly placed by Jimmy Simmons. United pressed for the winning goal; Simmons got the ball past Molyneux but it hit the grounded Walter Bettridge, then the goalkeeper barely got a touch on Wally Masterman's header, but it was just enough and the game ended 1-1.

United had to face problems for the replay against Oldham on March 13. Cook, English and Davies, who were all hurt at Boundary Park, did not play against Chelsea and now Utley was injured too. Fortunately the two full backs were declared fit to return, allowing Sturgess to step into the half-back line to replace Utley. It was all change again as Brelsford was a late withdrawal with influenza, but Utley had made a miraculous recovery. Whoever was in the team, the biggest Bramall Lane attendance of the season was anticipated, despite the withdrawal of all cheap train fares. Oldham were a dangerous team, but United had already beaten them comfortably at Bramall Lane in the League.

Although there were no special excursion trains, Oldham brought a fair following to Sheffield and contributed well to a large crowd of 43,157 that filled most of the ground. The 'big mound' (the Shoreham Street end) was a sea of faces and flat caps and the cricket pavilion and the Bramall Lane end held thousands more, 'very thickly gathered', wrote the *Sheffield Daily Telegraph*. Ideal pitch and weather conditions added to the occasion, which proved to be a repeat of the 3-0 scoreline by which United beat Oldham in December. This time, however, it was a rather flattering margin. United's victory was merited, but Oldham played well in the middle of the first half and the beginning of the second. Oldham's combination play was better, but United 'had a very great superiority in dash'. Dash overcame method. United's attacking play 'compelled success', but on occasion they had to recognise 'with gratitude the splendour of its defence'. English, who had been honoured with selection for the Football League to play the Scottish League the following week, and his partner Cook were magnificent. They both 'did wonderful work in tight corners, timing their rushes splendidly and kicking very cleanly'. Harold Gough was 'extended to the utmost more than once' and 'this triumvirate is earning, and deserving to earn, golden tributes from everybody just now'. Fred Hawley took his opportunity at centre half with great success, excelling in heading, foiling the Oldham attack repeatedly. Alongside him, Sturgess 'was a dominant figure in defence of his own goal' and Utley 'touched his finest form'. In attack, Fazackerley's touches deserved better reward, and Kitchen was 'a daring raider'.

Oldham might have scored first when Elliot Pilkington, 'right in front of goal and only a few yards away, steadied himself, and then driving in a hard shot saw Gough leap across and push the ball behind for a corner'. It was 'a dramatic save, cheered to the echo'. Gradually United gained the ascendancy and got a goal after thirty-five minutes, when 'Kitchen dribbled through, bearing away to the right, and Simmons, taking up the running, put the ball right into the goal mouth. [Goalkeeper Howard] Matthews only pushed it out, and the ball, striking Kitchen as he raced in, rebounded into the net.' Six minutes later it was 2-0 as Evans centred, the ball was partially cleared and Utley drove it back. Oldham defender Charles Roberts tried to trap it but he was sharply dispossessed by Fazackerley, who, with little of the goal to aim at, found it, 'amid tumultuous cheering'. Oldham rallied at the start of the second half as Roberts headed against the bar, then Gough saved from Joseph Donnachie. United survived, and sealed the tie with fifteen minutes remaining: 'Kitchen in his stride took one of Masterman's best passes, and going on evaded Cook's rush and, when well inside the penalty area, shot at great speed into the net.' Matthews challenged him as he struck the ball and both men were hurt, Kitchen having to leave the field for three minutes. Gough made two more saves and Gilbert Kemp missed a chance right at the end, but United were worthy victors, advancing to the semi final 'amid many signs of enthusiasm'.

United's progress in the Cup meant that League matches were now coming thick and fast. Four days after the replay they travelled to Middlesbrough and played out a 2-2 draw on a Wednesday afternoon, which restricted the attendance to just 5,000. United looked tired and 'did not show themselves the hard striking, dour combination of the Cup ties', the *Sheffield Daily Telegraph* remarking in their defence: 'It is charitable to suppose that they were not quite as fresh as they would have liked to be, and, as compared with the possibilities of Cup successes, League points did not make such an answerable call on either their powers or duties.' United were not in the picture at all in the first half but managed to reach half time level at 1-1, as only Middlesbrough's faulty marksmanship prevented them being three goals to the good. One shot from George Elliott struck the inside of the post and came out, then the same player missed by a foot. Eventually he had better luck, scoring from Urwin's centre. United drew level with a goal out of nothing, when Haworth made a poor headed clearance straight to Wally Masterman, who 'beat Davies with a shot which the latter never got a glimpse of'. United had a fairer share of the play in the second half but the home crowd shouted for a penalty when Fred Hawley's hands shot up, but he was not quick enough and the ball struck him full in the face. Evans and Fazackerley joined Hawley in the wars, both going off at the same time, leaving United temporarily with nine men. Pantling, Utley and Masterman were also 'damaged', though it was stressed that Middlesbrough's play was fair throughout. United survived to go ahead midway through the second half, when Kitchen managed only a half-kick at a right-wing cross but the ball rolled slowly into the net. The lead lasted until the eighty-ninth minute, when Elliott scored again, then it needed a fine save by Gough to preserve the point.

Next for United was Aston Villa at Bramall Lane on March 20, a game for which Jack English was unavailable as he was playing for the Football League against the Scottish League in Glasgow. The attendance for the Villa game was estimated to be around 18,000, which included 'an extraordinary amount of khaki'. They watched a 'dashing' performance from United and a convincing win. As important as the 3-0 result, however, was that a week before the semi final against Bolton Wanderers all eleven players 'ran off the field unhurt at the finish'. United's forwards were all in sparkling form, especially Masterman and Fazackerley, who supplied many fine passes to the wingmen, who were both 'nippy and clever'. Kitchen was 'magnificent in the centre' and was given a 'hearty ovation' at the final whistle. United thought they had scored when Fazackerley hit the bar and the ball bounced down to be cleared by goalkeeper Sam Hardy, the referee rejecting appeals that it was over the line. United took the lead after twenty-one minutes in similar circumstances to the Fazackerley effort. This time Masterman hit the underside of the bar, Hardy scooped it out, but this time the referee signalled a goal. Now it was the Villa players who had cause for complaint. Villa came out strongly in the second half and Gough was called into action to fling himself at a shot from Joe Bache and to fist away a free kick from Harry Hampton. United relieved the pressure with a splendid goal by Kitchen. He set off from the half way line, touched the ball over James Harrop and as Hardy came out, Kitchen lifted the ball over him and headed it into the net. Utley preserved the two-goal lead when he pulled off a remarkable hooked clearance, before

Kitchen got the third following another long dribble, a burst of extraordinary speed and a 'swift shot at close quarters'. A late save from Hardy denied Kitchen his hat trick. It was the perfect result before the semi final the following Saturday.

In the build-up to the semi final 'Looker-On' wrote in the *Sheffield Daily Telegraph*: 'After Saturday there will only be one event of outstanding importance to be decided in the world of football, namely, the Cup final, and then the curtain will be rung down, with no little satisfaction to everyone, upon the most extraordinary season that has ever been or is likely to be again.' He lamented the abolition of cheap railway fares, which had dealt a blow to those wanting to travel to the two semi finals. Only Bolton followers would find it easy, as they had to journey the short distance to Blackburn. It was unlikely that supporters of Everton or Chelsea would travel to Birmingham, but it was hoped that a good number of United supporters would use to the full 'special motor char-a-bancs' that were available to hire from Sheffield motor companies. A 'well-informed football critic' from Bolton then gave his views of his local team. They commanded respect but were by no means a great side, lacking the dourness of Sheffield United in defence, the artistry of Aston Villa or Newcastle in attack and the aggressiveness of Wednesday. Their main weakness was in goal, where none of three goalkeepers tried – Joe Edmondson, Edward Sidlow and Percy Toone – had made the position his own. Edmondson was the only one eligible to play in the semi final but he had been guilty of so many lapses lately that a section of the Bolton crowd had lost confidence in him. The half-back line did not generate much confidence either, though the forward line was strong. The veteran David Stokes, who had also felt the wrath of the crowd two years previously, had now won back their favour and Evan Jones, a Welsh international, enjoyed the Cup, scoring as many goals in this competition as in the League. The left-sided combination of

Joe Smith and Ted Vizard came with a big reputation, deservedly so. Overall, the Bolton team's morale was said to be 'hopeful but not sanguine'. If United's renowned defence could keep Bolton's forwards in check, they surely could do enough to score two or three goals and win the tie.

United's eleven was revealed two days before the match, the directors deliberating for some time over the composition of the half-back line, where four men possessed strong claims for inclusion. Fred Hawley was the unfortunate one who would travel only as reserve, as the management opted for the tried-and-tested trio of Sturgess, Brelsford and Utley. However, an unforeseen problem had arisen, which was nothing to do to with the team and everything to do with the recently introduced emergency railway measures. United had chartered a special train to transport them to Blackburn, but the Lancashire and Yorkshire Railway Company now informed them that they were unable guarantee arrival at Blackburn before 2.30pm on account of the number of special trains they were running from Bolton to Blackburn. The *Sheffield Daily Telegraph* sarcastically commented that this in itself was a striking tribute and assurance of the certain partisanship of the crowd on a ground that the Football Association was supposed to have selected as a neutral one. It seems ludicrous today that a team playing in a semi final would travel on the morning of the match and plan to arrive at the ground just an hour before kick-off, but these were different times. After some negotiation, the booking agents Messrs Cook persuaded the railway company to change the departure time of the charter train, which would also carry supporters, from 12.05pm to 11.30am, so that it could avoid the aforementioned traffic and arrive in Blackburn at 1.45pm. Another group was leaving Sheffield on a scheduled service at 8.35am; they would be tired as many of them had been working until seven o'clock in the morning.

News of the Bolton Wanderers team came through to the *Telegraph* by telegraph. Their directors had sprung a surprise by selecting two young full backs with little Cup-tie experience. The team was training quietly and a couple of days before the big game visited Winsford in Cheshire to partake of the town's famous brine baths. They would have a big following in Blackburn, a great many supporters travelling by chartered char-a-banc, by car or on foot. Those supporters would not travel with great confidence, their primary emotion being one of anxiety, not at the prospect of losing in the Cup but at the possibility of losing their place in Division One. If they had a choice, avoiding relegation was more important than winning the Cup. In the other semi final, bottom placed Chelsea were facing Everton, who were amongst the leading half-dozen in the League, but Chelsea's Cup results belied their League position, and included fine wins at Manchester City and Newcastle. Everton were undoubted favourites, preparing for the tie with relaxing visits to Southport and West Kirby.

The March 27 semi finals produced an expected result at one venue, an unexpected one at the other. At Ewood Park, Sheffield United managed to see off their Lancashire opponents at by a score of 2-1. United captain George Utley led out his men, balancing a football on his right hand. He was followed by Stanley Fazackerley, his pronounced centre parting dividing his greased scalp into halves, both men being watched closely by a heavily-overcoated policeman and thousands of flat-capped men, some of them sitting on the low perimeter wall by the players' tunnel. The team took the field to face a hostile crowd numbering some 22,500, reported to be nineteen-twentieths in support of Bolton Wanderers, but United overcame the partisan atmosphere – just – having to withstand Bolton pressure for thirty-five of the final forty-five minutes. In this period they were lucky when Ted Vizard's shot hit the foot of the post with Harold Gough beaten. However, luck evened itself out when Joe Kitchen broke clean through but missed the gaping goal by yards, explaining afterwards that the ball 'got up' just as he was shooting. United started the game well and could have been two goals ahead in the first ten minutes, Fazackerley and Jimmy Simmons going close. It was Simmons who scored the first goal after thirty minutes, 'ending a very smart sprint with a fast, oblique shot, which Edmondson tried to keep out, but only helped into his own goal'. Soon afterwards George Utley got the best goal of the match. He was challenged by Bob Glendenning and Billy Jennings, but he 'coolly and cleverly evaded the attentions of both, and then having run nearly thirty yards, he steadied himself and in front of Edmondson and with the utmost deliberation drove the ball into the net. It was a glorious goal, and quite the outstanding feature of the match.'

Bolton's half backs proved not to be the weak link they might have been, but their inexperienced backs had a sorry time, which could have been even worse had Bob Evans, Wally Masterman and Kitchen been on their best game. There was some excuse for Kitchen, who had been ill during the week. Bolton rallied after half time and pulled a goal back half way through the half when a header by Joe Smith from a pass by David Stokes found the net. After this United were 'on pins and needles', their team now apparently comprising a goalkeeper, two backs and eight half backs, so wrote the *Sheffield Daily Telegraph's* reporter. The attack 'vanished to nothingness' and it was left to the overworked (regular) half backs and backs to stem the tide. Often the retreating forwards got in the way of Bill Cook, Jack English and Gough, who were thankful when Fazackerley and Kitchen made breakaways. English's selection for the previous week's inter-league match had raised some eyebrows, but this game showed exactly what the selectors saw in him. He had an able partner in Cook, the pair covering each other's every movement. The defence pulled United through at the finish, as the forwards as a whole gave their worst display of any of the Cup ties so far. Fazackerley was hindered by twice being badly hurt, but Kitchen was not the daring raider of other matches and Masterman was strangely quiet. This had an effect on left winger Evans, of whom very little was seen. Utley played well, Bill Brelsford moderately, but it was noticeable that centre forward Frank Roberts preferred to avoid United's tough centre half than go near him. Sturgess did excellently against Vizard, but United's best men were the backs and the goalkeeper. In summary, if United had played their usual game Bolton would have been decisively beaten, but when the forwards stopped playing after going two goals in front it was a close-run thing. No matter, United were in the final for the first time since 1902. In the other semi final at Villa Park, Chelsea shocked Everton by pulling off a fine 2-0 win.

The victorious United team and their jubilant supporters had little time to celebrate their success, as the return train was due to depart less than one hour after the final whistle, leaving Blackburn at 5.55pm. The triumphant group of players and supporters was unceremoniously left to their own devices as the train terminated at Manchester's Victoria Station, forcing hundreds to find their own way across the city to the Central (Midland) Station in time for the 8.23pm departure to Sheffield. Having reached the Cup final, one imagines a joyous, if laborious, journey home, despite all that the railway companies and the Kaiser could do to spoil it.

United were back in action just two days later, taking on Manchester City at Bramall Lane. The result was a scoreless draw, but United's unbeaten record now stood at eighteen League and Cup games. The United players had not had time to fully recover from the strain of their fraught Cup win and were up against rivals who had not played on Saturday.

However, United neglected to take a number of chances in the first half and when the forwards understandably faded in the second half United once more relied on their noted defence to keep their goal intact. Jimmy Simmons, who was leading City's left back Eli Fletcher a merry dance, was United's outstanding player, beating his opponent regularly. Once Simmons got through but 'failed to secure the perpendicular', losing his balance as he shot wide. United's play fell off in the second half after Utley was kicked on the knee and had to go to outside left, with Evans moving to left half. City almost went ahead when Fred Howard 'drove in at top speed, the ball striking the under-side of the bar and being scrambled away'. Gough and his backs faced a busy time, but they managed to keep City out.

Easter was approaching, and United were now two matches into a hectic spell of five games in ten days. Good Friday, April 2, took them to Notts County, where they suffered defeat for the first time since another public holiday, Boxing Day. George Utley was out, still suffering from the kick on the knee he received against Manchester City, so Fred Hawley took his place. United wasted the chance to take the lead when Jimmy Simmons sent a penalty wide of the post. County took advantage to build a 2-0 lead at half time, before adding a third ten minutes into the second half. Unusually, Harold Gough was at fault for two of the goals. Three minutes after County's third goal Joe Kitchen reduced the margin but United's all-round failure and absence of keenness were discomforting in view of the upcoming Cup final. The attendance was around 10,000, mostly comprising men in khaki, and United did not lack support as many of them were members of the Hallamshire Reserve Regiment.

The next day United got back on track with a 3-2 win over Bradford Park Avenue. Rain fell all game and the ground was incredibly muddy, so good football was impossible. Two

penalties were squandered - one by each side. After Simmons'
miss at Notts County, right back Bill Cook was entrusted with
the kick, but he dragged it slowly on to Ernie Scattergood's
trailing leg.[37] Jimmy Bauchop then missed one for Bradford,
before Simmons shot United in front. Bradford equalised five
minutes later when Gough could only parry a shot from Jimmy
Smith and Bauchop ran in to head the ball over the line.
United regained the lead thanks to clever refereeing by Mr
Peers, who allowed play to proceed when Simmons was
tripped as he dribbled through. United's right winger managed
to stay on his feet and centred for Joe Kitchen to score with a
shot that went in off the bar. Then came 'the finest goal seen
on the ground for some time' as Wally Masterman, thirty yards
from goal, beat Scattergood with 'a glorious and very fast
shot'. Smith scored a consolation for Bradford near the end of
the game, but United were deservedly successful. Easter
Monday brought another point from a 1-1 draw with
Sunderland, when once again many thousands of soldiers were
in attendance. Stanley Fazackerley gave United the lead with a
first-time shot when Simmons's corner was kicked out to him
by a defender. A previously exciting game slackened off in the
second half as several players showed signs of tiredness, but
Sunderland drew level when Gough was beaten by a good shot
by George Holley.

On April 10 came a second trip to Oldham in four weeks
and, after United's highly successful result there in the Cup,
the home side was looking for revenge, which they achieved in
style with a comprehensive 3-0 win. It was a humiliating
experience for United; five minutes after the match one
Lancashire man was heard to say, 'It looks as though United
don't care tuppence what happened.' The *Sheffield Daily*

---

[37] At this time Cook was not to know that he would never score a goal for
Sheffield United in his 324 appearances for the club he continued to play for
until 1927.

Telegraph uncharacteristically chastised United, calling their performance 'distasteful'. It added that 'a canker-worm of indifference had ingratiated itself' and the task of the Oldham defenders was 'a pic-nic'. Only United's backs and goalkeeper emerged with any credit. In a rare example of stern criticism, the *Telegraph* suggested that the United players no longer cared about League points or win bonuses: winning the Cup was the only thing of importance to them now. They could play ninety per cent better without any risk of spraining ligaments and certainly could not have played worse had they striven to do so. Several members of the United team were on the field, but they did not play, wrote the *Telegraph*. It was a stinging attack from a normally very supportive newspaper. A Manchester newspaper concurred, stating that 'it was altogether a woeful exhibition'. If there was any excuse, it was that Oldham were top of the League and in good form.

Just two days later was another trip to Lancashire and another defeat, this time 2-1 to Liverpool, but at least United made a much better game of it than at Oldham. The pitch was very heavy after Sunday's rain and the wind was strong, but the sun shone brightly. United had plenty of shots, but none of them accurate enough and it was Liverpool who scored first, a brilliant goal begun by Thomas Fairfoull, who avoided English's charge and drew out Gough, then supplied Fred Pagnam to turn the ball slowly over the line from a tight angle. In the second half Jackie Sheldon missed one penalty, putting the ball wide, then converted another. Poor Bill Cook was the culprit both times, first for handball, then for a push on Donald McKinley. United, inspired by Utley, now 'set about' their opponents and got a goal when Kitchen's fine drive 'passed wide of [Elisha] Scott, who made a capital effort to prevent it passing over the goal line'. Davies then hit the bar, the ball coming straight down to Scott, but overall United's shooting was erratic and the defeat was deserved.

United had two games to play in the week before the final: Manchester United at home on Saturday April 17 and Tottenham Hotspur away on Monday, from which they emerged unscathed in terms of results and injuries. Manchester United were beaten 3-1, Utley scoring the first goal with a 'capital drive' from twenty yards, then five minutes later Evans added the second. Fazackerley headed against the post in the second half, but Enoch West scored for Manchester to make it 2-1. Towards the end of the game Masterman set off on a dribble, withstood a charge by James Montgomery and a buffeting by Walter Spratt and scored the third with a fine shot across goal. Two days later United travelled to London to play Spurs and managed a somewhat fortunate 1-1 draw. It was a fine spring evening and the pitch was firm, producing plenty of attractive football. United's goalkeeper and backs were once again prominent; Gough made 'many masterly saves' and Cook played 'a giant's part'. Gough was temporarily laid out when Bert Middlemiss struck a shot with so much pace that it burst through his hands and hit him in the face. United enjoyed a number of escapes and went in front against the run of play. Utley gave Evans a beautiful pass, the left winger then doing likewise to give the ball to Davies, whose 'transference to Fazackerley was the touch of an artist.' The United inside right beat goalkeeper Bill Jacques with an accurate low shot. Jim Fleming scored the equaliser after twenty-eight minutes of the second half, then Billy Minter skimmed the bar with a splendid shot, but United held on. United, and Chelsea, who had played at home to Manchester United the same evening, now had four clear days to prepare for the Cup final.

The decision had been taken before Christmas that the final would be held outside London, but it was not until the end of March, scarcely three weeks before the scheduled date, that the venue was selected. The final was to take place at Old Trafford, the ground of Manchester United FC, on April 24, with a 3.30pm kick off. The officials in charge were referee Mr H. H. Taylor of Altrincham and linesmen Mr J. F. Pearson and Mr G. Miller. Mr Taylor was a respected official who had taken charge of several big games in the past year, including a Scotland v Wales international, the Scottish League v the Football League and the Sheffield United v Burnley Cup semi final, also at Old Trafford. If a replay was necessary, it was to take place at the Everton FC ground on May 1. Removing the final from London meant the competition had 'lost something of its magnetism', wrote the *Lancashire Post*. The final had gained its immeasurable reputation from its grand setting at Crystal Palace, and there was always the added attraction of 'a jaunt to town' for supporters of provincial clubs. Crystal Palace gave the match 'an unconventional frame' and elsewhere, even at the magnificent Old Trafford, the match would be very much like any other, lacking its hitherto attendant 'colour'. If there was any benefit to be gained, it would be that the players would be more accustomed to the surroundings of a 'normal' football ground and would thus perform better. It was noticeable that in previous Cup finals the unfamiliar sense of spaciousness at Crystal Palace had prevented many players from doing themselves justice. There had been too many 'dull and dismal' finals at the Palace. It was to be hoped that Sheffield United and Chelsea would give an exhibition worthy of the occasion and the stake. But however well the two teams played and whoever won, it was announced that there would be no celebration or jubilation after the Cup was presented, a decision that was met with general approval all round.

CHAPTER FOURTEEN

JUST A GENERAL KICK-ABOUT

Newspaper reports and soldiers' letters from the front gave the British people at least a glimpse of what life was like in the trenches – the sufferings, the hardships, and the occasional distractions. At the same time, Britons were told how the German people were coping with the war. Whether or not the public realised it, whatever they read in the newspapers could not exactly be treated as the gospel truth, as propaganda and heavy censorship were applied to all reports and correspondence. Many such articles had football as a theme, some of them quoting letters from soldiers who wondered how football could continue at home as they endured unspeakable privations, but one or two were surprisingly dispassionate. The newspaper correspondents liked to engage a mocking tone when describing the Germans' attitude to sport, and football in particular, but at other times they wrote in deadly seriousness, realising that the state of preparedness and mind of Germany posed a real and immediate threat to the security of Great Britain and its allies.

One reporter warned of the German soldier's single-mindedness, in contrast to the almost happy-go-lucky demeanour of 'Tommy Atkins', who enjoyed singing songs and reading football match reports to keep his spirits high, complaining when the newspapers did not reach the trenches.

The Germans, on the other hand, preferred to concentrate on just the matter at hand – fighting, and winning, the war. They, wrote the reporter, thought of nothing but their country and the war. Other articles carried similar messages. The Bishop of Bangor warned that while Britain amused itself on pleasurable pastimes, the Germans were far more organised in building their military strength. They did not waste time watching football matches. Every man, woman, and child had their assigned place and job and were working together with one single aim - to conquer Britain and its allies. Germany's factories were working full time and every working man was trained, ready to fight if required.

Captain Frederick Guest, a member of the Parliamentary Recruiting Committee, exhorted British workers to do likewise, appealing to their comradeship and sense of fear, writing: 'In the production of war material every minute means another shell and perhaps the saving of another of these gallant lives. How can you stop for an instant to think of racing, football, cricket, holidays, or strikes while victory hangs in the balance and your mates are blown to bits? You must realise that our margin of strength is very narrow, and therefore every man should work and every woman should pray for the maintenance of that thin heroic line which stands between us and extermination.'

However, it cannot have been entirely true that every German not in the army was spending every available minute manufacturing the tools of war, as time could still found for sport and physical fitness, though football in Germany in the early part of the twentieth century was not a nationally popular game. Communal gymnastics, or *Turnen* in German, occupied the free time of much of the youth of the population. Competitive sport was viewed by many as something in which the English participated, dividing the country into winners and losers. *Turnen*, on the other hand, created unity and bonding, ideal traits in an age of Prussian discipline and order. German football was therefore born out of a degree of rebellion against the drudgery and boredom of what could conceivably be described as mass-participation aerobics.

The *Turner* (gymnasts) always believed that their drills and routines were undertaken to prepare them for war, so naturally they were among the first to enlist in the army. However, the 'rebel' (non-professional) footballers did not hold back and signed up in large numbers too, unlike their English (professional) counterparts. Most clubs thus lost the majority of their players, although matches did continue during the war. *The Times* reported that in Berlin: 'Riding exercise is taken by gentlemen in the *Tiergarten* every morning as usual. Sport is reviving, and there are a good many football matches. Two recently played were those between Berlin and Vienna and Berlin and Leipzig.' The Berlin newspaper *Lokalanzeiger* reported that football was in full swing in Germany, publishing details of forthcoming league matches and the prospects of the various teams, some of which had to rely on a completely new set of players to replace those who joined the army. Others had to merge to get eleven men on the pitch, such as great rivals Kickers Stuttgart and VfB Stuttgart. However, football had a hard time in another way too: when Britain's naval blockade bit deeply into Germany's food supply, the Kaiser ordered that all public open space should be used to grow potatoes. There was now a shortage of both players and pitches.

But football was growing in popularity in the country, so much so that German soldiers liked to play games at the front whenever conditions allowed. The *Berliner Tageblatt* reported that some German infantrymen captured two officers and three men of the Royal Scots – and their football. Delighted with their prize, the Germans attempted to play with it, much to the disdain of their prisoners, who took it upon themselves to teach their captors how to play under Association rules. The newspaper then suggested that having learned to play football properly, the Germans were getting more injuries in the game than in battle, the implication being that British military advances were being repelled easily by their own heroic soldiers. The propaganda did not end there: German newspapers, and German language newspapers in America, were quick to exploit the failure of recruiting at football matches in Britain, in their eyes proving that the British were 'unworthy champions..... of democracy'. The *Berlin Lokalanzeiger* gloated that 'if after a game of football in London which was attended by more than 100,000 spectators only three young men could be induced to enlist, one may rightly conclude that the youth of England has very little interest in a war which already has inflicted terrible losses upon the English troops'. Which match it was that attracted such a large crowd was not explained, and one suspects that an extra zero was added to the figure for effect.

That German soldiers liked to play football at the front was, according to *The Times*, simply because they were 'an imitative race' who only took up the game after watching the British play across the trenches. This opinion was contradicted by the *Berliner Tageblatt*. In reporting that 'the game of football is among the most popular and most widespread sports in the German army', it gave the following account:

> *In the 85th Infantry Regiment are a number of players, including a German international, who at the express command of his captain took his ball with him to the front. Great therefore was the joy of the 85th when, after a victorious fight with the English, they captured as booty the enemy's complete football outfit.*

German prisoners of war in England enjoyed football too. At Frimley camp, the prisoners were said to be 'contented and at ease in their compound'. Their 'Teutonic character' apparently made for 'resignation, not for cheerfulness in adversity' but they did sometimes take part in recreational activities. 'Games are played,' sarcastically wrote The Times, 'including football - German football, but still football.' Some Germans clearly liked football, but another reported episode from the battlefield suggested that others were not sure what the game was all about. When the German front lines saw British soldiers advancing whilst kicking footballs in front of them, they wondered if the spherical objects might be some new kind of grenade. This unreferenced incident could have been from the first day of the Somme offensive on July 1, 1916, when Captain Billy Nevill of the 8th Battalion, East Surrey Regiment, encouraged his men to go 'over the top' by promising a reward to the first of them to 'score a goal' in German trenches. Led by Nevill, they together kicked four footballs across No-Man's Land as they advanced. Many men were shot dead almost immediately, but their objective was gained. Nevill, however, was not amongst those who made it across, being killed before he reached the German wire. Their brave action was commemorated by a poem in the Daily Mail:

On through the hail of slaughter,
Where gallant comrades fall,
Where blood is poured like water,
They drive the trickling ball.
The fear of death before them,
Is but an empty name;
True to the land that bore them,
The SURREYS played the game.

If the Germans played football at the front, the British liked to think they played it more, and better. One report from the front told of how in a lull in the fighting, some British soldiers took advantage of the few hours of calm to indulge in the favourite British Saturday afternoon sport. While the artillery duel went on at the front line, the troops, who had been brought back to rest some distance behind the firing line, inflated several footballs and started to kick them about. Seeing the action, another battalion challenged them to a game and 'an exciting match followed'. Winter came early in 1914, snow falling before the end of November, but that did not discourage the troops, for as one soldier wrote back home: 'The spirit of our men continues excellent. Football has been very popular during this cold snap, and the game has been played by our men when within range of the German artillery. Uhlan[38] lances have done service as goal-posts.'

Another time, an unnamed officer matter-of-factly wrote:

The men are truly wonderful; some of the (censored) were playing football yesterday afternoon, three shells pitched among them, killing one and wounding nine. Within a quarter of an hour they were playing football again. Of course, it was unaimed fire, but it gives you an idea of the callous value of life.

In April 1915 it was reported in the *Sheffield Daily Telegraph* that an international football match took place 'within sound of the guns'. A letter arrived at his home in Matlock from J. T. Gregory, a driver with the Royal Field Artillery, but also one of the best outside lefts in West

---

[38] The Uhlans were Polish light cavalry, armed with lances, sabres and pistols.

Derbyshire, who had played for Derby County, Matlock Town and Darley Dale. Gregory wrote:

> *We had a match the other day between England and Scotland. England won 2-1. Jefferies, of Norwich City, scored both goals for England. I have been asked to play for the Territorials in a match, and a Scotchman and I have picked a team to play one of the other sections.*

Much myth and legend has built up surrounding the 'Christmas Truce' of 1914, when soldiers of both sides stopped shooting at each other and instead fraternised with the enemy, exchanging gifts and singing songs. The higher ranks were well aware of the damage to spirit Christmas in the trenches might bring. In early December General Sir Horace Smith-Dorrien issued an instruction to commanders of all divisions, stating:

> *It is during this period that the greatest danger to the morale of troops exists. Experience of this and of every other war proves undoubtedly that troops in trenches in close proximity to the enemy slide very easily, if permitted to do so, into a 'live and let live' theory of life. Officers and men sink into a military lethargy from which it is difficult to arouse them when the moment for great sacrifices again arises. The attitude of our troops can be readily understood and to a certain extent commands sympathy. Such an attitude is, however, most dangerous for it discourages initiative in commanders and destroys the offensive spirit in all ranks. The Corps Commander therefore directs Divisional*

Commanders to impress on subordinate commanders the absolute necessity of encouraging offensive spirit. Friendly intercourse with the enemy, unofficial armistices, however tempting and amusing they may be, are absolutely prohibited.

The directive was to no avail. On December 20 an informal truce occurred in an area manned by the 20th Brigade as German soldiers were seen taking British wounded to safety from No-Man's Land. Three days later the 23rd Brigade reported a similar situation. It was only a temporary respite. On Christmas Eve ninety-eight British soldiers were killed, many by sniper fire. That evening Christmas trees, candles and paper lanterns appeared on enemy parapets. Both sides began to sing carols and hymns and gradually an exchange of communication developed. Then, on Christmas morning a ceasefire commenced when the 20th Brigade and their German counterparts allowed each other to advance, unarmed, to collect and bury their dead. As they did so they mingled and began conversing with each other, resulting in joint burial sites and the passing over of food - the Germans provided *sauerkraut* and sausages, whilst the British gave them chocolate in return.[39]

An emotional letter to *The Scotsman* from Private John Robb of the 6th Gordon Highlanders described what he witnessed on Christmas Day and the preceding days: 'Our battalion is having a pretty hot time just now. We have lost a good many men. I have been very fortunate myself, thank God, although I had a very narrow shave last Friday night, as we had a charge, but none of our chaps were touched. The

---

[39] Elsewhere, the war went on as normal. Eighty-one British soldiers died on Christmas Day, many the victims of snipers. The 2nd Grenadier Guards were involved in heavy fighting and suffered losses.

Grenadier Guards and the Gordons lost a lot of men that night; the Germans were about thirty to our one. We shall require a large number of men out here yet to assist us, as we are outnumbered. We are four days and four nights in the trenches at a spell, and we are knee-deep in mud and water all the time. This being Christmas Day, both the Germans and us ceased firing the whole day, and our chaps left their trenches and went over to the Germans and wished them a merry Christmas. Our chaplain, the Reverend Esslemont Adams, went up to the firing line to-day, and had a talk with the Germans. One of the German majors gave him a cigar for a souvenir, and Mr Adams gave the major a small prayer out of his cap in return. He also read the burial service to seventeen Germans who were buried to-day. The major told him that they were quite fed up, and wanted to stop; so we commenced fighting at 5pm again. I wish it was all over, as the trenches are not quite the best, but we are sticking it with a right heart. I wish you a happy New Year and good luck.'

Other letters to the *Manchester Guardian*, under the headline 'Christmas Day In The Trenches – More About The Extraordinary Unofficial Armistice', gave further insights. One officer wrote: 'In the afternoon my attention was called to a large group of men standing up half-way between our trenches and the enemy's. So I went out with my sergeant to investigate, and actually found a large party of Germans and our people hob-nobbing together.' Private Higham of the Stalybridge Territorials wrote: 'I was a bit timid at first but me and a lad called Sterling went up, and I shook hands with about sixteen Germans. They gave us cigars and toffee, and they told us they didn't want to fight, but they had to. All the Cheshires and the Germans were together by this time, and we sang "Tipperary" for them, and they sang a song for us.' Others told of the joint burial ceremonies:

A truce had been arranged for the few hours of daylight for the burial of the dead on both sides who had been lying out in the open since the fierce night-fighting of a week earlier. When I got out I found a large crowd of officers and men, English and German, grouped around the bodies, which had already been gathered together and laid out in rows. I went along those dreadful ranks and scanned the faces, fearing at every step to recognise one I knew. It was a ghastly sight. They lay stiffly in contorted attitudes, dirty with frozen mud. The digging parties were already busy on the two big common graves, but the ground was hard and the work slow and laborious.

The British High Command was unimpressed, reiterating that such fraternisation must not go on. Smith-Dorrien even threatened disciplinary action against the officers of the units that took part. Propaganda decreed that the Germans had to be portrayed as 'evil Hun' and blood-lusting madmen, so reports of friendliness on their part had to be repressed. However, the letters home enabled news of the truce to escape. Some even included details of a football match played in No-Man's Land on Christmas Day. One such letter began:

The digging completed, the shallow graves were filled in, and the German officers remained to pay their tribute of respect, while our chaplain read a short service. It was one of the most impressive things I have ever witnessed. Friend and foe stood side by side, bare-headed, watching the tall, grave figure of the padre outlined against the frosty landscape as he blessed the poor broken bodies at his feet. Then, with more formal salutes, we turned and made or way back to our respective ruts. Elsewhere along the line I hear our fellows played the Germans at football on Christmas Day. Our own pet enemies remarked that they would like a game, but as the ground in our part is all root crops and much cut up by ditches, and as, moreover, we had not got a football, we had to call it off.

A diary entry, made by a soldier in the Royal Warwickshire Regiment, said: 'A quiet day. Germans shout over to us and ask us to play them at football, and also not to fire and they would do likewise. At 2am (Christmas Day) a German band went along their trenches playing "Home Sweet Home" and "God Save The King", which sounded grand and made everyone think of home. During the night several of our fellows went over No-Man's Land to the German lines and were given drink and cigarettes.'

There is still much conjecture about exactly where and when the match (or matches) took place, but enough evidence exists to support the claim that football was indeed played between the two warring sides. A letter to *The Times* from a Major in the Royal Army Medical Corps informed readers that on Christmas Day: 'The (censored) Regiment actually had a football match with the Saxons, who beat them 3-2!' This account is backed up by the regimental records of the 133rd Saxon (German) regiment, which also record a Christmas Day game ending with a 3-2 scoreline in favour of the Germans. A member of the London Rifle Brigade then wrote: 'On Christmas Eve the Germans burned coloured lights and candles along the top of their trenches, and on Christmas Day a football match was played between them and us in front of the trench.' However, it has been suggested that the two '3-2' references must be coincidental, as the unnamed Major's regiment was separated from the 133rd Saxons by the River Lys (Leie in Flemish), but it could be, of course, that the Major heard about the match, perhaps from a wounded soldier, and did not actually witness it himself. Indeed, why would he make it up or miscommunicate what he had been told? If he wanted to do that, surely England would have won?

In 1983, Great War veteran Ernie Williams, a former Territorial of the 6th Cheshires, claimed that he had taken part himself in this or another match, saying: 'The ball appeared from somewhere, I don't know where, but it came from their side - it wasn't from our side that the ball came. They made up some goals and one fellow went in goal and then it was just a general kickabout. I should think there were about a couple of hundred taking part. I had a go at the ball. I was pretty good then, at nineteen. Everybody seemed to be enjoying themselves. There was no sort of ill-will between us. There was no referee, and no score, no tally at all. It was simply a melee - nothing like the soccer you see on television.' In a contemporary account, the 6th Cheshires' Company Sergeant Major, Frank Naden, told the *Newcastle Evening Mail*:

> *On Christmas Day one of the Germans came out of the trenches and held his hands up. Our fellows immediately got out of theirs, and we met in the middle, and for the rest of the day we fraternised, exchanging food, cigarettes and souvenirs. The Germans gave us some of their sausages, and we gave them some of our stuff. The Scotsmen started the bagpipes and we had a rare old jollification, which included football in which the Germans took part. The Germans expressed themselves as being tired of the war and wished it was over. They greatly admired our equipment and wanted*

*to exchange jack knives and other articles. Next
day we got an order that all communication and
friendly intercourse with the enemy must cease
but we did not fire at all that day, and the
Germans did not fire at us.*

Williams and Naden's unit has been traced to Wulverghem,
just north of Ploegsteert in Belgium, suggesting that an
impromptu, informal, match took place there (and possibly in
other locations too), but evidence is scant that organised game
(s) were played there or elsewhere on the front. This location
is also not too far distant from the River Lys, either side of
which were stationed the Major in the Royal Army Medical
Corps and the 133rd Saxon regiment.

Regardless of the truth or myth of the 'Christmas Day
football match,' what is commonly accepted to have happened
is an amusing incident on April 1, 1915. *The Times* takes up
the story:

*The First of April was not allowed to pass without
one practical joke being played on the enemy. An
airman flying over the Lille aerodrome dropped a
football. It fell slowly through the air, and the
Germans could be seen hurrying from all
directions to take cover from what they evidently
thought was a bomb. That it bounced to an
enormous height from the ground without
exploding was probably taken to be due to a
delayed-action fuse, for it was not till the ball
finally came to rest that they emerged from their
shelters to examine it. On it was written 'April
Fool! Gott strafe England!'*

The message, meaning 'May God punish England,' was a sarcastic rejoinder to the German army's use of badges and posters bearing this slogan. The *Manchester Guardian* also printed the story, elaborating on the jape by writing: 'The wisdom of the jest lies in the fact that it embodies what is so very much the best way of acknowledging this gloomy, elaborately drilled Teutonic fury, if it has to be acknowledged at all. This "Quip Modest" is vastly more effective than any retorts in kind, if only because the Germans have so abundantly proved themselves incapable of it.'

Even in 1915 the Germans did not have a sense of humour.....

CHAPTER FIFTEEN

THERE WAS ONLY ONE BALL & WE HAD IT MOST OF THE TIME

Twice previous winners and once runners-up, Sheffield United had made it through to their first English Cup[40] final since 1902. Either side of the turn of the century United were one of the most dominant forces in English football, taking the Football League Championship in 1897/98 and finishing second in 1899/1900. They also lifted the Cup in 1898/99 and 1901/02 and lost the final in a replay in 1900/01, thus making five consecutive seasons in which the players collected medals.[41] But following the decline or departure of many players, including such prominent men as half back and

---

[40] The full title of the Cup is 'The Football Association Challenge Cup Competition'. First played for in the 1871/72 season. It was variously known under its complete name, as The Football Association Cup, The Association Cup, The Association Challenge Cup, The Challenge Cup, The English Cup or simply The Cup. It didn't become commonly known as 'The F.A. Cup' until later, possibly as late as the 1960s. The first Cup final programme front cover to announce itself as for simply 'The F.A. Cup Final' appears to be 1987. The final was also known as 'The Final Tie' until the 1960s: the first final programme front cover to omit the word 'Tie' appears to be 1966, but 'Tie' reappeared as a one-off for the 100th final programme front cover in 1981.

[41] Wednesday won the League in 1902/03 and 1903/04 and the Cup in 1896 and 1907. The years around the turn of the twentieth century brought a period of success for the city of Sheffield never since replicated.

captain Ernest Needham, goalkeeper William Foulke, full back Harry Thickett and forwards Walter Bennett, Fred Priest and Bert Lipsham, the team rarely threatened to challenge for honours for the next decade, their highest League placing being fourth in 1906/07. There were also embarrassingly early exits from the Cup at the hands of Blackpool, Swindon Town and Darlington, all at Bramall Lane. First or second round Cup defeats became the norm, none of them more unfortunate than the tie against Huddersfield Town in 1913. United were leading 2-1 after seventy-five minutes when the game was abandoned in a snowstorm, losing the rearranged match 3-1 four days later.

But the arrival of a group of players who were to give United many years' service heralded a period that the club hoped would bring a repeat of earlier successes. William 'Billy' Gillespie (563 appearances), Albert Sturgess (512 appearances), Bill Brelsford (417 appearances), Joe Kitchen (342 appearances), Harold Gough (335 appearances), Bill Cook (324 appearances), Jimmy Simmons (301 appearances), George Utley (240 appearances), Bob Evans (220 appearances) and Stanley Fazackerley (143 appearances) signed for United between 1907 and 1913. All except the injured Gillespie played in the 1915 Cup final. The 1914/15 Sheffield United team was therefore well stocked with players at or nearing their peak, and newer signings such as Harold Pantling, Jack English, Fred Hawley, Wally Masterman, David Davies and Jack Thompson were expected to improve and compete for regular places over the coming years. The 1913/14 season at last brought signs of recovery as United reached the semi final, losing out 1-0 to Burnley in a replay at Goodison Park following a goalless draw at Old Trafford, so the club was delighted to go one better the following season.

The commanding Utley was proving to be the key: he was the captain, left half and the man around whom the team revolved. At last United had found an on-field leader and inspirational figure to replace the great 'Nudger' Needham, the 'Prince of Half Backs'. Utley had played in Barnsley's Cup win in a replay at Bramall Lane in 1912. The Sheffield United directors liked what they saw and offered his hometown club a British record transfer fee of £2,000 for his services. Some directors were said to be of the view that no footballer was worth that sort of money (an opinion with which Utley himself agreed) and that he would never last the term of his engagement, but he proved them wrong, despite initially not being keen on the move because he was due a long-service benefit at Barnsley. A five-year contract and the promise of a benefit at the end of it were enough to sway him. United's run to the 1914 semi final brought in over £13,000 in gate receipts, more than enough to cover Utley's transfer fee and wages, and also help towards much-needed ground developments at Bramall Lane, but in later years his favourable contract terms caused unrest, even rebellion, in the United dressing room.[42] It had been known for some time that the traditional venue for the final was unavailable. Other than four replays, every Cup final between 1894/95 and 1913/14 had been staged at London's Crystal Palace (the site of the current National Sports Centre and athletics stadium), with attendances regularly higher than 70,000 and three times topping 100,000. The 1912/13 final between Aston Villa and Sunderland attracted a massive crowd of 121,919.[43] But the stadium was requisitioned by the Admiralty for military training purposes

---

[42] Utley's contract allowed him to take the entire gate receipts for one match as his benefit, a clause that was not available to other players. He chose a match against Sunderland in 1920, which produced net takings more than twice the £500 other players received for their benefit. He was the last player in English professional football to enjoy such a perk.

[43] Other sources claim the attendance at this game was 120,081. Whichever is correct, it was a world record gate for a football match at the time.

and closed to the public in February 1915. The Crystal Palace club had been forced out too, playing its remaining fixtures at the nearby Herne Hill running track. There was also the potential disruption to travel in the capital for the Football Association to consider in its deliberations over the choice of an alternative venue. The final was therefore moved north for the first time since the early 1890s, to be played on April 24. The relatively new ground used by Manchester United in the Trafford borough of the city had successfully held the final replay between Bradford City and Newcastle United in 1910/11 and was thus considered suitable for the 1915 final. On its opening in 1910, a contemporary journalist described Old Trafford as 'the most handsomest, the most spacious and the most remarkable arena I have ever seen. As a football ground it is unrivalled in the world'. With a capacity of around 80,000, it was not much of a step down from the vast Crystal Palace in terms of size and facilities. It would prove more than adequate for what was to be the lowest Cup final attendance (other than for replays) for twenty years. Had these been normal times, however, a new record crowd could quite reasonably have been expected at Crystal Palace, especially with the rare sight of a team from the capital in the final. Chelsea were said to represent the whole of London and so would have brought followers from all over the metropolis, whereas clubs like Tottenham and Arsenal attracted support only from their local areas.

Chelsea had had a poor season in the League, finishing in nineteenth place, one point above bottom team Tottenham Hotspur. They did not manage an away League win all season. However, the Cup was a different matter and they pulled off some excellent, and unexpected, results. In the first round they drew 1-1 with Second Division Swindon Town, winning the replay 5-2, both games being played at Stamford Bridge. Chelsea then came out on top 1-0 in a tight all-London game against Second Division Arsenal. Harold Halse scored the only goal after forty minutes:

> *Halse, behind his mates and inclined to the left side of the field, raised the ball over the heads of the contending forces at considerable velocity. The drive hit the underside of the bar and turning inwards the ball fell over the line and inside the netted space. What a fine goal and what a chorus of cheers!*

Chelsea then put their League form to one side to pull off a surprise 1-0 win at League championship challengers Manchester City in round three. City had the better of the match and Chelsea goalkeeper Jim Molyneux saved well from an excellent shot by the Sheffield-born Horace Barnes. Chelsea then scrambled away a Tommy Browell header, surviving to get the winner with ten minutes left when centre forward Bob Thomson scored 'with a fine oblique shot which gave [Walter] Smith no chance'. In the fourth round Chelsea were held 1-1 by Newcastle United at home, when over the two hours some of the players became so tired that they could not do themselves justice. Thomson scored first for Chelsea when he 'very smartly dashed between [Frank] Hudspeth and [Bill] McCracken to hit in a low shot which completely beat [Jimmy] Lawrence' but Tommy Goodwill equalised when he shot hard and low into the net. Newcastle were strong favourites in the replay but Chelsea recorded another shock, winning 1-0 at St James's Park with a Harry Ford goal in extra time. It was 'a fine victory, well merited after a most exciting struggle', wrote the *Sheffield Daily Telegraph* Newcastle set up a series of early attacks but found Molyneux in fine form behind a determined defence. Chelsea had more of the play in the second half but at the end of ninety minutes the game was goalless. Ford scored early in the extra period, after which Chelsea were hard pressed to hold on. Angus Douglas and Goodwill nearly scored for Newcastle and Molyneux was made to work hard in the Chelsea goal as the home half backs joined their forwards. They could not overcome a stubborn defence and Newcastle had to admit defeat.

Another difficult tie awaited Chelsea in the semi final, against another League title challenging team, Everton at Villa Park, but once more Chelsea succeeded against the odds, winning 2-0. It seemed that Everton were beaten before they started, as goalkeeper Tommy Fern and back John McConnachie were absent, leaving their rearguard looking distinctly uneasy at the outset and disturbed as the game proceeded. Their whole team was thrown out of gear, as the halves did not trust the backs, who in turn had no confidence in their goalkeeper. Chelsea were without their usual half back Laurence Abrams, but his replacement Andy Walker did a better job than Everton's substitutes. Fern's deputy Frank Mitchell made a 'fearful blunder' for Chelsea's first goal, whilst Bobby Simpson, in for McConnachie, was outwitted by Halse in the build-up to the second goal. Jimmy Croal profited from Mitchell's mistake as 'McNeil centred, Mitchell ran out to catch the ball. But before he could relieve himself, Thomson charged him and the ball fell on the ground. Croal gained possession without trouble and quickly shot it on the ground in an oblique direction into the net.' Halse's second goal might have been prevented had Mitchell 'shown more intuition'. Chelsea had their share of luck when Everton's Bobby Parker evaded an attempted trip and was heading straight for goal when the referee stopped play to give a free kick to Everton, which James Galt hit firmly but it was deflected for a corner. Molyneux came out to catch the flag kick but missed it, and Joe Clennell's shot hit Walter Bettridge in front of an otherwise unguarded goal.

Chelsea were through to the final because they 'were not quite as bad as Everton', according to the *Sheffield Daily Telegraph*, in a game in which good football was hard to find. The 20,000 crowd, made up mainly of Birmingham people, regarded proceedings with absolute indifference. At half time even the optimists were talking of extra time and a replay, but the mistakes of the Everton defenders altered that prognosis. The *Sheffield Daily Telegraph* could not see how Chelsea could hope to beat Sheffield United, as goalkeeper Harold Gough and his defensive colleagues would not yield goals so simply as the Everton defenders did. However, Chelsea were accustomed to being the underdog throughout the later stages of their impressive Cup run. To beat Sheffield United they would have to breach the second-best defence in the League, but in Chelsea's favour, throughout the season United had found it difficult to score goals. In fact, Chelsea had scored more often, despite being near the bottom of the table.

Chelsea had earned the nickname 'The Beanstalk Club' due to their rapid rise to prominence. Formed as recently as 1905, the Stamford Bridge ground was put at its disposal and the new club applied to join the Southern League. However, this league gave them the cold shoulder, and regretted it ever after. Instead, Chelsea became a rare southern member of the Football League, joining its Second Division. In under four months they put together an excellent team at a total cost of less than £500, their most notable signing being the mighty goalkeeper William Foulke, whom they bought from Sheffield United for £50. They also signed several Scottish players, a trend they continued to follow, and which significantly influenced the club's style of play. Scottish football had a reputation as being more cerebral and skilful than the English game, an approach the Scots took with them to London. Chelsea secured promotion in their second season, were relegated in 1910, but regained their First Division status in

1912. In normal times they attracted sizeable attendances to their large and well-equipped ground, bringing in an average of £25,000 per year in gate receipts. Now they were in their first Cup final.

As the day of the final neared, there was nowhere near the usual excitement and press coverage because of the constant shadow of war that hung over Britain. In fact, one newspaper published a cartoon suggesting that Germany's Kaiser Wilhelm ought to present the Cup to the winning captain as the continuation of football in England had assisted the war efforts of his country. The cartoon showed the winning captain saying: 'Thank you, sire.' The Kaiser responded: 'On the contrary, thank you.' The day before the Cup final the poet Rupert Brooke, serving as a temporary Sub-Lieutenant in the Royal Naval Volunteer Reserve with the British Mediterranean Expeditionary Force, died after developing sepsis as a result of an infected mosquito bite. The day after the final the British Mediterranean Expeditionary Force made first landing at Gallipoli in modern-day Turkey. Two days prior to the final the Second Battle of Ypres began as German forces tried to re-take the town the British had held since November. Fighting continued well into May, but allied forces pushed back the German offensive, despite facing the horrors of poison gas, used for the first time on the Western Front. During the month-long series of exchanges the British, French and Canadians suffered 60,000 casualties, the Germans 35,000. Such a number of dead and injured would have more than filled the terraces and stands of Old Trafford.

The build-up to the final was therefore understandably low key, the war having dampened the usual eager anticipation. The mood of the Sheffield United players was low key too. When asked about the final they did not flicker an eyelid, not from a sense of indifference but one of calm confidence. They were said to be 'keen as mustard' and proved it by twice being

246

driven by motor car into Derbyshire before walking back to Bramall Lane. Prior to the final United captain George Utley gave a big hint as to his team's intended tactics, saying: 'If we are foolish enough to make the mistake of trying to play Chelsea at their own game they will beat us. They are cleverer than we are, as far as pretty football is concerned, and if we allowed them to settle down to the Scottish style of attack they adopt we would be laying up trouble for ourselves. The game that we play best is the wide swinging variety, the type that wins Cup ties as a rule, and because that is our natural game, and because it is probably the best paying game in Cup ties we shall play it. There is plenty of room at Old Trafford for anybody, and whatever happens Chelsea won't be able to say that they haven't had a "run" for their money.' United's defence and half backs could always be relied upon, so their prospects largely depended upon the virility of their inconsistent forwards. If they were on song, United would be hard to beat. A *Sheffield Daily Telegraph* reporter asked various Football Association dignitaries the night before the final whom they thought might win. They were all of the view that it would be Sheffield United. The only person who refused to express an opinion was Mr H. H. Taylor – but he was the referee!

If Chelsea needed encouragement, the match programme noted that the underdog had won six of the last ten finals and that the only previous London club to lift the Cup did so in Lancashire, when Tottenham Hotspur beat the favourites – Sheffield United no less – in a replay at Burnden Park. A full-page article entitled 'The Last Act' congratulated the Football Association for selecting the 'splendidly equipped and commodious' Old Trafford for the final, adding that it was an appropriate venue because Manchester was in easy reach of the densely populated townships of Lancashire, Yorkshire, the Midlands and the Potteries. It sympathised with the 'adherents' of Chelsea that the final had been banished from the capital the very year one of its teams reached it, but remarked that had Crystal Palace been available, Sheffield United supporters would have faced similar travel difficulties. Another column entitled 'Topics of the Day' commented that either club was worthy of holding the trophy, and wished that the losing team would have the opportunity to redeem their failure a year later, a wish that remained unfulfilled.

The programme was produced by hosts Manchester United FC, with a special version printed on silk for presentation to the players and officials. The front cover encouraged readers to visit Beaty Bros outfitters on Market Street and Oldham Street to purchase 'New Goods for Spring' in the shape of suits for 31/6, 42/-, 52/6 or, top of the range, 63/-. Other pages featured advertisements for Jackson's of Howard Street, Stockport, and their 'Famous 3/9 Hats, 10/6 Boots, 21/- Macintoshes and 30/- Raincoats – If You Are Not Wearing Them You Are Losing Money'; Manchester Brewery Company's Milk Stout; Oxo; Dewar's White Label whisky; the *Athletic News*; Harrop's furnishing stores, Piccadilly; and 'Dri-Ped', the 'Super Leather For Soles', ideal for the footwear of Tommy in the trenches.

The Manchester Hippodrome (Oxford Street) and the Ardwick Empire (Ardwick Green) picture houses received one-line advertisements at the top and bottom respectively of several pages, their entertainment elaborated upon on page thirteen. The Ardwick Empire was presenting 'A Year in an Hour', starring comedian Nixon Grey, entertainer Thornley Dodge and 'Scotch' comedian Jack Lorimer. It also promised to show the latest war news and pictures. The Hippodrome was showing Albert Hengler's 'great water comedy "Very Soft"', boasting an all-star company. The following week Miss Christine Silver was to appear in J. M. Barrie's play 'The Will'. The back page of the match programme was devoted to

The New Palace, Oxford Street, whose entertainment included a 'tartan revue' entitled 'All Scotch', and 'The Inebriate on the Slack Wire', Harry Lamore. Next week would see the arrival, direct from the Aldwych, London, of Lady Constance Stewart-Richardson, who was to appear in a 'Greek Ballad Dance' called 'The Wilderness'. However, Lady Stewart-Richardson would not be present at matinees, when 'suitable deputies will be provided'.

The programme also included a page detailing each team's route to the final, and 'Who's Who' guides to the players of the two teams. United's 'Who's Who' included Fred Hawley, Chelsea's Vivian Woodward and Laurence Abrams, none of whom played in the final. On page eight the players' names were displayed in team formation and numbered from one to twenty-two, despite there being no numbers worn on shirts at the time. Sheffield United were to wear red and white shirts and black knickers, Chelsea royal blue shirts and white knickers. The teams lined up as follows:

Name	Position	Birthplace	Height	Weight
Sheffield United				
Harold Gough	Goalkeeper	Chesterfield	5'10"	12st 6lbs
Bill Cook	Right Back	Usworth	5'7 1/2"	10st 7lbs
Jack English	Left Back	Hebburn	5'8"	11st 7lbs
Albert Sturgess	Right Half	Etruria	5'11"	11st
Bill Brelsford	Centre Half	Sheffield	5'8"	11st 9lbs
George Utley	Left Half	Elsecar	5'10 1/2"	13st
Jimmy Simmons	Outside Right	Blackwell	5'7"	10st 9lbs
Stanley Fazackerley	Inside Right	Preston	5'11"	11st 6lbs
Joe Kitchen	Centre Forward	Brigg	5'7"	11st
Wally Masterman	Inside Left	Newcastle	5'11"	12st
Bob Evans	Outside Left	Chester	5'10 1/2"	11st 7lbs

Chelsea

Jim Molyneux	Goalkeeper	Port Sunlight	5' 9"	11st 9lbs
Walter Bettridge	Right Back	Oakthorpe	5' 8"	10st 3lbs
Jack Harrow	Left Back	Mitcham	5'8 1/2"	11st 11lbs
Fred Taylor	Right Half	Rotherham	5'8 1/2"	12st 5lbs
Tommy Logan	Centre Half	Barrhead	5'11"	13st 4lbs
Andy Walker	Left Half	Dalkeith	5'10 1/2"	12st 7lbs
Harry Ford	Outside Right	Fulham	5'7 1/2"	11st 4lbs
Harold Halse	Inside Right	Leytonstone	5'7"	10st 10lbs
Bob Thomson	Centre Forward	Croydon	5'6"	11st
Jimmy Croal	Inside Left	Glasgow	5'8 1/2"	10st 7lbs
Bob McNeil	Outside Left	Springburn	5'7"	10st 10lbs

It is noticeable that all the Sheffield United players were northern men (but just one from Sheffield), and that there were only four from London and its surroundings in Chelsea's line-up. They too relied heavily on players 'imported' from the north, four of them from Scotland. Another highly noteworthy aspect of the game, and probably of football and society of the time, was the heights of the players. None of them were six feet tall and Chelsea's forward line was particularly small, by today's standards at least. The days of the 'typically English big centre forward' were yet to come.

Chelsea's best player, the famous amateur footballer and England international Lieutenant Vivian Woodward, who had missed most of the season on army service, had been given leave to play in the final, withdrawing from the Footballers' Battalion team that lost 2-1 to the 2nd Sportsmen's Battalion a couple of days before. However, Woodward sportingly declined his usual inside right position, allowing centre forward Bob Thomson, scorer of the winner at Manchester City and five goals overall in the Cup, to keep his place. Thomson had helped the team reach the final, so he should play in it, insisted Woodward. The gentlemanly amateur did not wish to deny a professional the chance of a medal. If Woodward had played, Harold Halse would have moved to centre forward and Thomson would have missed out. However, Thomson himself was doubtful, having suffered a dislocated elbow ten days earlier in a League game at Bolton, but he was declared fit. Thomson was used to playing with a handicap, as he was blind in his left eye, but that never seemed to bother him. Harrow, with a crushed instep, and Logan and Halse, both with sprained ankles, were also carrying injuries, but they too recovered sufficiently to play. It was reported in the *Sheffield Daily Telegraph* that Chelsea would have the support of 'a goodly number' who were willing, and wealthy enough, to pay the regular London to Manchester return fare of £1 10s 11d, a figure comparable to the average weekly pay at the time. During the trip the Chelsea supporters would be able to enjoy 'several exclusive corridor carriage parties'.

Both teams adopted the then standard '2-3-5' formation of two backs, three half backs and five forwards. The primary job of the backs was to mark the opponent's wingers and they scarcely ventured forward. Contemporary newspaper match reports often mentioned that a back had had a good game because he 'kicked well', suggesting that when he got the ball he got rid of it quickly and lengthily. Goalkeepers, meanwhile, had to release the ball rapidly once they had caught it, otherwise they would be barged over or have it kicked out of their hands, either event producing a high risk of conceding a goal, and sustaining an injury. Indeed, Chelsea's first goal in the semi final came from such an incident. There was little or no protection for goalkeepers. The half backs watched the opposing inside forwards and centre forward, but when in possession of the ball their task was to supply their own forwards. The centre half, in contrast to the role he has today, played a key part in organising his team's attacks as well as shadowing the other team's centre forward when they had the ball. The inside forwards often dropped back to collect the ball from the half backs, before then playing it to the winger on their side of the pitch. Each winger's task was to send in crosses to the centre forward and the onrushing inside forwards. Designed plays from corners and free kicks were rare or non-existent, save for trying a hard shot from a free kick within thirty yards' range. The five forwards were expected to score the bulk of the goals, and in Sheffield United's case they certainly did. Of the sixty-one goals the team registered in League and Cup in the 1914/15 season, fifty-six were scored by forwards, just four by half backs and none by backs (one was an own goal).

It was a very restrictive and regimented style of play but it was all that was known at the time, having been in common use for more than twenty years. Innovative thinking such as that of the great Huddersfield Town and Arsenal manager Herbert Chapman (incidentally, a South Yorkshireman and former Sheffield United player) was still a decade into the future. Chapman was amongst the first to realise that the 1925 change in the offside law[44] provided an unforeseen opportunity to adapt his team formation to best advantage, resulting in a period of dominance for his club Arsenal. Yet slight variations in tactics were in existence in 1914/15: Chelsea, strongly influenced by the Scotsmen in their team, were known to favour a method of play involving attacks made up of a series of short, pretty, zig-zag passes, which was sometimes overdone. This approach was sometimes called 'drawing room football' as it could theoretically be played in a confined space. In contrast, Sheffield United's game was based on hard running and rapid movement of the ball, termed by the *Sheffield Independent* as a 'get there quick' style. They relied

---

[44] From now on, for an attacking player to remain onside, only two opponents had to be nearer the goal line when the ball was played forward, rather than the previous requirement of three. Chapman developed a 3-2-2-3 formation, which later came to be known as the 'W-M' formation, in which the central half back moved in line with the two full backs, therefore into a more defensive position.

on speed and sudden, rapier-like thrusts, rather than the 'pattern weaving' preferred by the Londoners. Some might argue that little has changed. Chelsea were seen as a clever side with little end product, whereas United were a well-drilled team in the true sense of the word, rather than an association of individuals.

There was an eerie atmosphere in Manchester for the final, partially brought about by the general depressing circumstances, but also by the unseasonably dull and drizzly weather, more akin to November than April. The people of Sheffield must have held mixed feelings about the game. Many thought that it should not be played, while one writer in the *Sheffield Daily Telegraph* claimed that United were 'bringing shame on themselves and the city' by participating in such a grand sporting event at this time of death and destruction. Some 49,557 disagreed, parting with gate receipts of £4,012 to back their opinion. Spectators packed on to the large uncovered terraces opposite the grandstand and behind each goal sheltered as well as they could under all manner of hats and umbrellas. Also in attendance were large groups of soldiers in uniform, some on leave, a number sporting bandages protecting injuries suffered at the front. They pulled their hats down low and their greatcoat collars up high to keep out the miserable drizzle. It was the sight of so many uniforms in the crowd that gave rise to the term 'The Khaki Final', one of the few Cup finals to be given its own nickname (the *Sports Special Green 'Un* of April 24 may have been the first publication to use this term). The troops present had travelled from all over Britain, though many of them would be killed in the trenches over the next three and a half years. The 'Sheffield Pals' Battalion' was well represented, being given leave to attend by their commanding officer Colonel Mainwaring. They were to lose 513 of their number on the first day of the Somme offensive just over a year later. The

Manchester Guardian pointedly commented that those in attendance who were not in uniform should have been. The *Sheffield Daily Telegraph* correctly predicted: 'There will, it is safe to say, never again be a Cup final played so long as the country is engaged in such a world war as that which is now in progress.'

Despite the lack of special excursion trains, *The Times* reported that 'a good deal of Yorkshire was coming to see the match'. Soon after breakfast all trains from Sheffield to 'Cottonopolis' from both the Midland and Victoria Stations were packed, several having to be run in duplicate. It was estimated that three thousand people journeyed over the Pennines by rail. One party travelled overnight from Cumberland, paying full fare. At an early hour, thanks to enterprising Sheffield hotel proprietors and posting houses, hired motor charabancs and other road vehicles began to leave the city *en route* to Manchester. A steady stream continued west out of Sheffield for some time on a journey that must have taken some three hours on primitive cross-Pennine roads.

Spectators were advised in advance by the *Sports Special Green 'Un* of the difficulties of travelling the two-and-a-half miles from Manchester city centre to Old Trafford. Taxi or other independent vehicle was the best option, as trams met a renowned bottleneck some distance away, which was a common cause of complaint amongst local people, although there was an alternative – the Salford line, alighting at Trafford Park, five minutes' walk away. Once close to Old Trafford most spectators would have to cross a railway bridge of inadequate width, which would cause more trouble after the match than before it as thousands tried to use it at once. The situation could be improved if the railway companies decided to open the 'cricket and football station',[45] a few minutes'

---

[45] Now the Old Trafford Metrolink Station on Brian Statham Way.

walk from the ground, so people coming from Sheffield would not have to travel into the city centre. As important as travel information was, as the *Green 'Un* put it, 'lining the inner man' - in other words, where could food outlets be found? Many restaurant keepers closed early on Saturday afternoons so 'the invaders who do not know the runs are in danger of being left on the wrong side of a meal'. If food could not be found near the ground before kick off, the advice was to make a flying start when the post-match exodus began and make for the centre of the city, where more eating establishments would be open.

Fed or unfed, those present inside the ground were greeted by a murky day with drizzly fog hanging over the ground, making visibility difficult. It was somehow appropriate that the weather should be so. Some observers doubted that the game would finish in such poor light. One writer described the scene as 'a Whistlerian monotone in grey'. The glow of thousands of cigarettes and the flicker of lighted matches punctuated the semi-darkness. However, the downbeat mood, if not the gloom, was lifted as the Irwell Old Prize Band, conducted by Mr J. W. Higham, provided musical entertainment. Lord Derby, who was to present the Cup at the end of the game, arrived, receiving 'a very hearty welcome, which the band, having just concluded a selection, mistook as an appreciation of their efforts'. The drizzle stopped just in time for everyone in the ground to rise and enthusiastically sing 'God Save the King' moments before the teams entered the field for the half-past-three kick off. The Chelsea team arrived first and were 'cordially cheered, but the roar which saluted them was as nothing compared with that which greeted Sheffield United a moment or so later', wrote the *Sunday Pictorial*. United captain Utley, dark haired and of rugged northern appearance, shook hands with his Chelsea counterpart Jack Harrow, also dark haired but of slighter build, and bandaged at the knee, as the match ball sat between them on the oversized centre spot.[46] No pennants or mementoes were exchanged by the two captains. Beside Utley the referee Mr Taylor stood attentively, his left hand in the pocket of his blazer, his shorts extending down below the knee. He looked no older than the two players. All around them the pitch surface was more rolled mud than grass. *The Times*, for once reneging on its policy of refusing to include in its pages full match reports, remarked that 'the preliminaries were more exciting than the game'. The report continued: 'It must be candidly set down as a poor football match, but it was an interesting spectacle.' The pitch was tacky but not really wet, so the ball became neither heavy nor slippery, and as there was no wind to blow away the murk, conditions for football were quite favourable.

Chelsea lost Harry Ford to injury in the first few minutes after a collision with Utley; while he was off they won a corner and a couple of free kicks yet when he returned, repaired, it was Sheffield United who took control. Kitchen raced away but Jim Molyneux saved his shot, Jimmy Simmons, Stanley Fazackerley and Kitchen then combined but a dangerous-looking attack was spoiled when Wally Masterman handled. Next, Harrow, standing by the post, kicked away a Kitchen shot with Molyneux beaten, then Masterman shot wide from a good position. The *Sunday Pictorial* described the early action: 'Sheffield United played fast, robust football, keeping the ball always on the move and, as a matter of fact, showing considerably more combination than the Londoners' front line'. The *Sports Special Green 'Un* reporter later wrote; 'Ten minutes after the start I put down my pencil and remarked to a colleague, "There is no need for excitement over this game. The Cup is won."' He was right. A

---

[46] The match programme lists Fred Taylor as Chelsea's captain, but all other sources found state it was Harrow.

London reporter believed Chelsea were bothered by the weather, writing; 'They looked up at the thick yellow pall in apprehensive fashion, but the Sheffielders, being quite used to that sort of thing at Bramall Lane, took no notice of it.' What nonsense, replied the *Green 'Un*; southerners apparently believed two things regarding the weather – that the sun never set on the British Empire, and it never shone on Sheffield.

The poor weather had little to do with United's dominance, but it was surprising that it took thirty-six minutes to score the first goal. The United half-back line of Albert Sturgess, Bill Brelsford and Utley was in total control and the forwards were quickly switching the ball from wing to wing. Such a move produced the first goal, scored by Simmons. Harrow was forced to pass back to Molyneux in order to break up an attack, the goalkeeper hurriedly kicking the ball out of play. From the throw-in:

> *The ball was lifted high over the centre by Utley.*
> *Bouncing behind Harrow, who vainly tried to*
> *head away, it went to Simmons, who from an*
> *oblique angle put in a swift, rising shot, the ball*
> *striking the far post and rebounding into the back*
> *of the net.*

After the goal Molyneux and Harrow were seen to argue. It seemed that Harrow expected Molyneux to come out and catch the ball, whereas the goalkeeper expected Harrow to head it away. Chelsea had their best chances just before half time when shots from Harold Halse and Tommy Logan were saved by Harold Gough and Ford struck one wide. So it was 1-0 at the interval, during which the band marched and played 'Tipperary', the song adopted and sung by the British troops as they marched off to war. There was also a collection on behalf of the East Lancashire branch of the British Red Cross Society, undertaken by soldiers, many of whom were Boer War veterans wearing South African army colours, including one who had lost an arm. They held up khaki-coloured sheets into which spectators threw pennies, 'something after the manner of firemen catching one who leaps from a window', reckoned *The Times*.

As the second half began the fog became thicker and more yellow, preventing a good view of the pitch from the stands and terraces. *The Times* commented that 'this was no great loss for it was not much worth seeing'. Referee Mr Taylor now seemed to be the most active person on the field, rushing to keep up with play just so he could see what was going on. For a spell the play of both sides was poor, Chelsea's especially so. Their forwards' passing was awry and they were often easily robbed of possession by United's halves. Molyneux made a number of good saves and Masterman had the ball in the net but was given offside. It was becoming clear that United had the measure of their opponents and should win, unless there was an unforeseen disaster. The Chelsea forwards were so much in the pocket of Utley that Halse and Bob Thomson swapped positions to try to escape the United captain's attentions, but to no avail. The fog cleared somewhat towards the end of the match but the light was fading on a dull day as United finally got the second goal their dominance deserved:

> *Seven minutes from the finish came a slashing attack, started on the left by Utley. It resulted in a stinging shot being sent in. The ball struck the cross-bar, but, as it rebounded, Fazackerley dashed in, and headed it into the net clear of Molyneux.*

If there was any doubt as to the outcome, this goal ended it. A minute from the end Kitchen sealed a 3-0 victory with a great goal:

Gaining possession near the half way line and in making a straight dash for goal, he kept Bettridge off, drew Molyneux out of his fortress and placed the ball in the net after a dribble of forty yards at the least.

Some of the crowd promptly came on to the pitch, thinking the game was over. 'A number of over-excited youths and men rushed on to the ground, wrung the hands of Kitchen and Utley in fine frenzy, and looked as though they meant to stay there,' reported the *Sheffield Daily Telegraph*. They were followed on to the pitch by others from the terraced side of the ground but the referee reacted by getting the game going again as quickly as possible, with 'the irrepressibles meanwhile dodging the players in a rush for the edges of the field'. The game concluded with spectators crowding the touchlines.

Apart from Chelsea's short spells of ascendancy, in the first few minutes and after United's first goal, it had been a one-sided match. United appeared to possess superior pace and fitness throughout and only a good performance from Molyneux in the Chelsea goal prevented the scoreline becoming even more decisive. Chelsea's forwards were poor, playing 'without any conception of combination work'. One writer remarked: 'It was not their [Chelsea's] day at any time,' whilst the Chelsea captain Jack Harrow commented: 'We lost to the better team on the day. They gave us no rest and little chance.' George Utley's view was concise and precise: 'There was only one ball, and we had it most of the time.' Referee Mr Taylor, who diplomatically made no comment before the match, admitted now that 'I think the better team won'. The

Athletic News reported that 'United simply brushed Chelsea aside as if they were novices', and the *Sports Special Green 'Un* wrote: 'If United had won by five goals, they would not have been flattered.' *The Times* agreed with the general sentiment of these reports, stating that United's two late goals gave them a lead 'more commensurate with their merits'.

Various southern newspapers were grudging in their praise of Sheffield United, but the *Sheffield Daily Telegraph* declared their opinions worthless anyway, considering they had chosen to neglect the existence of professional football for most of the season. This was the first match on which many of them had reported for several months; they were mocked for showing total disregard for their avowed policy of ignoring football when the Cup final, involving a London team, arrived. 'We are asked by some of these newly-born critics to imagine that it was a poor final,' wrote the *Telegraph*. 'Well, we have seen well on for a score of such now, and fail to remember one which produced more honest and clean play, or cleverer football. If it be a crime for United to squelch the fritter and glitter of the Chelsea men, then United were criminals of the deepest dye, and if the southerners are to be commiserated with upon having their preconceived plans dashed to nothingness, then they have all our sympathy.' If some believed that the game did not approach the level of a Crystal Palace final, they were accused of viewing proceedings 'through London-smoked glasses'. The *Telegraph* also delighted in the fact that the Cup was won by an all-English team, not one populated by Scots, and speculated that United could be the first club to hold the Cup for two years, as there was likely to be no football in 1915/16. The newspaper was wrong: it turned out to be five years.

It had been a well deserved but, despite the *Telegraph's* words, hardly a glorious victory, one based on the commanding play of United's half backs, particularly captain

Utley, whose influence was incalculable. Indeed, he was praised for his 'omniscience'. He controlled Chelsea's right wing, where Ford, after his early injury inflicted by Utley, was 'fairly mesmerised' by United's captain, and inside right Halse fared no better. Centre forward Thomson, who seemed to be constantly wary of his elbow injury, found Brelsford 'insuperable' and Sturgess made Croal and McNeil on Chelsea's left look ordinary. This was sweet revenge for Sturgess, who had been given the runaround by Croal in an England v Scotland international a year earlier. To the rear of this solid trio was another line of stalwarts, formed of only two men - Cook and English - who were 'lightweights in poundage but giants in effectiveness'. Behind them, wrote the *Sheffield Independent*: 'Gough in goal was – Gough. One of his clearances meant the laying out of a couple of his own men. He did the double trick. It was to Gough, "the only way." He who hesitates is lost. Gough did not hesitate.' United's forwards were generally 'enterprising and speedy', the best of them being Simmons, whose 'dazzling runs delighted the crowd', Fazackerley, who passed well and unselfishly, and Kitchen, who swung the ball out to his wings with certainty and accuracy and was always on the spot when a chance presented itself. The sole topic of argument amongst commentators was whether Utley or Simmons was United's star man; most agreed it was Utley. There had also been little or nothing in the way of ill-temper in the match, the only heated moment coming when a Chelsea player 'took a mean and cruel advantage of his opponent, and a "bunch of fives" was threateningly uplifted in response'. A sharp word from the referee quickly calmed the players down. The players involved were unidentified in reports, but the most likely Sheffield United candidate was Bill Brelsford, given his reputation of being one not to back away from confrontation.

The Cup was presented to Utley by Lord Derby, whose speech was difficult to hear as he attempted to address the players over the noisy crowd. His words have been variously (if similarly) reported,[47] but all versions agree that the tone of his speech suggested that the time for games was over; now everyone should concentrate their efforts on fighting for the safety and security of Britain and its Empire. He was sure his appeal would not be in vain; every man must face his duty and do his best.

Sheffield United had won the Cup for the third time in their history, but it was no time to celebrate. It was a hollow triumph. The accepted custom of filling the Cup with beer or champagne and sharing it around the players was not followed by the United team. Instead, a muted meal was taken by directors, players and friends that evening at the Exchange Restaurant in Manchester, where the Cup, draped in red and white, enjoyed a prominent place on the top table. Chairman Tom Bott congratulated the team on their victory and their general conduct. They were gentlemen on and off the field, he declared. Charles Clegg also spoke, thanking the players for the good, clean game they had played. It was a pleasure to be associated with them, he said, wishing every one of them prosperity during the trying times ahead. In response to the critics he stated:

> *There has been some talk of disgrace being attached to winning the Cup this year, but I do not hold with that opinion. I take the victory to be an honour to Sheffield. So far as I am concerned, I*

---

[47] Lord Derby was reported to have said: (a) 'Join together and play a sterner game for England'; (b) 'It is now the duty of everyone to join with each other and play a sterner game of football'; (c) 'It is now the duty of everyone to join with each other and play a sterner game for England'; or (d) 'You have played against one another for the Cup, play with one another for England now.'

take the responsibility for the statement that the action which the Football Association took at the outset would be repeated were the same crisis to arise again. We have suffered more than usual from ill-judged criticism, and people who criticise sometimes get their popularity in proportion to their ignorance, but I think, after all, we acted wisely – having regard to our knowledge of all the circumstances – when we had to come to a decision. That, at all events, was the opinion of the Sheffield United Club, and we did not trouble about the opinion of the critics. I am as proud as anyone that we have won the Cup. It is sheer twaddle talking about disgrace. The disgrace lay with those who made such a suggestion, and not with the players or the club.

Whether honour or disgrace was the correct description, there would be no celebratory dinner or triumphal carriage ride around the city. Understandably and correctly, nobody was in the mood for jubilation over the Cup final result, not even United followers in Sheffield who believed it was right to play the match. Some 1,500 to 2,000 supporters gathered outside the Midland Station to welcome the victorious team back to the city when their train arrived at 10.15pm, despite there being no announcement of its time of arrival. Around forty police constables were on view, but not the Cup, which was taken away almost in secrecy. The players were hurried into taxis and sent home, 'to the accompaniment of considerable enthusiasm'. United had one more League game to play, away to Bolton Wanderers two days after the final. They won 1-0 to finish a respectable sixth in the table, trailing champions Everton by three points. Oldham Athletic were second, one point behind Everton, followed by five clubs on forty-three points, separated by goal average. The last-placed of those five clubs was Wednesday, finishing one position below United by 0.065 of a goal.

In the days after the final, criticism that the match had been played at such a time was still pronounced. Opinion was certainly divided. The *Sheffield Independent* backed the club, stating that the match and the scene had 'nothing but the best British gold about it'. Football people were supportive, congratulating United on their success. Defeated Chelsea chairman William Claude Kirby sportingly wrote: 'Kindly convey to your directors, officials and players the hearty congratulations of my co-directors and myself on your club's victory in the F.A. Cup last Saturday.' The Wednesday directors hid their envy well, writing: 'The directors of the Wednesday Football Club desire to congratulate the directors and players of the Sheffield United Football Club on their success in again winning the Football Association Challenge Cup, and in once more bringing home the trophy to the original home of Association football.' Other congratulatory letters came from Grimsby Town FC, Rotherham County FC, Everton FC, Glasgow Celtic FC, Bradford Park Avenue FC and Notts County FC. Notably, several 'well done' postcards were received from soldiers at the front.

Whether it was right or wrong to play the final was now irrelevant: the fact was it had been played and Sheffield United had won the Cup, which remained in the club's committee room in the John Street stand for most of the next five years. It was given a couple of public airings soon after the final, first in the window of Messrs Fosters' tailor's shop on High Street in Sheffield city centre, then on May 1 at the final of the Wharncliffe Cup, played at Bramall Lane between the reserve teams of United and Wednesday, a game the visitors won 4-1. 'There were quite 6,000 people present,' wrote the *Sheffield Daily Telegraph*, 'and the Football Association Cup was carried round the ground during the game, causing much enthusiasm.' A couple of photographs were taken of the winning United team, one with trainer George Waller and another with Waller and the entire club committee, posing with the Cup. No one in either shot looked particularly happy. There were no smiles; grim faces were the norm. No real celebration could take place until the war was over. Then, a dinner was held in the Bramall Lane cricket pavilion dining room, five years to the day after the victory over Chelsea. As a stark reminder of what was happening elsewhere in the world, a few days after the Cup was shown to the crowd at the Wharncliffe Cup final, the unarmed ocean liner RMS Lusitania, *en route* from New York to Liverpool, was sunk off the Old Head of Kinsale, Ireland, by a German submarine. The ship went down in just eighteen minutes, taking some 1,198 people with her, including almost a hundred children.

CHAPTER SIXTEEN

I WISH THE GERMANS COULD COME AND THROW A FEW BOMBS ON THIS CROWD

The Cup and League winners had been decided; the 1914/15 football season was over. Not before time, said many, who complained that it was a national disgrace that sporting events had been allowed to go on so long. Although football had finished, the flat racing season had just commenced, and it was alleged in the House of Commons that soldiers attempting to board troop trains destined for Southampton docks had been delayed at Waterloo Station by large crowds of racegoers using special trains provided by the railway companies. One MP complained of 'hundreds of char-a-bancs, motor cars, and all sorts of vehicles taking able-bodied men - so far as I could see, nine out of ten were able-bodied – to Epsom to see the races. I think these men could be better employed just now than going to races. I do not know whether anything of a special character has been done to mobilise this type of man. If not, something ought to be done.' There were also complaints in Parliament that valuable telegraph facilities were being taken up for amusement and pleasure - transmitting racing results - when the operators were badly needed for commercial business and for serving the needs of the army and the navy.

As had been the case the previous August, there were vehement appeals for racing to be abandoned. The cricket authorities had decided months earlier that there would be no 1915 County Championship. If racing was to be discontinued, football was sure to follow. However, the *Athletic News* was certain football would continue in 1915/16, writing: 'Football will go on unless something unforeseen and unexpected happens. Football will go on but there will not be next season a single player who can be described as unpatriotic or a shirker.' This assessment of the situation proved accurate, as it implied that players would no longer be full-time professionals but would also have to take jobs in industry. When questioned in the House of Commons in mid May about the likelihood of legislation being introduced to forbid the holding of race meetings, Home Secretary Reginald McKenna replied, amid cries of dissent:

I fear that legislation prohibiting race meetings is too contentious to be proposed at the present time...... if I may judge from that expression of opinion which the House now gives, that answer might reasonably be altered.

Two days later, Prime Minister Asquith was asked the same question and gave a similar answer, stating that he did not believe legislation was necessary. The debate soon turned to football, to which Harold Tennant MP, Under-Secretary of State for War, contributed, his frustration obvious as he stated:

With regard to football, I myself have taken a great interest in it, and have made speeches on the subject, in which I thought it was desirable in the great struggle in which we find ourselves that such sport as a regular and professional undertaking ought to be abandoned, and I told the Football Association so. I made some impression, I am glad to say, upon the Football Association. I think they were genuinely impressed, so much so that the chairman was quite of my way of thinking. But I was informed after the meeting had taken place with representatives of all the leagues throughout the country, that if we as a Government were to forbid, under the Defence of the Realm Act, or some legislation such as we might introduce to stop football, the only result would be the leagues would play exactly the same matches, and another cup would be given by some generous donor; that the people in the districts where football is so popular would insist upon having some match that they could watch; and that, therefore, it was perfectly futile for the Government to embark on such a policy. After that had taken place I did not see any useful purpose could be served by prolonging the controversy, and, therefore, I was reluctantly compelled to abandon my point of view.

Sir Joseph Walton, Liberal MP for the football and working-class stronghold of Barnsley, argued surprisingly strongly against the continuation of football in the 1915/16 season:

It is a perfect scandal that either [football or racing] should go on in this time of dire distress and war as they would in peace time, and what is needed is a strong lead from the Government on this matter. Lord Derby said that the Jockey Club would stop all racing in twenty-four hours if they had the word from the Government that they should do so, and he added that if racing continued, upon the Government would rest the sole responsibility. I press those words upon the attention of my Right Honourable friend, and I submit that the time has come when the naval and military authorities of the country should make it clear, in emphatic terms, that in their judgement both racing and football injure recruiting and are calculated to hinder the full production of munitions of war. There are thousands and thousands of men who, when there is a football match, cannot deny themselves the pleasure of going there; but if these matches were not held next winter, then in all probability many thousands of these men would be induced to remain at work in producing munitions of war. This is no small matter. I think we ought to consider the feelings of our men in the field. Some wounded men were recently at a great football match [possibly the Old Trafford Cup final], *and one of them said, 'I wish the Germans could come and throw a few bombs on this crowd; it would waken them up and would make them realise what war is.' I am fond of a football match, but I felt it my duty not to attend football matches during this winter, even when pressed to do so. I think this is no time for athletic footballers to be kicking a ball about. Men like them, who are in the pink of condition, have a duty to enlist and go and fight for their King and country at the front. I have not hesitated to tell that straight to my own constituents. I, therefore, would urge upon the*

War Office and Admiralty to speak out with no
uncertain voice, and let us for the duration of the
war have a complete cessation both of racing and
football.

Despite the arguments, racing was not abandoned, and indeed carried on - with restrictions as to the number of meetings permitted - throughout the war.[48] One major concession was that because the Epsom Downs course was being used to house prisoners of war, the Derby was moved to Newmarket and temporarily re-named the New Derby Stakes.

As regards football, now a bigger decision had to be taken. If Admiral (Retired) W. Henderson had his way, football should be stopped for an entirely different reason to those of morals, recruitment or money. In a letter to *The Times* he declared that football pitches and other open and recreational spaces should be 'put under the plough' for the cultivation of vegetables. He did not get his way, at least as far as professional football grounds were concerned. Official moves to consider what might happen to football had been made before the end of the season, when on March 29 the Football Association Council gave itself the power to suspend the game either partially or entirely, if it was considered desirable to do so. The next day the Football League held a special general meeting at the Connaught Rooms, Great Queen Street in London's Holborn district. The objective of the conference was to formulate rules for the registration of players for the 1915/16 season. The following rule changes were agreed:

---

[48] In the spring of 1917 the Government wished to ban horse racing as there was a severe shortage of cereals in Britain, but changed its mind after strong representations from the industry, which persuaded the Government that racing's breeding programme was necessary to supply the army with suitable horses. Thereafter racing was restricted almost entirely to Newmarket. Other professional sports that continued throughout the war included billiards and boxing.

- All professional players who were re-engaged or transferred were to forfeit their wages from May 1, 1915, until they reported for training on August 2 at the earliest.

- For the season 1915/16 new players were not to be signed to a contract whereby wages were payable before training commenced.

- Wages payable during the nine months from August 2 to April 30, 1916, were not to exceed seventy-five per cent of the amount the player would normally have received. Any payment in contravention of this directive was to be regarded as an illegal payment, punishable under the appropriate rule.

- No new players could be signed until August 2. Any registration before that date would be illegal. No wages were to be paid before August 2.

- The maximum basic wage was to be £156 per year, reduced from £208, although after two years' continuous service at one club a player's wages would rise by £26 per year, and an additional £26 per year every two years of continuous service after that, to a maximum of £260 per year. Any increments were to be in £26 stages every two years.

- The League was to arrange with such leagues as they thought necessary that all players registered by the clubs of the various leagues should be respected as retained players until August 2.

All the rule changes were endorsed at an extraordinary general meeting of the Football Association later in the day. The poor players were therefore to receive no pay for the three months of the summer and would have their wages cut by at least a quarter the following season - if it was to take place at all. A standard contract of the period lay almost entirely in favour of the employing club. A player had to agree 'to play in an efficient manner and to the best of his ability'; he must 'do everything necessary to get and keep himself in the best possible condition prior to and during the season so as to render the best possible service to the club'. He could be given fourteen days' notice of termination if he was 'palpably inefficient' or was guilty of serious misconduct or a breach of club disciplinary rules. For this he was paid a maximum of £4 per week - but most were on far less – from when he reported to training at the beginning of August or from the start of the season a month later, until the end of April. During the summer players received a lower wage than during the playing season, assuming they were to be offered a new contract. Even if the club did not offer a player a new contract it retained his registration until it could be sold, or transferred, to another club. This became known as the 'retain and transfer' system and although it had been the subject of a legal challenge in 1910 by former Aston Villa player Herbert Kingaby, the court ruled in favour of the present system. If a player was offered a new contract and he did not like its terms, hard luck. He had no recourse to a 'hold-out' or renegotiation. It was take it or leave it, and if he left it his club still retained his registration so he could not be transferred. If he did not sign, he did not play and he did not get paid. His only alternative was to go and play in another country (including Scotland), but that rarely happened.

Well before the end of the 1914/15 season players were aware of what was coming regarding their contracts, as rumours circulated as early as February. Players suspected that in future their wages and club rosters might be cut. They knew that staying in the Cup as long as possible would be financially beneficial to them and their clubs; nonetheless they would have to economise and save for darker times ahead. Clubs would have to reduce the number of players they employed, so there was an incentive for players to maintain their best form to the end of the season, regardless of League position. As for the clubs, some were in a deplorable position. One Southern League club had to borrow money from the League in order to travel to an away match, and the Football League decided to help clubs by paying the expenses of club representatives attending League meetings. Midland League clubs were relying on the generosity of their supporters to get them through the season.

The situation was seen by some as 'the end of a Golden Age'. Clubs were now being compelled to consider football more from a business point of view, rather than carry on with the absurdity of many decisions they had previously taken in order to try to compete with each other. Nothing had seemed likely to stop the 'mad plunging for players', as the *Sheffield Daily Telegraph* termed it, but now war had done that. As for the players themselves, they would now have to seek useful employment in the summer, and perhaps for some time beyond. Some players might even no longer be deaf to the call of the country. They would not be paid between the end of April and the beginning of August but they were expected to keep themselves fit and ready for a resumption of action in four months, sixteen months, twenty-eight months or whenever it might be. The Players' Union, so vigorous when it was formed in 1907, had meekly accepted the contractual changes imposed upon them. Perhaps it feared a repeat of what happened in 1909 when threatened strike action over the maximum wage was met by the Football Association banning *sine die* those associated with the Union. The players backed down from their stance over the maximum wage, instead negotiating a bonus system to supplement wages, and official recognition for the Union by the F.A.

Five years later the Union had now done so little that rumours circulated that it had ceased to exist. Eventually it made a protest, after everything was settled. The Players' Union was a toothless body, for which the players had to take the blame for not sticking together. The Football League responded angrily to the Union's late protest, stating:

> *We dissent* in toto *from the resolution of the Management Committee of the Players' Union. The allegation that the alterations made in the League rules are too drastic is contrary to the facts, whilst the suggestion that the players, as the earning factor, should have been consulted in the matter is a mere flattering platitude to the players. We regret that our past experience of conferences with the representatives of the Players' Union have irrevocably convinced us that the management of the latter body is indisposed to be of any practical assistance to clubs and governing bodies. Through the distressing trials in the early days of the season – when it was apparent that the difficulties would grow rather than diminish – the Players' Union adopted a policy and attitude calculated to hinder us in our purpose to keep the game going and complete our competition. Secure of their contracts, the Union failed to realise the grave risks the players ran that the competition would prematurely end. The Union representatives raised objections to all our proposals to adopt a scheme for the good of the game, and left us to fight the battle for existence without lending the*

least assistance. Whilst it may be true (as stated by the Management Committee of the Players' Union) that 'the majority of players have shown a lack of interest in their own welfare,' it is undeniably true that the Players' Union has shown no interest in the welfare of the game and its continuance on such lines as would ensure the completion of the League competition. If the attitude of the Players' Union to the game is accurately reflected by the manifesto issued by its Management Committee, then we can never imagine the Union being of any practical service to the game.

By late April no definite decision about the future of football had been arrived at; Football League president John McKenna stated that nothing in that respect had yet been decided or discussed. The various Leagues decided to meet again in July, when their future action was to be guided by the military situation at that time. Prior to this conference of Leagues, the Football League management committee met at the South Shore Hotel in Blackpool, where they decided to propose a three-division competition for 1915/16, along with a subsidiary competition devoted to charity.

In Parliament, the Under-Secretary of State for War remained non-committal, preferring to leave the decision about the continuation of football in the hands of the football authorities, stating: 'Although the measures which were taken last year did not realise all that was hoped, in the main the results obtained were satisfactory, and I should like it to be known that the Government look with confidence to those responsible in this matter to restrict the programme of football matches in accordance with the general feeling of the public.' He was forced to reiterate the Government's standpoint later in the month, when he said: 'I am afraid this is not a matter upon which the Government can issue definite instructions.'

Tennant and the Government were probably relieved that they did not have to issue any definite instructions, as the all-important decision was duly taken by the football authorities. The scheduled July meeting of the English, Scottish, Southern, and Irish Leagues was held at the Winter Gardens in Blackpool. The agenda contained two main items: the playing of League football the following season, and the registration of players. One anticipated problem was that if there was to be no football, would clubs be able to retain players until it was resumed? However, that question apparently became irrelevant when it was unanimously - and somewhat surprisingly - decided that 'the best interests of the nation and those engaged in the war and preparing the munitions of war, will be best served by the continuance of the game'. On the face of it, such a statement may have led some to believe that football would carry on just as before, but that was not the case. Each League was to decide whatever programme suited its own needs. In addition, each League was to approach its national association to consider the desirability of the discontinuation of professionalism for the 1915/16 season. Here was the catch. Football would still be played, but no one would get paid for playing it. If this step was approved, all former professional players would therefore automatically become amateurs. The pronouncements were described by the *Sheffield Daily Telegraph* as 'sensational', but the newspaper was happy that at least it was now final – there would be football, but not 'League football as generally understood'.

The *Telegraph's* sports and pastimes columnist 'Looker-On' took his usual well-considered and balanced view of the future of the game. In his opinion, the enforced modifications would bring long-term good. Throughout previous seasons and the current troubled campaign, he and a few other writers had:

.....*supplied the small chorus of protest against the absurd limits to which professionalism was dragging the game, but practically without any support or response from those who considered that nothing could happen to put a brake on the impetuous pursuit of success. Some of us wondered whether anything could ever bring clubs to a proper sense of the evils which were springing up, for so long as the crowds grew so long were the sensational bids for players. Money alone appeared to be the one thing rung into one's ears from week to week, and how it could be applied to the end of capturing players and winning honours. Then the great war broke out, and the whole structure of professionalism as pursued to absurd limits comes tumbling down like a pack of cards. The question now arises whether the solution will be seized to bring out of chaos order and commonsense methods, in the engagement of and treatment of professional players, and thus bring back thousands who have felt they could not give countenance to the pastime so long as it was absolutely saturated with the money element. Candidly, we believe there is a promise of a better day. It seems almost impossible with the serious times ahead, that players will ever again be able to command such payments as shall make them independent of work.*

However, it was to be a false hope. By the early 1920s, wages and transfer fees were once more on the rise.[49]

The idea of imposing amateur status on all players was sure to be problematical. Would players who up to now had no reason to take up work outside football during the winter risk injury on the field of play for no remuneration at all, especially when the clubs were pocketing all the gate receipts? Would amateurism remain unblemished? With the best of intentions there would always be some prepared to resort to 'veiled professionalism' and the paying of players 'under the table'. It might be better to pay them something, even if it was half of what they received before. Clubs could easily afford to pay players £1 per match, although some players had already expressed disdain at the prospect of playing for such a sum. Critics suggested that they needed to get it into their heads that the country was engaged in a terrible war and that clubs had lost thousands of pounds during the 1914/15 season just to keep the game going and their players in employment. It was now up to the players to influence which way football might go – they could either retain their popularity amongst supporters by adopting a reasonable attitude to their clubs, or they could lose it should they remain intransigent. Once again the players had to take some of the blame for the situation they were now in. Had they given the Players' Union their full support earlier in the season when the wage deduction scheme was proposed they would now be in a stronger position to take part in the current discussions. An unidentified player was quoted in *Sporting Life* as saying:

> *So far as I understand the proposals, the clubs will have their football, the public will pay to*

---

[49] The maximum wage was raised to £8 per week in 1922. The first £5,000 transfer fee came the same year, the first £10,000 fee in 1928.

watch it, and the whole of the takings will go to the clubs. We players are to give our services for nothing, although football is our living, and there is not much doubt that if we are not ready to play for nothing we shall have to suffer in the future. Why should we give up the whole of our income and scrape along as best we can? It is true that most of us are in the army or engaged in Government factories, but we don't earn anything like the amount we have been getting for playing, and we expected when next season came along that we should be able to get back to our average income. We thought that we should be able, perhaps, to keep at work, and that we should not get less from the clubs. We are not greedy. We don't think the clubs can afford to pay as much as they have been doing, but there is a vast difference between knocking off fifty per cent and sweeping wages away altogether.

There was some sympathy for the dilemma in which the anonymous player and his colleagues found themselves, but they had little choice than to prepare themselves for a culture shock.

The Southern League had already decided to abandon its competition and advised its clubs to play only friendly matches by the time the Football League's annual general meeting was held on July 19 at the Connaught Rooms in London, prior to which joint discussions were held with the Football Association and the Southern League. The conferences would determine whether any football at all would be played under the Football League's name in 1915/16 and, if so, what rules would apply for the registration of players and the structure of competitions. The meetings extended from ten o'clock in the morning to six o'clock in the evening, with only a brief interval in the afternoon, following which the F.A. issued the following resolution:

- *Considering the present and future prospects of the game, and recognising the paramount duty of every man to help to carry on the war to a victorious issue at the earliest possible moment, and not to do anything that will in any degree postpone or hinder the desired result, resolve that, for the present, the following regulations shall be observed:*

- *That no international matches or the Challenge Cup and Amateur Cup matches of this Association be played during next season.*

- *That Associations, Leagues, and clubs be allowed to arrange matches, without Cup medals or other rewards, to suit local conditions, provided that they do not interfere with the work of those engaged in war work.*

- *That clubs may join any combination of clubs which may be convenient to them.*

- *That matches be played only on Saturday afternoons, and on early closing and other recognised holidays.*

- *That no remuneration shall be paid to players, nor shall there be any registration of players, but clubs and players shall be subject to the rules and conditions applicable to them on the 30th April, 1915.*

- *That agreements with players for service after 30th April, 1915, shall be suspended until further order.*

The Football League's AGM that followed the joint conference then ratified earlier proposals that its 1915/16 competition should be suspended. The League also formulated its own rule changes, one of which was that clubs should issue a list of retained players, and players open to transfer, by July 26, 1915. Such lists would stand until the next regular League competition was staged, whenever that might be. The League then outlined how its revised competitions, and player eligibility regulations, would be structured:

> *For the period of the war, the management committee seeks to arrange a number of competitions, which may include clubs in membership of the League, and other clubs in the respective localities, so that there may be, throughout the country, as far as possible, football played which will meet the requirements of the people, provided always that any Football League club has liberty to refuse to participate in any such competition. All League players shall be allowed to play for any club they please, without any transfer being necessary, whether in membership with the League or not, and shall revert to the ordinary rules governing the League competitions, when all the players shall automatically revert to the club holding their League registration. No payments shall be made to players in respect of existing agreements, the League promising to support any of their clubs should litigation ensue.*

A vote had previously been taken amongst the forty League clubs concerning the payment of players. No discussion was permitted as to whether they could be paid a lesser amount; it was a straight choice – pay or no pay. Twenty-one clubs voted in favour of continuing payment, nineteen were against (Sheffield United voted for payment, Wednesday for non-payment). There was hardly a convincing case for either position. Ironically, most of the twenty-one were Second Division clubs, eighteen of which earlier in the season had need to apply for assistance from the Football League relief fund. This poll was taken not to come to a definite conclusion about professionalism, but to provide the League's management committee with a sense of the overall feeling of its clubs before entering into conference with the Football Association and the Southern League. A near fifty-fifty split gave them no mandate in either direction. It was during this three-way conference that the decision was taken to cease payment of players.

For the few players, Sheffield United's George Utley amongst them, who had been fortunate enough to secure multi-year pre-war contracts, there was to be some compensation – but not of a financial nature. Their contracts would not be cancelled, but suspended, to be brought back into effect on the resumption of 'normal' football at some undetermined future date, yet how could anybody possibly know when that might be? Players might be dead or too old by then. Such an imposition probably could not be legally enforced, but any player wishing to take his club to court would receive no public sympathy whatsoever, and any club subject to a legal claim could rely on the full financial support of the Football League. There might also be a difficulty with the insurance of players. As they were no longer paid employees, they would not be covered by the regulations of the Federation of Insurance. Furthermore, if players were injured playing football they may be unable to work in the supply of munitions, and would therefore receive no wages at all. Thus a rule was later introduced to use a portion of pooled gate money for the purpose of remunerating players who could not work as a result of a football injury. They would receive their full wage until such time that they could resume work. One unanticipated result of the new regulations was that with well-known footballers now working in the manufacturing industry, the football teams of those factories might benefit as there was nothing to prevent such players turning out for any number of teams as they pleased.

To replace the existing Football League structure, two groups of clubs were formed to play competitive matches amongst themselves, arranged on a geographical basis to reduce the requirement for extensive travel. If nothing else, teams would experience the novelty of playing clubs they had not recently encountered and small clubs would get a rare opportunity of playing against the major names. During the break in Football League business while the Football Association/Football League/Southern League conference took place, the club representatives were asked to get together and come up with some plans for the regional sections. Here Sheffield United's secretary John Nicholson took control and had the Yorkshire group finalised in no time, such that when League secretary John McKenna returned to the room he seemed very pleased, and remarked: 'This is some business.'

Group 1 was to comprise Wednesday, Sheffield United, Bradford Park Avenue, Bradford City, Notts County, Nottingham Forest, Derby County, Leeds City, Huddersfield Town, Barnsley, Hull City, Grimsby Town, Lincoln City and Leicester Fosse. Group 2 was made up of Manchester City, Manchester United, Liverpool, Everton, Bolton Wanderers, Bury, Burnley, Stockport County, Oldham Athletic, Blackpool and Preston North End, plus two or three as yet unnamed others. It was further decided that if other groups of clubs, such as the five League clubs and the six Southern League clubs in London, arranged a competition among themselves, they would all be under the control, for the time being, of the Football League. As was their right under the current conditions, Aston Villa, Birmingham, Wolverhampton Wanderers and West Bromwich Albion decided not to play any competitive matches and would participate only in friendly games for charity. They stood firm against playing any organised football at all, as Frederick Rinder, the Aston Villa chairman, remarked that having to travel to away games outside the midlands would prevent players from working in munitions factories on Saturday morning. The north-east clubs adopted a similar standpoint, which made things easier all round for the clubs from Yorkshire and Lancashire as it cut down considerably on travel. Blackburn Rovers had already gone a stage further, previously deciding not to take part in any football at all. Their directors decreed that 'it was most undesirable that adult football should take place until the war is brought to a successful conclusion'. They further stated that Blackburn would compete only if compelled to do so; the Football League was in no position, or mood, to compel any club to do anything.

Players were not to be paid, but referees and linesmen could not be expected to provide their services for free; referees were to receive half a guinea per match, linesmen five shillings, and would be reimbursed the cost of third-class rail fare. Clubs were permitted to pay players a meal allowance of a maximum of 2s 6d, plus travel expenses. The Scottish Football Council, which had not been party to the discussions in London, did not concur with the introduction of amateurism; it agreed to allow professionalism to continue, but players would receive just £1 per week and would be engaged during the week in munitions work.

The Football League AGM also had some normal football duties to perform. The Football League Championship trophy and winners' medals were presented to the representative of

Everton FC and the Second Division Shield given to Derby County FC. Leicester Fosse and Glossop North End, the clubs that finished in the bottom two places of the Second Division, had to put themselves forward for re-election, alongside Football League aspirants Stoke City, South Shields, Chesterfield and Darlington. Leicester Fosse topped the poll with thirty-three votes, followed by Stoke with twenty-one, and were duly elected to the League. When they would be able to compete was unknown. Poor Glossop, the smallest town ever to host a Football League club, had suffered from pitiful attendances and a severe shortage of funds, and received just a single vote, probably from themselves.

Most of the Sheffield United players found jobs in reserved occupations in the local area, such as in collieries, engineering works and munitions factories, work that usually exempted them from conscription when it was introduced in March 1916.[50] In mid August 1915 United advertised for new players to apply to the club, but a number of the pre-war professionals continued to turn out in the reduced League competition. However, some, such as Stanley Fazackerley, were often unavailable as they were on active service. Ironically, Fazackerley appeared for Chelsea when he was passing through London, helping out the team he did a great deal to defeat in the Cup final.[51] United were fortunate in that nine of

---

[50] Harold Gough worked at Fryston Colliery near Castleford, Jimmy Simmons at Blackwell Colliery in Derbyshire. Bill Brelsford, Albert Sturgess and Harold Pantling played for the Thomas Firth National Projectile Factory (Templeborough) team in 1917 (Brelsford was captain), so it is fair to assume they worked there. The trio would have been a formidable half-back line in works football. There was a Gillespie in the Hadfeld's Ltd works team in 1917, but it has not been ascertained whether this was Billy. David Davies, who did not play in the Cup final, returned home to work in a Welsh coal mine. Reserve winger Jack Thompson was the first United player to enlist, joining the Royal Engineers.

[51] Fazackerley played for Chelsea three times in late November and December 1918, soon after the cessation of hostilities in Europe.

the Cup winning team were available - work permitting - for the start of the new season, the exceptions being Bob Evans, who had returned to his native Cheshire to work in a shipyard, and Albert Sturgess, who had not yet been in contact with club secretary John Nicholson, so his plans were unknown. One player who had missed almost the entire 1914/15 season was Billy Gillespie, whose return to action would be welcomed by all. Several guest players working locally had also committed themselves to the club.

The football authorities had taken heed of the general mood of the country, also taking into account the financial predicament of many of its clubs. For example, although they won the Cup, Sheffield United lost over £2,000 during the season, despite a receiving a payment of £757 11s 4d from the Football Association as their share of the receipts from the semi final and final ties. Only 1,300 season tickets had been sold (compared to 2,000 the previous season) and the average attendance at Bramall Lane plunged from 21,503 in 1913/14 to 14,947 in 1914/15. Other clubs were similarly badly - or worse - off: Bradford City lost £3,736, Bradford Park Avenue £1,330, Barnsley £2,399 10s 3d, Sunderland £2,084 and Oldham Athletic £1,025 11s 3d. The Football League itself lost £386, whilst Wednesday issued an appeal to shareholders to raise money to pay off debts of some £10,000. Oldham's financial figures were ruinously telling: they remained near the top of League all season and had a good run in the Cup. Their average takings per League match were £221, their lowest since joining the League, and season ticket receipts fell by £882. Without Cup income of £1,800 they would have been in severe difficulty. As it was, their debt stood at £2,074 12s 2d. The Southern League was a rare bright spot; it made a profit of £201, but some its clubs, in enduring the bitterest of criticism from the London press - which itself made money out of the game in the good times - were on the brink of going out of existence. And to think critics complained that football clubs were insistent on keeping the game going merely for profit! Several years later Charles Clegg continued to defend the decision not to abandon the professional game during the 1914/15 season, stating: 'On the amateur side of the game, of which there were approximately 20,000 clubs, football ceased to be played. On the professional side, of which there were only about 400 clubs, only such matches were played as were deemed to be expedient as a means of relief both to the mind and the body. Although adversely criticised, the action received general approval.'

The 'Khaki Final' remains a poignant moment in football history, even a watershed. It signalled the end of an era, the conclusion of a period of massive growth in the popularity of the game since it became properly organised and structured in the 1880s. No one could predict how long the war would last and how the country would recover in economic and social terms at the end of it. On a purely football scale, it could reasonably be argued that had the war not intervened Sheffield United could have dominated competition for the next few years. They had a settled side with many players at or nearing the peak of their powers and they had the inspirational Billy Gillespie to return to strengthen the team further. The *Sheffield Daily Telegraph* believed that United could have become 'one of the foremost teams in the League' and might 'achieve further successes in the Cup'. It was a great shame they were denied the opportunity to attempt to relive the glory days of Needham and Foulke, but there were far more important considerations to be taken into account.

The 1914/15 Sheffield United team was unique. They continued to play competitive football and lifted what was then the biggest prize in the game while tens of thousands of men of similar age were being slaughtered at the front. Right or wrong, it was not their fault, it was not their decision. They were just doing their job, under contract to do so. The tragedy of the millions who died cannot be underestimated and should never be forgotten but, in the relatively insignificant terms of professional football, it was sad too that the players who were experiencing the highlight of their careers were not able to properly celebrate or enjoy it. But, apart from unfortunate teammate Jimmy Revill, at least they still had their lives.

APPENDIX

The Sheffield United men who played in the final

Harold Gough - Signed from Castleford Town in 1913 but a Derbyshire man. Replaced the injured Ted Hufton and kept his place thereafter. Described as calm, efficient, brilliant and reliable, letting nothing worry him. One writer said of him: 'If he was coming out for a ball, it was his.' Reckoned to be United's best goalkeeper since William Foulke, no mean accolade considering that the excellent Joe Lievesley preceded him. Some thought Gough to be the best goalkeeper in England at the time, but he had to be content with just one international cap, won in 1921. During the war he worked at Fryston Colliery before joining the Royal Navy. Left United in 1925 when he took a public house, thus breaking the terms of his contract. Died in 1970.

Bill Cook - Signed from Hebburn Argyle in 1912. Two footed, a crisp tackler, cool, never flustered and sound of temperament. Never knew when he was beaten. His method was also described as romantic and cavalier. He was both a contortionist, which might explain some his unlikely clearances, and a comedian. Formed a great partnership with fellow north-easterner Jack English. Did not score a goal in his long United career, but missed a penalty in 1914/15. Returned to the north east to work during the war. Collected a second Cup winner's medal in 1925. Died in 1974.

Jack English - Signed from Watford for £500 in 1913 but a man of the north. Neat, stylish, intelligent and polished full back with a fine sense of anticipation and good distribution. In comparing English and Cook, the *Sports Special Green 'Un* wrote: 'If there is any difference between them, they both have it.' Like partner Cook, during the war he worked in a north-eastern shipyard. Did not re-sign for United after the war. Died in 1953.

Albert Sturgess - Signed from Stoke City for £350 in 1908. England international, totally reliable anywhere in defence or in the half-back line. Versatile, good in the tackle, consistent and an industrious competitor. Tall, slim and rangy, nicknamed 'Wiry' or 'Hairpin' due to his build. Took over in goal on several occasions, therefore known as 'the one-man football team'. Left United in 1923. Died in 1957.

Bill Brelsford - Signed from Doncaster Rovers in 1909. Born in Darnall, Sheffield, tough and uncompromising, never shirked a tackle. Good header of the ball. The only real weakness in his game was passing the ball. Often involved in 'dust-ups' with opponents, especially those of Wednesday and Leeds. After one such incident when he suffered a broken nose, he remarked: 'I don't know what caused the bother. Something went wrong and bang went the apple cart.' Two of his brothers played for Wednesday. The *Sports Special Green 'Un* wrote about him: 'Bill has got some shoulders, and he uses them. If anyone gets in the way when he wants to use them, then much the worse for the would-be trespasser.' Left United in 1922 but returned as a coach in 1925, remaining at the club until 1939. Died in 1954.

George Utley - Signed from Barnsley for a British record £2,000 in November 1913 on a five-year contract. Played in two Cup finals before 1915, losing one and winning one, so seen as a Cup specialist. Authoritative, dominating and commanding presence, a natural captain. He gave confidence to his teammates, who all appeared to 'shine in the reflected brilliance'. Trainer George Waller said he was 'a tower of strength, particularly in a Cup tie, and a clever leader of men'. He proved a worthy successor to the great Ernest Needham. Long throw expert, but it was said he threw the ball with one hand. A fine cricketer, he also played for Sheffield United CC. Left United in 1922. Died 1966.

Jimmy Simmons - Signed from Blackwell Colliery in 1908. Talented, two footed, fast and tricky, slightly built but said to have a heart as big as the body of his celebrated uncle, the gigantic William Foulke, who was from the same Derbyshire village. His uncle once stated that he did not think 'the little beggar had it in him'. Played for Blackpool in the war whilst on honeymoon in the town. Worked at Blackwell Colliery during the war before joining the forces in 1918. Left United in 1920.

Stanley Fazackerley - Signed from Hull City for £1,000 in 1912. Exceptionally clever and stylish, with extraordinary tricks that sometimes baffled teammates as well as opponents. Difficult to knock off the ball and a cool finisher. Tall and graceful. Favourably compared to Sunderland's England international Charles Buchan. Left United in 1920. Died in 1946.

Joe Kitchen - Signed from Gainsborough Trinity in 1907. Individualistic, dashing and exciting, known for his penetrating solo bursts and dribbles. A great crowd favourite and the dressing room comedian and morale booster. His best form came in 1909 when he was close to playing for England but, according to the *Sports Special Green 'Un*: 'I think somebody must have told him how good he was, and it didn't improve him,' but 1915 saw a return to his best. Left United in 1920.

Wally Masterman - Signed from Gainsborough Trinity in 1914. Tall, ran with his head down and the ball seemingly tied to his foot, but he had the knack of choosing the right moment to pass. Possessed a powerful shot. Left United in 1920. Died in 1965.

Bob Evans - Signed from Aston Villa for £1,100 in 1908. He had already won international caps for Wales when United found out he was born on the English side of the border near Chester, so he later represented England. Ran with a long, raking stride and hit a fine shot, though he was sometimes criticised for not being forceful enough. Once described as 'the best winger England and Wales ever had'. The *Sports Special Green 'Un* suggested that if he was arranging a family crest, it should picture a phoenix accompanied by the motto 'Come Again', as in 1915 he seemed to have renewed his youth. He worked as a carpenter at a shipyard in Saltney, Cheshire, and at a petroleum company in Ellesmere Port during the war. The Cup final was his last professional football match, as he broke his leg playing works football in December 1918. Died in 1965.

Others who played in the Cup run

Ted Hufton - Signed from Atlas & Norfolk works team in 1912, displacing long-serving goalkeeper Joe Lievesley. Broke his nose in a trial match at the start of 1913/14 and lost his place to Gough. Renowned penalty saver, keeping out eleven of the eighteen he faced in his career. Left United in 1919 and played for West Ham United in the first Wembley Cup final in 1923. Wounded during the war serving in the Coldstream Guards. Died in 1967.

Fred Hawley - Signed from Ripley Town in 1912. Powerfully built half back, not a first choice but the first man called upon if any of the regular half backs were injured. He missed the start of the 1914/15 season with injury. He played many League games but was the unfortunate twelfth man not picked for Cup final. The *Sports Special Green 'Un* wrote about him: 'It can be said, as has been said of the average husband, that he's a good man to have about the place.' Left United in 1919. Died in 1954.

David Davies - Signed from Stockport County in 1913. Welsh international with excellent ball control and made tricky runs. A great trier and fans' favourite, he stood in admirably for other forwards but was always the one to drop out when the regular player regained fitness. Left United in 1919.

Jimmy Revill - Signed from Tibshelf in 1910. One of the fastest wingers in the game, strangely dubbed 'old aeroplane legs'. He once told an opponent: 'I've been greased all over today and you'll never catch me. I'll give you the biggest doing of your life.' Limitless enthusiasm, but he could not dislodge the more consistent Bob Evans. Once, on a Bank Holiday when there was no public transport, he walked to Bramall Lane from his home in Chesterfield. Died in the war in 1917.

Secretary/Manager

John Nicholson – Served the club from 1899 to 1932, when he was killed in a car accident. Nicholson was not the team manager in the modern sense of the word, as signings and team selection were the responsibility of the directors. The trainer was responsible for training and physical fitness. The secretary/manager role was more of an administrative task, an intermediary between the committee and the football staff.

Trainer

George Waller - Joined United in 1892, he became first team trainer in 1896 and held the post until 1931, during which time he oversaw one League title and four Cup wins. Died in 1937.

BIBLIOGRAPHY

Books

Alexander, Jack (2003); *McCrae's Battalion: The Story of the 16th Royal Scots*, Mainstream Publishing, Edinburgh

Armstrong, Gary with Garrett, John (2006); *Sheffield United FC – The Biography,* The Hallamshire Press, Sheffield

Bailey, John (1999); *Not Just on Christmas Day: An Overview of Football During the First World War*, 3-2 Books, Upminster

Bell, Matthew and Armstrong, Gary (2010); *Fit & Proper? Conflicts and Conscience in an English Football Club*, Peakpublish, Calver

Brown, Malcolm and Seaton, Shirley (1999); *Christmas Truce,* Pan Books, London

Clarebrough, Denis (1989); *The Official Centenary History - Sheffield United Football Club - The First 100 Years,* Sheffield United Football Club, Sheffield

Clarebrough, Denis (2001); *100 Greats – Sheffield United Football Club*, Tempus Publishing Ltd, Stroud

Clarebrough, Denis and Kirkham, Andrew (1999); *A Complete Record of Sheffield United Football Club 1889-1999*, Sheffield United Football Club, Sheffield

Clarebrough, Denis and Kirkham, Andrew (1999); *Sheffield United Football Club – Who's Who*, Pauline Climpson, Criccieth

Dewar, George A. B. (1921); *The Great Munition Feat, 1914-1918*, Constable and Company Ltd, London

Foley, Michael (2007); *Hard As Nails – The Sportsmen's Battalion of World War One*, Spellmount Limited, Stroud

Gibson, Ralph and Oldfield, Paul (1994); *Sheffield City Battalion – The 12th (Service) Battalion York and Lancaster Regiment – A History of the Battalion Raised by Sheffield in World War One*, Leo Cooper, Barnsley

Harman, Ruth and Minnis, John (2004); *Pevsner Architectural Guides: Sheffield*, Yale University Press, London

Harris, Clive and Whippy, Julian (2008); *The Greater Game - Sporting Icons who fell in the Great War*, Pen & Sword Military, Barnsley

Hesse-Lichtenberger, Ulrich (2003); *Tor! The Story of German Football*, WSC Books Ltd, London

Hobsbawm, Eric and Ranger, Terence (1984); *The Invention Of Tradition*, The Cambridge University Press, Cambridge

Jensen, Neil (1990); *The Khaki Final*, The Association of Football Statisticians

Mason, Tony (1980); *Association Football and English Society 1863-1915,* Harvester Press, Brighton

Matthews, Tony; Clarebrough, Denis and Kirkham, Andrew (2003); *The Official Encyclopaedia of Sheffield United*, Britespot Publishing Solutions Limited, Cradley Heath

Pollard, Sidney (1959); *A History of Labour in Sheffield*, Liverpool University Press, Liverpool

Riddoch, Andrew and Kemp, John (2008); *When the Whistle Blows: The Story of the Footballers' Battalion in the Great War,* J. H. Haynes & Co. Ltd, Yeovil

Sparling, Richard. A. (2009); *History of the 12th Service Battalion York and Lancaster Regiment*, Naval and Military Press, Uckfield

Tweedale, Geoffrey (1995); *Steel City - Entrepreneurship, Strategy and Technology in Sheffield, 1743-1993*, Clarendon Press, Oxford

Vasili, Phil (2000); *Colouring Over The White Line: The History of Black Footballers in Britain*, Mainstream Publishing, Edinburgh

Vasili, Phil (1998); *The First Black Footballer: Arthur Wharton 1865-1930 – An Absence of Memory*, Frank Cass Publishers, London

Vasili, Phil (2009); *Walter Tull, (1888-1918), Officer, Footballer: All the Guns in France Couldn't Wake Me*, Raw Press

Vignes, Spencer (2007); *Lost in France: The Remarkable Life and Death of Leigh Richmond Roose, Football's First Play Boy*, The History Press Ltd, Stroud

Ward, Geoffrey C. (2005); *Unforgivable Blackness – The Rise and Fall of Jack Johnson*, Pimlico, London

Wilson, H.W. and Hammerton, J.A. (Editors) (1914); *The Great War - The Standard History of the All-Europe Conflict, Volume 1*, The Amalgamated Press Limited, London

Young, Percy M. (1981); *Football in Sheffield*, Dark Peak Ltd, Sheffield

Newspapers

Athletic News
Berlin Lokalanzeiger
Berliner Tageblatt
Daily Mail
Edinburgh Evening News
Frankfurter Zeitung
Lancashire Post
London Evening News
Manchester Guardian
Morning Post

Newcastle Daily Chronicle
Newcastle Evening Mail
Sheffield Daily Telegraph
Sheffield Independent
Sporting Life
Sports Special 'Green 'Un'
Sunday Pictorial
The Sportsman
The Times
Yorkshire Post

Periodicals and Magazines

Field
Flashing Blade
Punch
The Cricketer
When Saturday Comes

Other Sources

The Imperial War Museum North, Salford Quays
http://hansard.millbanksystems.com/
http://archive.timesonline.co.uk/tol/archive/
http://pws.prserv.net/Roger_Wright/Norris/SL14SD.htm
http://www.spartacus.schoolnet.co.uk/FWWfootball.htm
http://www.wikipedia.org/
http://1914-1918.invisionzone.com/forums/index.php?act=idx
http://www.1914-1918.net/
http://www.firstworldwar.com/
http://www.ww1westernfront.gov.au/essex-farm/flanders-fields.html
http://www.cwgc.org/
http://www.chrishobbs.com/

http://www.nfa.dept.shef.ac.uk/jungle/index.html

http://www.independent.co.uk/

http://www.soccer-history.co.uk/footballersbattalion.pdf

http://www.givemefootball.com/

http://www.fa-cupfinals.co.uk/

http://www.victoriacross.co.uk/

http://www.patriotfiles.com/index.php?
name=Sections&req=viewarticle&artid=7132&page=1

http://www.historylearningsite.co.uk/
christmas_1914_and_world_wa.htm

http://www.christmastruce.co.uk/football.html

http://archive.scotsman.com/

http://cylchgronaucymru.llgc.org.uk/

http://www.corshamref.org.uk/files/offsidehistory.pdf

http://www.cricketarchive.co.uk/Archive/Seasons/
1914_ENG.html

http://www.sheffield.gov.uk/libraries/archives-and-local-
studies/publications/world-war-one

http://www.sheffieldforum.co.uk/

http://www.sheffieldhistory.co.uk/

http://picturesheffield.com/

http://www.sbg.org.uk/

http://www.s24su.com/

http://www.omnesamici.co.uk/
MemoriesSomeNotableDays.html

http://www.theoldestfootballgroundintheworld.com/
history.html

http://www.measuringworth.com/ppoweruk/

INDEX

Bramall Lane (stadium), 5-6,
19-20, 22, 41, 57, 70, 75-76,
92-93, 95, 98, 103, 127-128, 133,
177, 179-180, 206, 209, 211, 214,
219, 240-241, 247, 257, 264-265,
286, 293

Brearley, Harry, 8, 12, 204

Brelsford, Bill, 66, 93, 173, 177,
181, 186, 206, 210-211, 216, 219,
240, 249, 257, 261, 290

Brighton and Hove Albion FC,
114, 142, 150, 156

British Expeditionary Force, 60,
73, 151

British Mediterranean
Expeditionary Force, 246

Buckley, Frank, 156, 163

Burn MP, Colonel Charles,
113-114, 119

Burnley FC, 102-103, 149, 173,
186, 224, 240, 283

Čabrinović, Nedeljko, 26, 106

Charrington, Frederick, 79-84,
88-89, 108-109, 114, 125-126,
137-138, 187

Chelsea FC, 62, 94-95, 113, 142,
152-153, 156, 158, 188, 209-211,
215, 217, 219, 223-224, 242-245,
247-253, 255-261, 264-265, 285

Clapton Orient FC, 62, 152-153,
156, 158, 162

Clegg, Charles, 63, 65, 135-138,
172, 262, 287

Conan Doyle, Sir Arthur, 83, 89

Cook, Bill (Sheffield United FC),
95, 173, 183, 185-186, 206, 209,
211-212, 218-219, 221-223, 240,
249, 261, 289-290

Croal, Jimmy, 244, 250-251

Croydon Common FC, 152, 156

Crystal Palace (stadium), 175,
224, 241-242, 248, 250

Crystal Palace FC, 70, 152-153,
156, 175, 242

Daily Mail, 229

Davies, David, 73, 75, 77-78,
93-95, 103-105, 127, 135,
173-174, 178, 181, 184-186,
208-209, 211, 222-223, 240, 293

Derby County FC, 100, 168, 231,
283, 285

Dietrich, Kapitanleutnant Martin,
199

Edinburgh Evening News, 165

Elphinstone, Captain Alexander,
159

Glasgow Celtic FC, 165, 170, 176, 264

Glasgow Rangers FC, 171

Gough, Harold, 61, 65, 74, 93, 102-105, 127, 129-130, 173, 176-178, 180-181, 183-184, 208, 212-214, 218, 220-223, 240, 245, 249, 257, 261, 289, 292

Grace, W. G., 39

Grantham, Colonel Charles, 153, 158, 160, 162

Guest, Captain Frederick, 226

Hadfield, Sir Robert, 201

Hallam FC, 5, 21

Hallamshire Football Association, 22

Halse, Harold, 210, 243-244, 250-251, 257-258, 261

Harrow, Jack, 250-251, 256-257, 259

Hatfield, Dr William Herbert, 194

Hawley, Fred, 61, 66-67, 129-130, 177, 186, 208, 212-213, 216, 229, 240, 249, 292

Hayes Fisher MP, William, 153, 155, 157

Heart of Midlothian FC, 164-165

Hendren, Patsy, 57, 163

Hillsborough (stadium), 21, 65, 77, 102, 178

HMS Aboukir, 94-95

HMS Amphion, 33

HMS Bulwark, 140

HMS Clan McNaughton, 206

HMS Cressy, 94-95

HMS Formidable, 178

HMS Hogue, 94-95

HMS Pathfinder, 78

Hobbs, Jack, 53-54

Hobsbawm, Eric, 23-24

Hufton, Ted, 178-180, 289, 292

Huntsman, Benjamin, 204

Ilić, Danilo, 106

Jellicoe, Admiral Sir John, 108

Johnson, Jack, 35-36

Jonas, Sir Joseph, 202-204

Jovanović, Mihaijlo, 106

Joynson-Hicks MP, William, 152-154, 157, 159-160, 163

By Matthew Bell & Gary Armstrong

Fit and Proper? Conflicts and Conscience in an English Football Club
Author: Matthew Bell and Gary Armstrong
ISBN: 9781907219115

Based on years of research by its two authors, Fit and Proper? details the history of the boardroom of Sheffield United Football Club, focusing particularly on the foibles of the men who over three decades from 1980 tried, and largely failed, to turn the 'Blades' into a profitable business and a successful club

About Dr. Gary Armstrong

Gary Armstrong is a Reader in the School of Sport and Education, Brunel University, London. He previously lectured in Criminology at the University of Westminster and the University of Reading. His research into sports-related matters has produced various publications including: Football Hooligans: Knowing the Score, Blade Runners: Lives in Football, and Sheffield United FC: The Biography.

Other Peak Platform Titles

Paying on the Gate: A Bantam's journey into the heart of lower league football
Author: Jason McKeown
ISBN: 9781907219252

They say you should never change your football team; but when Jason McKeown happens to stumble upon his local club, Bradford City, he instantly finds greater enjoyment from swapping the so-called glamour of Manchester United for the deeper substance of lower league football. As he grows up from excitable teenager to young adult, the strong bond with the Bantams proves both a hindrance and help in shaping his future.

Paying on the gate celebrates the virtues of supporting your local, less glamorous football club as opposed to the superficial nature of following one that wins more often, but with whom you have no relationship. The glory may be in short supply, but Jason's decision to break the golden rule helps him learn what being a football supporter is really about.

'A Catalan Dream: Football Artistry and Political Intrigue'
Author: Tim Hanlon
ISBN: 9781907219153

In 2003, Barcelona was in full crisis on and off the pitch with the team struggling in the league and the protests of fans leading to the resignation of the president. A new radical board led by the charismatic Joan Laporta was ushered into power and a dramatic recovery began to unfold. The enigmatic Ronaldinho instigated the turnaround and helped the club to European success before he was superseded by home grown players like Leo Messi and Andres Iniesta, led by coach Pep Guardiola, the iconic figure of Cruyff's side.

About Tim Hanlon
Tim Hanlon is based in Barcelona and has been covering Spanish football for the national news agency in the UK, the Press Association, and other British media on a freelance basis, for the past seven years. As the only British reporter to regularly cover training practices and speak to players, Tim has been in the ideal position to write about the dramatic events as they have unfolded at the Barcelona club.

I Hate Football: A Fan's Memoir
Author: John Firth
ISBN: 9781907219021

It is easy to support a successful football team, but it takes guts, loyalty and a whole heap of stupidity to follow one of the also-rans. "I Hate Football" is the story of such a group of fans who are unfortunate enough to follow Sheffield Wednesday. It is a record of the fortunes of the club from 1970 through to 2009, as seen through the eyes of the fans; fans that live and breathe every kick. This is the autobiography of almost every fan in the country - a must read for all football fans.

About John Firth
John Firth grew up in Sheffield and now lives in Wakefield. He is married with a seven year old boy who has Autism. When his son was diagnosed with Autism, he resigned his position to give the care and support that their son desperately needed. He then started up a plumbing business that is now flourishing. What precious spare time that he has is taken up by writing and obviously following Sheffield Wednesday, which is a huge passion in his life.

Playing For England: England Supporters Band Early Years
Authors: John Hemmingham & Stephen Holmes
ISBN: 9781907219108
Format: Hardback

In the spirit of 'Fever Pitch', 'The Full Monty' and 'Brassed Off' this is the story of the Sheffield based England Band This inspirational band, aged between 10 and 80 plus, play with passion in support of their country and have now 'Played for England more times than Beckham'. Richard Branson personally persuaded them to sign up for their first chart making record deal and the Band have since released many others plus three singles and an album for the World Cup 2010. They have made numerous TV and Radio appearances.

About John Hemmingham
'Give me the child until he is seven and I'll give you the man'. So it was that as a seven year old boy growing up in Sheffield within sight of his team's ground, John was already obsessed with football and playing the bugle, in that order. In typical style John took a bugle to a match in 1993 'just for a laugh'. The mystery bugler was identified and asked to form a football terrace band. Then in 1996 John and the band were given the honour of being asked to play for England.